Nations in Turmoil

Nations in Turmoil

Conflict and Cooperation in Eastern Europe

Janusz Bugajski

Westview Press
BOULDER • SAN FRANCISCO • OXFORD

[redacted]

[redacted]

This Westview softcover edition is printed on acid-free paper and bound in library-quality, coated covers that carry the highest rating of the National Association of State Textbook Administrators, in consultation with the Association of American Publishers and the Book Manufacturers' Institute.

Published in 1993 in the United States of America by Westview Press, Inc., 5500 Central Avenue, Boulder, Colorado 80301-2877, and in the United Kingdom by Westview Press, 36 Lonsdale Road, Summertown, Oxford OX2 7EW

Library of Congress Cataloging-in-Publication Data
Bugajski, Janusz, 1954–
Nations in turmoil : conflict and cooperation in Eastern Europe / Janusz Bugajski.
p. cm.
ISBN 0-8133-1626-X
1. Europe, Eastern—Politics and government—1989–
2. Nationalism—Europe, Eastern. 3. Europe, Eastern—Ethnic relations. I. Title.
DJK51.B84 1993
940'.09717—dc20 92-24761
CIP

Printed and bound in the United States of America

The paper used in this publication meets the requirements of the American National Standard for Permanence of Paper for Printed Library Materials Z39.48-1984.

10 9 8 7 6 5 4 3 2

To Aimee,
my inimitable colleague and friend,
for making it all possible

Contents

Acknowledgments

This book is the culmination of two years of extensive travel to all the countries, old and new, in eastern Europe. I would like to thank all of the organizations that helped to sponsor my trips and the colleagues who shared my adventures. Indispensable research assistance for various parts of the project was provided by a host of students, including Elizabeth Krzysik, Lesley Seplaki, John Lazas, Olga Milosavljevic, Michelle Heald, Christopher Beecroft, Allan Hoffman, Kim Brinck-Johnsen, Elena Ciura DeCastris, Natasha Mylroie, Becky Siahaya, Sean Harris, Eric Bruder, Gisele Grayson, Anne Nisenson, Sarah Despres, Ann Horvath, Marianne Oglo, Susan Penksa, John Kenny, Karin Orsic, Dimitry Osipov, Nancy Oglo, and Viden Nedialkov. My special gratitude—for help above and beyond the call of duty—must go to my research and administrative assistants at the Center for Strategic and International Studies in Washington, D.C., Aimee Breslow, Darcy Zajacek, and Anne Truslow.

Janusz Bugajski
Washington, D.C.

EASTERN EUROPE: States, Regions, and Nationalities

Introduction: The Liberation of Eastern Europe

The east European region has undergone breathtaking changes since the Soviet empire began to unravel at the close of the 1980s. The rapid disintegration of the unpopular and illegitimate Communist regimes was accompanied by a democratic upsurge in each state. But the painstaking process of reform and reconstruction heralded a prolonged period of political turbulence, economic uncertainty, and international instability. Ethnic and nationality tensions also resurfaced throughout the region, as the new governments grappled with the aspirations of disgruntled minorities and the problem of implementing independent foreign policies and devising new security arrangements. This book attempts to establish the contours and dimensions of international conflict and cooperation in eastern Europe during the early post-Communist period. It explores the roots and branches of ethnic and nationality relations throughout the region and focuses on the most contentious internal and inter-state issues. To place the subject matter in context, it is valuable to begin with an overview of political and economic developments in the region since the collapse of Communist Party rule and the demolition of the Soviet bloc.

With the dismantling of the one party state, systemic political and economic reforms were launched in each country, although with varying degrees of intensity. Structural transformations were deemed essential for rescuing the region's bankrupt economies, building sound and durable political institutions, enhancing public participation, and gaining Western financial assistance and foreign business investment. Each new administration drew upon diverse constitutional and legislative procedures from the Western democracies, and its own independent pre-Communist traditions in constructing a democratic parliamentary system of government. A broad assortment of political parties and coalitions replaced the crumbling one-party systems throughout eastern Europe. They were formed on the basis of the nation's existing social constituencies, interest groups, and emerging ideological trends. But as political and government controls were eliminated from virtually all spheres of public life, new social tensions have been generated as a result of deteriorating economic conditions and the unsteady emergence of pluralistic political systems. In some cases, disputes were also sparked over domestic divisions based on ethnicity or regionalism, as well as over the foreign policies of the newly elected governments and their evolving relations with neighboring states.

Given this context, four important variables must be considered in order to understand eastern Europe's current predicament and to trace the evolution of international relations in the region since the fall of Communism: domestic political developments, market-oriented economic reforms, ethnic and nationality relations, and changing international conditions.

Some states have moved faster than others on the political front, even though each country has held multi-party general and local elections during the past two years. The first national elections had the character of a plebiscite to legitimately break the Communist stranglehold on power; forthcoming ballots will help to crystallize the political constellations and profiles of each state. Most of the Balkan countries have remained at the rear of the democratization process, although political pluralism has clearly taken root and the reformed Communists are unlikely to retain or regain exclusive power anywhere in the region. Nevertheless, the dislodging of the old political apparatus from each important institution, particularly at local administrative levels, has proven to be a slower process in Romania, Bulgaria, and Albania than in the central European states of Poland, Hungary, and the Czech and Slovak Federal Republic. Yugoslavia has occupied an intermediary political position, as the pace of democratic change has differed between the country's six republics and this in turn, has also contributed to undermining the existence of the multi-national federation.

While democracy has remained only partially embedded in the institutional fabric of most of these sovereign nation-states, power struggles have continued to be waged both inside and outside the new political structures. Such contests are evident either between the former oppositionist activists and the ex-Communist reformers, who have adapted to the new political landscape (observable in Bulgaria, Albania, and Romania), or within the former dissident circles (as witnessed in the fracturing of Poland's Solidarity, the Czech Civic Forum, and Slovakia's Public Against Violence). These conflicts have been partly ideological and programmatic, but often involved a marked degree of personal ambition and mutual animosity. To fully decipher these political conflicts, analysts needed to look beyond the theories of democratic transformation by examining the biographies and personalities of the leading political actors.

Political competition may, of course, be a healthy process if it does not imperil the process and progress of democracy, and the competitors remain publicly accountable and subject to a system of laws and regulations. However, a clear danger in eastern Europe is the likelihood that political life will remain splintered into a broad spectrum of minute, weak and uninfluential parties. This would make stable governments difficult to sustain. Political parties are still constructed largely around personalities and friendship connections rather than distinct programs and platforms, and the majority of organizations lack a solid material foundation. The ideal solution would be the emergence of a handful of reasonably strong parties, spanning the traditional political spectrum and representing the interests of specific sectors of society. In fact, many of the new mini-parties are likely to fall by the wayside, others will coalesce, and a few will expand substantially. In the interim, unsteady governing alliances, hastily arranged between a plethora of small parties, may remain hesitant or hamstrung in undertaking or pursuing any significant economic and foreign policy initiatives.

For the foreseeable future, each east European government will remain preoccupied with crisis-management as it attempts to contain and resolve a bewildering array of domestic problems. Restructuring policies that dramatically increase unemployment and deepen material inequalities could ignite clashes between social classes, occupational groups, regional interests, and state bodies. Some sectors of society will also prove susceptible to manipulation by militant or populist left-wing or right-wing forces. In addition, while public commitment to and identification with distinct political parties remains fragile or absent, widespread alienation and frustration manifested in disengagement from the political process could damage domestic reform programs and further undermine national stability.

Renewed turmoil could, in turn, paralyze a government and lead to rearranged coalitions, resignations, and early general elections. A strong executive may therefore prove crucial in some instances, to ensure a sufficient degree of administrative equilibrium where weak democratic governments prove unable to cope with economic difficulties and escalating social unrest. But there exists an equal danger that a strong President or head of state could assume extra-parliamentary dictatorial powers with or without some degree of military participation. Calls for increasing the powers of the presidency have already been heard in Poland, Czechoslovakia, and among the Balkan states. Presidential prerogatives gained during a national emergency, possibly with sizeable public support, may not be easily revoked or curtailed once a measure of stability is restored in the country. Such a scenario could herald a dictatorial interlude or a prolonged period of unsteady authoritarian rule, that some have dubbed a process of "Latin Americanization." It may also trigger new political and social struggles between distinct interest groups that the newly constructed institutions may prove unable to contain or resolve.

Developments have not been uniform throughout the east European region, and some countries may prove more prone to dictatorship, whether of a civilian or quasi-military variety. In some cases, this could be backed by substantial popular support, particularly where its stated purpose is the restoration of order and stability at a time of intense turmoil and growing public uncertainty. Furthermore, new authoritarian regimes may not necessarily seek to reimpose totalitarian state controls over society and could prove more corporatist and protectionist rather than socialist in their economic orientations.

To avoid any potential drift toward dictatorship in the region, successful institution building remains imperative and must include the ripening of a sound political infrastructure from the capital down to village level. The first series of multi-party national and local elections did not signal the culmination of the democratization process but only its raw beginnings. Communist methods of operation and the mentality of subservience and time serving still need to be expunged from all national bureaucracies and public bodies. This may prove a much slower and laborious endeavor in some countries than the initial dislodging of Communist leaders from the most powerful and prominent positions. The restoration of democratic procedures will mean the dismantling and replacement of some bureaucracies and the culling and rationalization of others. In most instances, the mass purge of functionaries appointed by the ousted regimes has been studiously avoided. Instead, the new governments will probably continue to incrementally thin out the bloated bureaucracies and introduce the principles of competence and competition to absorb the former *nomenklatura* into a more productive management structure. Furthermore, stable constitutional arrangements must be introduced, with a legitimate and balanced separation of powers between the organs of central government to preclude any future authoritarian temptations.

The pace of economic transformation has differed significantly between the east European states. It has been determined partly by the depth of economic crisis in each country, by official concerns about possible social upheaval, and by the programmatic propensities of the new governments. All countries in the region have faced similar if not identical economic problems and imbalances, including industrial obsolescence, stagnant productivity, foreign indebtedness, and the non-competitiveness of their products. They have all inherited distorted and inefficient centrally planned economies that were grossly unresponsive to market stimuli.

Each administration has faced a difficult dual task: to transform the command economy into a market system while simultaneously maintaining a sufficient measure of social tranquility to avoid capsizing the reform process. Market reforms must involve the scaling down of state subsidies to industries and consumers, alongside an extensive privatization of the economy. But such policies invariably create widespread unemployment, as inefficient enterprises become bankrupt before a significant number of private businesses are established to soak up the surplus labor during the industrial reorganization. Rising unemployment results in a severe psychological shock to a society nurtured on lifetime job security, and this trauma is further exacerbated by a lack of geographical mobility or work retraining opportunities. Structural reform also means a comprehensive fall in living standards until the economy starts to rebound. Prices have to rise substantially in order to adjust to normal market levels, while wage increases are constrained as firms have to become independent and competitive entities. Such economic difficulties have deflated early public expectations for a swift material improvement, and could, in turn, foster disillusionment, apathy, or even radicalism. The region will therefore continue to undergo a difficult economic transition in the midst of an often unsteady development of political pluralism.

Poland initially made the most far-reaching commitment to dismantling the state-controlled system. Hungary and Czechoslovakia trailed somewhat behind Warsaw, purportedly in search of a smoother, more gradual, and less painful transition to a fully capitalist economy. But all three states have undertaken important steps to privatize their economies and disassemble the state system, realizing that half-measures would simply prolong public agony and deepen economic decline. By contrast, most of the Balkan countries have proceeded more tentatively in introducing marketization and privatization programs. They remained constrained by the bureaucratic apparatus, and by serious manifestations of social and political instability that were aggravated by even more severe economic deterioration.

Economic developments in the region during the past two years have therefore resulted in a growing differentiation between the central and south east European countries. The former appear to be more advanced in developing a rudimentary capitalist economy and have obtained more significant Western assistance and business investments. This developmental gulf will remain a contributing factor to ongoing Balkan instability. An additional concern in the region is the probability of uneven economic development between urban and rural areas, and between central and peripheral regions of specific countries. This could also increase public polarization and radicalization, particularly if it is intermeshed with existing ethnic, religious, and cultural cleavages.

A key economic objective in each country is the creation of a sizable middle class of productive and imaginative entrepreneurs. Compared to the western states, eastern Europe started off at a severe historical disadvantage. Centuries of foreign domination and economic underdevelopment were compounded by the deliberate thwarting of private enterprise under decades of Communist central planning. Destroying capitalism certainly proved to be an easier proposition than restoring it. The essential preconditions must now be met for private businesses to flourish, including appropriate legislation, credit availability, tax relief, and infrastructural development. An important beginning has been made, especially in central Europe, but the middle class remains small, fragile, and often frustrated by legalistic confusion and bureaucratic obstruction. Moreover, social disquiet has been generated by often justifiable popular perceptions that former Communist managers have unfairly benefitted from the market reforms by establishing private businesses with illegally acquired assets, while a new small group of entrepreneurial embezzlers have profited from the capitalist revival.

The political honeymoon in eastern Europe is clearly over and all the new governments need to implement tough economic decisions. Long-term economic success in constructing market economies will not gain any administration short-term popularity. It may even result in widespread unrest, as sectors of the population remain prone to populist rhetoric and millenarian appeals reinforced by a growing gap between rich and poor and by an uncertain economic future. This danger was evident during Poland's presidential elections in December 1990, when an unknown émigré businessman defeated the incumbent and widely respected Prime Minister by offering a mirage of prosperity without presenting a viable economic package. Similar populist forces are lurking in the background across the region. Each administration must therefore weather the social storms that accompany the return of capitalism, while concurrently satisfying Western creditors and multilateral institutions and encouraging foreign investors. Some vision of the future must also be offered by state leaders to the general public, a vision that neither promises unreachable targets nor drives the citizenry to gloom and doom. In overall terms, although economic conditions remain poor in eastern Europe they are not as severe as in the 1920s and 1930s, when they undermined the region's young democracies, and they will gradually improve.

In addition to the difficulties of political development and economic transition, some states will be preoccupied with cultural, religious, and ethnic tensions. In the post-Communist era, nationalism has resurfaced throughout the region, although it is a less dangerous phenomenon than in the inter-war period as no large outside powers with expansionist territorial designs are currently encouraging national conflicts in eastern Europe. In practice, resurgent nationalism may be either a positive or a negative force. It is positive where it helps to restore previously suppressed cultures and encourages self-determination and pluralism, and it is negative when it becomes exclusivist, assertive, and chauvinistic at the expense of vulnerable minorities.

Simple distinctions between East and West in their handling of nationalism should be avoided. In general, the west European nations have been able to freely develop their distinct identities and cultures during the course of this century. This luxury enabled them to achieve a measure of self-confidence that dispelled nagging fears about supranational European integration. By contrast, most of eastern Europe has only experienced sporadic periods of independence during centuries of foreign occupation and domination, in which national identities, cultures, and languages were threatened with extinction. In the past half century, the region has also borne the brunt of two variants of totalitarianism that have sought to terminate all national differences. The current nationalist resurgence is as much an assertion of group identity, pride, and self-respect as it is a restoration of political self-determination and independence.

However, in the ethnic mosaic of eastern Europe, national self-assertion can also lead to inter-ethnic conflicts. States such as Poland, Hungary, and Albania seem to have a head start in avoiding the most intense domestic hostilities, primarily because they form more ethnically homogeneous and compact national entities. But in the multinational federations of Yugoslavia and Czechoslovakia, cultural, linguistic, religious, and regional differences have fanned friction, particularly where economic conditions have deteriorated and political decentralization has failed to satisfy leaders of the constituent republics. Romania and Bulgaria define themselves as uni-ethnic states, even though both contain large and vibrant minorities aspiring toward cultural and political self-determination and fearful of assimilation and ethnic extinction. These inbuilt contradictions, as well as the potential for state repression and inter-communal disputes, will continue to spark controversies and ignite hostilities even as democracy and capitalism take root. Paradoxically, the open expression of ethnic, religious, and other grievances in a pluralistic setting may actually aggravate domestic and international conflicts.

One central problem revolves around the distinction between individual civil rights and collective group rights within any single state structure. Not all administrations that may firmly guarantee the former for all citizens will necessarily recognize any deep commitments to the latter. Government officials may fear that bestowing special privileges or implementing affirmative action programs for national minorities may actually aggravate inter-communal divisions. Such policies could breed resentment among the majority population in a deprived economic climate, while arousing far-reaching but unacceptable aspirations for territorial autonomy and even separatism among the minority group.

On the international arena, Soviet leaders and their successors concluded during the last four years that relations with the new east European governments will henceforth need to be based on pragmatic mutual national interests rather than enforced ideological and political commitments. This has led to a genuine rapprochement with the central government in the post-USSR and the development of direct relations with the independent post-Soviet republics. However, the process of forming new international relationships is unlikely to be predictable or unproblematic. The ongoing disintegration of the USSR will have a major impact on all the east European states. Continuing turmoil on the territory of the former Soviet Union, whether manifested in a complete collapse of central authority or in renewed coup attempts by hard line autocratic, nationalistic, or military forces, would have a major spillover effect throughout the region. It could result in an even more severe disruption of important energy supplies and trading networks, precipitate an influx of refugees that seriously exacerbate economic and social problems, and even instigate armed incursions and border violations by military or paramilitary forces.

Dormant and often unresolved inter-state problems, and divergent or sometimes antagonistic national ambitions, have already engendered conflict within and between several east European countries. The defunct Communist regimes operated on the premise that social classes and not nationalities were the principal actors in socio-economic development and foreign affairs. National borders were redrawn after World War Two, largely to coincide with Moscow's geopolitical interests and to placate some local national yearnings. Under the Stalinist tyranny and the Brezhnevite *status quo,* most national demands were depicted as "bourgeois relics" that would disappear as the proletarianized citizenry gradually merged into a transnational "socialist" culture.

The Kremlin became the final arbiter in any international disputes and sought to prevent any regional conflicts among its satellites from upsetting its hegemonic "internationalist" goals. Although nationalism was relegated by Communist ideology to a secondary phenomenon, it was nevertheless recognized in practice as a powerful mobilizer of public opinion. It was therefore often manipulated by local Communist leaders as a legitimizing device in their post-Stalinist "national roads to socialism," and in order to divert public hostility toward the capitalist Western states. More fervent nationalist positions were adopted by Communist regimes that obtained varying degrees of political independence from the Soviet Union, particularly in Albania, Yugoslavia, and Romania.

The unraveling of the Soviet bloc has released previously submerged national ambitions and stimulated the formulation of new foreign policies and security doctrines among all the east European states. Emerging nationalisms in the post-Communist period are unlikely to replicate the often destructive nineteenth century and inter-war disputes. Nevertheless, diverse state interests and traditional ethnic or religious animosities may in some instances fester and grow. Government officials and political leaders searching for popular credibility in the midst of severe social disruption may seek to capitalize on nationalist passions against foreign or "alien" domestic scapegoats. Moreover, extremist political groups will also attempt to take advantage of public disorientation and frustration during the destabilizing and unpredictable economic reform process. In a liberated political climate, radical nationalist groups generally have the freedom to operate and organize, and some will seek to exploit unresolved ethnic, cultural, religious, and racial antagonisms to increase their influence over the public and the government.

In other cases, long suppressed national minority aspirations will continue to surface amid growing demands for cultural, linguistic, and religious rejuvenation. This in turn could inspire calls for regional autonomy, territorial independence, or even complete secession from the dominant state if grievances are not addressed and resolved. The proliferation of numerous national minority demands could thereby figure highly on domestic political agendas and they must be contained within the emerging parliamentary systems if serious conflicts are to be averted.

Nationality disputes linked with various political and economic grievances will also have important international reverberations. Unsettled conflicts that were simply subdued during the Communist period will continue to strain relations between a number of states in the region. Moreover, the disintegration of the multinational federations of Yugoslavia and the Soviet Union may significantly heighten irredentist and annexationist ambitions and other political claims by neighboring countries, and could have a ripple effect through the region. The republics of Macedonia and Moldova are two poignant examples of such trends that may embroil a number of bordering states in conflicting historical and territorial claims.

The evolution from a simple bi-polar to a complex multi-polar European system will seriously effect the stability and the security of the continent. Some observers have pointed out that a multi-polar system is inherently more unstable, given the emergence of several power centers, the loosening of prior international alliances, and the erosion of the pacifying effects of nuclear deterrents that balanced East-West relations during the Cold War era. The east European states no longer fear that their actions will precipitate a superpower confrontation, and hence may be less restrained in their foreign policy objectives and initiatives. Although the possibility that some local armed conflict may involve the two superpowers have been significantly reduced, limited wars over borders and minorities also have the potential of escalating among neighbors, reshaping and recreating conflictive regional alliances, drawing in some of the west European states, and triggering destabilizing wider confrontations.

In the light of the political, economic, and nationality problems evident in the post-Communist transition, this study provides a comprehensive investigation of the sources, manifestations, implications, and prospects for international conflict throughout eastern Europe. It explores the significance of historical antagonisms and continuing political discords between specific nationalities and states in the region. These are manifested in territorial disputes, ethnic cleavages, minority frictions, secessionist demands, irredentist claims, ideological and religious animosities, social, economic, and environmental problems, and the emergence of conflictive sub-regional alliances. Scenarios are then explored in which current disputes may escalate into more damaging confrontations, including armed clashes of varying intensity. The last part of the book assesses the development of international cooperation both within eastern Europe and between east and west European states since the collapse of the Soviet bloc. It evaluates the progress and prospects for east European integration into the multinational pan-European political, economic, and security institutions; a process that can help the new democracies to overcome their profound internal and external problems.

1

A History of Upheaval

For centuries eastern Europe was dominated or controlled by rival expansionist empires. It remained a highly volatile region constructed from a mosaic of ethnic groups, religions, and cultures. The dividing line between Catholic and Orthodox Christianity fractured the area, and substantial pockets of Islamic and Protestant populations added to the region's diversity. After the disintegration of the large imperial states, several east European nations gained their independence and statehood. But during the 20th century, the region was subjected to two totalitarian ideologies, Fascism and Communism, that severely retarded progress toward a liberal democratic capitalism. In addition, statehood and national territory did not always coincide, as some nationalities had sizable populations left outside their state borders. These developments provoked disputes over territories, minorities, and resources, and prevented the emergence of secure and durable international alliances. During the past half century, eastern Europe has also been occupied by the Soviet Union, which subdued but did not resolve long-simmering ethnic and national conflicts, and in some cases Moscow contributed to exacerbating these disputes. Any assessment of contemporary east European nationality conflicts, and the prospects for international cooperation in the post-Communist era, must begin with an overview of the region's history and a reflection on its complexity. In addition, the phenomenon of nationalism must be explored, as this elusive ideology is likely to dominate developments in the region throughout the next decade.

A Troubled History

In the first nine centuries of the Christian era, the central and eastern parts of Europe experienced extensive migrations by an assortment of ethno-linguistic groups.[1] Among the reasons for their movements westward were population pressures in their traditional areas and the availability of better grazing and agricultural lands in the European heartland. By the seventh century, various Germanic tribes dominated much of the area north of the Rhine and Danube rivers.[2] The next major group to gradually push west were the Slavs, who were primarily sedentary agriculturalists.[3] Other peoples that did not make a long term impact on the region, or were absorbed culturally and linguistically, included the pastoralist Huns and Avars, while the Turkic Bulgars merged with the Slavic groups in the southeastern Balkans.

By the eighth century, the Slavs had settled much of central and eastern Europe. They were sub-divided into three main groupings—western Slavs (Czechs, Slovaks, Poles, Wends), eastern Slavs (Russians, Belarusans, Ukrainians, Ruthenes), and southern Slavs (Serbs, Croats, Slovenes, Montenegrins, Bosnians, Macedonians, Bulgarians). But in the ninth century, Germanic tribes reversed their westward migration and started to penetrate the Slavic territories. At about the same time, Magyars or Hungarians moved into the Danubian Plain from the eastern steppes and conquered a swath of territory in central Europe, thus splitting the north and south Slavs and extending their presence into formerly German areas. The origins of the Romanians are less clear, despite indigenous claims of ethnic continuity from the Dacians and the Romans who settled in the Danube Delta in the second century AD. Meanwhile, the Albanians probably have the most credible claim to residential longevity in the Balkan region. According to available historical evidence, they are linguistically, ethnically, and culturally the descendants of Illyrian groups who established a kingdom on the Adriatic coast in the third century BC.

The extensive migratory period in eastern Europe was largely over by the tenth century, when new kingdoms and chiefdoms became territorially stabilized. However, their borders were often fluid and their internal ethnic composition remained changeable. The ethno-linguistic mix was further complicated by an uneven process of assimilation and cultural mergers, and by the settlement of other diverse groups often at the invitation of local princes. Over the centuries these included communities of farmers, traders, merchants, manufacturers, or soldiers, whose ethnic origins included German, Jewish, Armenian, and Greek.

The early tribal groups practicing indigenous religions came under Christian influence and missionary activity from about the fifth century onwards. Christianity was often spread and enforced by kings, princes, and chieftains, who accepted the new faith because it offered economic advantage and buttressed their political control. Two main Christian centers, Rome and Constantinople, generated a strong influence in eastern Europe, and a clear territorial and cultural division developed between the Western Catholic and the Eastern Orthodox religions.[4] The Catholic faith spread primarily in the central and northern areas, among Poles, Czechs, Slovaks, Hungarians, Slovenes, and Croats, while Orthodoxy took root in the southern and eastern areas among Russians, Romanians, Serbs, Bulgarians, and Macedonians. The Protestant Reformation in the 15th and 16th centuries created sizable pockets of Lutherans, Calvinists, and other smaller sects, while the Catholic Counter-Reformation regained some territories for the Vatican. The Muslim religion also spread after the fifteenth century, once the Ottoman Turks conquered Constantinople and proceeded to expand Turkish control throughout the Balkans.

Older European empires became overstretched, internally weakened, and eventually disintegrated when subjected to sustained external pressures. For example, in the south east the Byzantine empire was overrun by Ottoman Turks during the fourteenth century. In the west, the Holy Roman Empire, a loose confederation of mostly German feudal states, gradually collapsed by the eleventh century. In the east, Mongol armies conquered the Russian territories in the eleventh century and penetrated the east European area before they were militarily stopped and retreated. The region became fractured into a number of independent or quasi-sovereign states that owed their existence largely to their neighbors' weakness.

Several state-kingdoms endeavored to expand their dominions between the tenth century and the rise of the imperial Central Powers in the 17th century. The most significant powers included the Duchy of Lithuania and the Kingdom of Poland, which federated in the 14th century. It became the largest state in Europe, that by the 16th century controlled a wide stretch of territory from the Baltic Sea to the Black Sea. A Czech state, established during the 7th century, was absorbed by Greater Moravia by the tenth century. A Magyar kingdom was created south of the Carpathian mountains, in the Danube Basin and Transylvania, and Croatian and Slovenian kingdoms were formed in the 10th and 11th centuries but soon fell under Magyar control. The first Bulgarian empire collapsed in the 11th century. The second Bulgarian empire was forged by the Turkic Bulgars who merged with local Slavs in the 12th century, but it was not a dominant power in the Balkans. The Serbian kingdom, which dominated the western part of the Balkan peninsula in the 13th and 14th centuries, was destroyed by the Turks as Ottoman rule began to spread northward toward central Europe.

Between the 15th and 17th centuries, the entire area of present day eastern Europe, aside from the most mountainous areas of Montenegro in present day Yugoslavia, fell under the control of outside powers and imperial states. The diverse political, economic, and religious systems of those empires added to the process of diversification throughout eastern Europe. The major imperialist players at this time became the Habsburgs (Austrians), the Ottomans (Turks), the Prussians (Germans), and the Russians.

The Habsburg dynasty underwent a dramatic expansion from the 16th century onward, principally through marriage with local monarchs rather than outright conquest. From their heartland in Austria, the Habsburgs gradually acquired Hungary, Transylvania, Romanian Bukovina, Polish Galicia, and parts of the Dalmatian coast, in addition to Bohemia, Moravia, Slovakia, and Slovenia.[5] Hungary achieved a privileged status in the Habsburg empire compared to the other kingdoms. The Habsburg emperor was also declared the king of Hungary, while the aristocratic Magyar landowners remained reasonably content with Austrian rule as their economic interests were protected in return for their political loyalty to Vienna. Hungary itself maintained control over Transylvania, Slovakia, and Croatia.

The turmoil of the Reformation, Counter-Reformation, and the Napoleonic Wars during the 17th and 18th centuries gradually transformed the absolutist monarchies and empires of western Europe into nation-states, with many having their own imperialist and colonialist designs outside the continent. By contrast, the Habsburg, Ottoman, and Russian empires remained as essentially autocratic monarchies and multi-national empires in the heart of Europe. They became increasingly racked by internal conflicts and troubled by nascent national liberation movements, in the midst of rapidly changing economic conditions.

Nationalism developed in western Europe as an essentially bourgeois conception for promoting national integration; it thereby preceded the birth and expansion of nationalist sentiments throughout eastern Europe. The region was dominated by outside powers and the elementary cohesion of cultural communities had not given way to a strong ethnic-national consciousness. Few national leaders emerged until the 19th century and the population structure remained primarily agrarian. There was also a division between the so-called "historic" and "non-historic" nations; the latter had little tradition or experience of independence and statehood to draw upon from the pre-imperial era.

The nationalist revolts of 1848-1849 shook the Habsburg empire to its foundations. They resulted from an assortment of tensions and trends: anti-absolutism, growing national and ethnic consciousness, an economic and agricultural crisis, and the emergence of a fresh generation of frustrated intellectuals searching for new ideologies and bases of power. But the Habsburgs survived these initial convulsions because the revolts were dispersed and uncoordinated, while Emperor Franz-Joseph proved to be a determined and astute ruler. Vienna also obtained assistance from Russia which feared that its own imperial position was under threat in the region. The Habsburgs initiated a land reform program that largely helped to neutralize the peasantry. They also applied a policy of divide and rule, playing off one nationality against another by providing selective economic and political benefits. This aggravated inter-ethnic resentments and animosities among some burgeoning east European nations. Although the 19th century "springtime of nations" proved short-lived, Austrian policy merely subdued national aspirations without satisfying them, and reactionary state policies simply fueled ethnic frustrations.

Some compromises were again reached by Vienna with Budapest in 1867, when the *Ausgleich* (compromise) was arranged. Austria-Hungary became a "dual monarchy," amidst complex administrative arrangements, and the empire was divided into two parts. This new structure intensified hostilities between Budapest and the subordinate Romanian, Slovak, and Croatian populations. In fact, the *Ausgleich* failed to satisfy most of the smaller nationalities and the Hungarians themselves increasingly sought full independence as well as far-reaching economic and social reforms.

The Turks crossed into the Balkans in the middle of the 14th century. Their crushing defeat of the Serbs at Kosovo in 1389 opened the way for the subjugation of south eastern Europe and initiated several centuries of Ottoman rule.[6] In general, Turkish overlordship did not destroy the ethnicity, culture, and religion of the subject peoples, and the overwhelming majority maintained their Christian faith. Only the Slavic Bosnians and Albanians converted to Islam in large numbers. Pro-Turkish local leaders were given substantial estates and provided soldiers and services to the Sultan in times of war, while the peasantry did not become serfs on the pattern of western Europe's Middle Ages. One important consequence of Ottoman rule was that most Balkan peoples did not develop a native class of aristocratic landowners or subsequently a strong bourgeois class.

The northernmost expansion of Turkish power reached southern Russia, Ukraine, and Hungary. The Turks defeated Magyar forces at the battle of Mohacs in 1526, after which they occupied Transylvania and most parts of Hungary. But after the Turkish advance was stopped at Vienna in 1683, with help from Polish contingents, the Ottoman's European empire began to contract. Turkish rule was increasingly resented as alien and unprogressive, especially after the rise of European nationalism during the 18th and 19th centuries. The Turkish empire continued to weaken from within as its war machine lost momentum, its economy deteriorated, and its central authorities grew increasingly corrupt.

The Ottoman empire underwent substantial shrinkage in the 18th and 19th centuries. By 1887, several Balkan states had gained independence from the Turks, including Greece, Romania, Serbia, and Montenegro.[7] Albania, Macedonia, and Bulgaria remained under Turkish tutelage but indigenous national movements were slowly expanding. During the 19th century, the new or reformulated states received assistance from either Russia, France, Austria, or Britain, each of which maintained their own imperial interests vis-à-vis the Ottomans. For instance, the Russians exploited pan-Slavic and pro-Bulgarian or pro-Serbian policies to expand their influence throughout the Balkans. But the Russian Tsars did not hesitate to betray any of their provisional allies if this coincided with their long-term imperial ambitions.

In the 17th and 18th centuries, the German lands were divided into several dozen duchies and principalities. The strongest state, aside from the Austrian Habsburgs, was Prussia whose ruler Prince Otto von Bismarck united the German lands during the 1870s.[8] Prussia also swallowed up western Poland during the course of that country's 18th century partitions. After the accession of Bismarck and the rise of German nationalism in the late 19th century, a policy of germanization was launched in Prussia's Polish dominions, particularly in the religious, educational, linguistic, and cultural realms. After the 1870s, Prussia-Germany became the dominant German power in Central Europe and the Austrian Habsburgs had to partially subordinate their interest to those of Berlin.

Following the gradual disintegration of Mongol and Tartar domination, from the 15th century onward, Russian princes in Kiev, Moscow, and St. Petersburg began to build a highly centralized, unified, autocratic, and expansionist empire. This was at a time when an unstable Polish Commonwealth began to dissolve from within and other ethnic groups had not developed sufficiently strong state and military structures to challenge Russian-Muscovite expansion over the vast eastern steppes.[9] During three partitions, in 1772, 1793, and 1795, Russia, Prussia and Austria carved up Poland and erased the country from the map. The Russian section was initially loosely administered, but after unsuccessful Polish revolts in the 1830s and 1860s, the Tsars clamped down and ruled Poland as another Russian province.

In the late 19th century, Austria increasingly feared Russian pre-dominance in south eastern Europe as well as the emergence of a large south Slav state following the disintegration of the Ottoman empire. Vienna annexed the province of Bosnia-Hercegovina and applied increasing pressures on an independent Serbia. After the assassination of Austrian Crown Prince Ferdinand by Bosnian terrorists in 1914, Vienna threatened Serbia, the Russian army mobilized, Germany lined up with Austria, and World War One was launched. The war lasted for four years, during which time the shape of eastern Europe changed dramatically. The defeated Central Powers (Germany and Austria), and their allies such as Hungary and Bulgaria, as well as revolutionary Russia, lost a great deal of territory in the post-war peace settlements while their military and economic power was severely constrained.

As German, Russian, and Austrian forces retreated, an independent Polish state was recreated in central Europe. The new country was smaller than pre-partition Poland as it had permanently lost large portions of its former eastern provinces. The Versailles peace treaty emasculated Germany, and this grievance was used as a major pretext by German nationalists during the 1920s and 1930s, for the purposes of renewed expansion eastward. Meanwhile, the collapse of Tsarist authority and mass unrest in the Russian army and throughout society provided fertile ground for revolution. In 1917, as governmental authority collapsed, Lenin's Bolshevik Party staged a *coup d'etat* and began to impose a Communist dictatorship in a newly formed Soviet Union which incorporated most of the former Russian empire. During the 1920s and 1930s, the Soviet Union went through traumatic state-induced disasters; these included civil war, forced collectivization, mass purges, and the enforced transfer of entire nations. A ruthless dictatorship was established that, in essence, continued the expansionist imperial objectives of Tsarist Russia.

During World War One, Austrian forces suffered serious military defeats in the Balkans. The Habsburg empire disintegrated and Vienna sued for peace, relinquishing enormous territories in central and southern Europe. The new state of Czechoslovakia was created, consisting of the historic lands of the Bohemian Crown (Bohemia, Moravia, and Austrian Silesia), and the formerly Slovak and Ruthenian areas of northern Hungary. Budapest lost about two thirds of its territory under the Treaty of Trianon in 1920, as punishment for its alliance with Austria and Germany; the abandoned areas included Slovakia (which reverted to Czechoslovakia) Transylvania (assigned to Romania) and Croatia-Slavonia (transferred to Yugoslavia). Romania was greatly enlarged, acquiring Austrian Bukovina, all of historic Transylvania and parts of the Banat (from Hungary), Bessarabia (from Russia) and southern Dobrudja (from Bulgaria). A new state of Yugoslavia (or land of the South Slavs) also emerged after World War One. It included an enlarged Serbia, Croatia-Slavonia and Slovenia (from Austro-Hungary), Bosnia-Hercegovina, Dalmatia, Montenegro, and Macedonia. Bulgaria lost some of its territories, including parts of Macedonia to Yugoslavia, as well as all of western Thrace to Greece, because it sided with Austria and Germany during the war and lost the Second Balkan war that it had launched in 1913.

All the east European states sustained enormous damage during the war, in terms of manpower and material losses. The crashing defeat of all the major empires that had dominated the region for centuries resulted in an enormous power vacuum that was haphazardly filled by the newly created nation-states. Two types of states existed during the period between the two World Wars: states that had acquired more or less what they wanted territorially and were determined to preserve their new frontiers (Poland, Czechoslovakia, Romania, and Yugoslavia), and states that had lost substantial territories in post-war treaties and sought to eventually regain them (Hungary and Bulgaria).

Germany and Russia were only temporarily weakened. During the interwar period both powers began to prey on the instabilities of the young east European governments and exploited many of the long-standing animosities between the newly liberated nations. The new administrations inherited largely undeveloped economies in which rudimentary forms of agriculture predominated. In fact, outside of Czechoslovakia, about 80% of the population was engaged in agriculture, and apart from Czechoslovakia all of them lagged behind western Europe in terms of technology and productivity. The class structure in most states had not been greatly affected by the industrial revolution. Industry remained underdeveloped and regionally confined to the capital and a few urbanized locations, while the bourgeoisie and the industrial proletariat remained small. The bulk of the farming communities either consisted of self-sufficient small homesteads or peasants entrapped in tenancy relations with medium and large landowners. Much of the countryside also suffered from overpopulation and a chronic absence of technical modernization.[10]

All the east European economies were hit by the Great Depression in the 1920s, as well as by the upheavals in the international division of labor and the severe lack of Western investment. This exacerbated the problem of capital shortage and of poor access to foreign markets. Moreover, there was little regional economic cooperation, while each government practiced some form of import protectionism. During the 1930s, the region's economies were increasingly tied to Germany through various trading arrangements, as Berlin pursued its long-term plan to integrate eastern Europe into a pan-German Third Reich.

Throughout the 1920s and 1930s, the initially democratic administrations of eastern Europe descended into authoritarian quasi-dictatorships, whether of the political, military, or royalist varieties, which sometimes bordered on fascism.[11] The one exception was Czechoslovakia, where democratic traditions survived largely intact. But these were not systematic or totalitarian fascist regimes, as in Germany, Italy, or Spain, because political pluralism was generally tolerated, human rights were not comprehensively violated, and there was no radical rightist ideology to mobilize the masses in service of the Party-state. Under increasing German influence, several states assumed more fascist and racist leanings, particularly those that had felt most aggrieved by post-war peace settlements or saw their chance for independent statehood under German and Italian protection; these included Hungary, Slovakia, and Croatia.

As Nazi Germany and Soviet Russia revived their strength and resuscitated their expansionist ambitions during the 1930s, the east European states found themselves weak, fragmented, vulnerable, and isolated. In the inter-war years, they had failed to achieve any meaningful regional solidarity or a system of common security to defend themselves against large, predatory neighbors. The west European powers were also unwilling to provide them with meaningful political and security guarantees. The Little Entente between Czechoslovakia, Romania, and Yugoslavia was designed as a defensive cordon against Hungary; but Poland refused to join and the association did not provide for mutual assistance against Germany or Russia. The Balkan Entente between Romania, Yugoslavia, Turkey, and Greece was directed against Bulgaria; it also failed to engender long-term cooperation or significantly contribute to regional unity. Increasing German pressures pushed several countries toward accommodation with Berlin, in the absence of viable Western protectors and a lack of regional unity. The states that did resist German pressure or stayed neutral were invaded and crushed by the Nazis at the outset of World War Two. In fact, by 1941 all the east European countries were either under direct Nazi control—Poland, the Czech lands, Serbia-Yugoslavia, and Albania—or had become Axis dependencies—Hungary, Slovakia, Romania, Croatia, and Bulgaria.

The Communist regimes installed in eastern Europe by the Red Army at the close of World War Two operated on the premise that social classes and not nationalities were the moving forces and principal actors in socio-economic development and foreign affairs.[12] This meant that national aspirations had to be submerged in the interests of the "internationalist" interests of the proletariat, in actual fact, the interests of the ruling Leninist vanguard Parties that took their orders from Moscow. State borders were, in some cases, redrawn to coincide with Soviet geopolitical interests and to placate some latent national yearnings. Several nations, including Poland, Czechoslovakia, Hungary, and Romania, lost territories to the USSR. A few states gained some lands at the expense of neighbors, but domestic and international disputes were not resolved but simply submerged and suppressed. Purges and campaigns were also periodically launched to eliminate "national deviations" or pro-independence sympathies among nationalists, minority groups, and various "class enemies." Under the Stalinist tyranny and the Brezhnevite *status quo,* national aspirations were depicted as "bourgeois relics" that would disappear as the proletarianized citizenry rapidly merged into a trans-national socialist nation.

The ruling Communist Parties implemented policies designed to overcome inequalities based on national origins while forging supra-national political, economic, and class interests. Some of the minority groups with grievances against the pre-war systems were also employed by Moscow as loyalist cadres willing to implement Communist policies. The Kremlin became the final arbiter in any international disputes and sought to prevent any regional conflicts among its satellites from upsetting its hegemonistic "internationalist" goals.

While the Soviet presence reduced possible secessionist and irredentist demands among the east European states, some traditional animosities were clearly manipulated by Communists where it suited Moscow's objectives. For example, the potential or imaginary German threat was constantly exploited, especially vis-à-vis the Poles and Czechs, in order to portray the Red Army and local Communists as protectors of national sovereignty. But the Soviets clearly failed to forge some supra-national consciousness in eastern Europe or to instill a sense of voluntary loyalty to the Soviet Union. Although nationalism was relegated by Communist ideology to a "secondary phenomenon," it was nevertheless recognized as a powerful mobilizer of public opinion. It was, therefore, often employed by local Party leaders after Stalin's death in 1953, in pursuit of their self-proclaimed "national roads to socialism." More fervent nationalist positions were adopted by Communist regimes that obtained some measure of political independence from Moscow and who were not dependent on Soviet military power, particularly in Albania, Yugoslavia, and Romania.

The Specter of Nationalism

The collapse of the artificial Soviet bloc alliance at the end of the 1980s, liberated all the east European states and released various ethno-nationalist aspirations. Nationalism consists of an extremely flexible, elusive, and variable system of values and objectives. It can be combined with various ideologies and is an expression of diverse interests, grievances, and goals. Ethnic nationalism may be a positive or a negative force, it can be aggressive or defensive, and it contains both rational and emotional elements. It may be consistent or unpredictable, it has moments of intensity and periods of relative passivity, and it is often contradictory.[13] Nationalism may be a binding, cohesive, motivating force for asserting ethnic identity, regaining national sovereignty and statehood, and limiting the influence of outside powers. It may instill a sense of patriotism, community loyalty, pride in ethnic history and cultural achievements, and a willingness to defend deeply held principles. During especially traumatic and revolutionary periods, shared ethnicity often provides an important anchor of stability and continuity. A sense of communal identity compensates for feelings of confusion and uncertainty in a rapidly changing world.[14]

In eastern Europe several ethnic groups had some form of state structure before the advent and expansion of multi-ethnic empires such as the Ottoman, Austrian, Prussian, and Russian. But some nationalities were more easily digested, as their national identities were embryonic and lacked a solid organizational foundation. In some cases, nationalism was actually born and strengthened during the closing stages of the imperial era. Several ethnic groups gained a distinctive national consciousness under foreign occupation, particularly during the revolutionary "age of nationalism" in the 19th century. Although nationhood and statehood became separated and submerged within Europe's multi-national empires, varying degrees of ethnic identity were preserved through distinct languages, religions, and culture, alternative educational and religious systems, and separate social organizations. East European nationalism grew partly in response to foreign domination and it became a movement of protest, particularly among ethnic groups that had lost their political sovereignty.[15]

Ethnic nationalism, as an ideology, is not necessarily a xenophobic phenomenon. Indeed, during the 19th century, nationalism developed into an international revolutionary creed aimed at destroying the power of ossified autocratic empires and liberating the subject peoples. It was advocated by leading intellectuals in both western and eastern Europe, and nationalists from one country sometimes fought for the national independence of other groups. Nationalism was also used to transcend class differences and served as a bond between rulers and ruled and between an assortment of socio-economic groups. It crystallized into a loose ideology that could mobilize populations for specific objectives, where a foreign government was unable to elicit such commitments. It ensured prolonged sacrifices for patriotic causes that could be either positive or negative in their effect; for instance, they could help preserve an oppressive system or radically liberalize the political structure.

Nationalism may become a negative force where it assumes a pronounced ethnocentric bias, asserting the superiority of any one culture, language, or religion. In trying to forge a common political unit and strengthen national identity vis-à-vis outsiders, nationalist leaders may deliberately exclude or discriminate against non-ethnics who are depicted as disloyal alien elements.[16] They operate on the axiom that a perceived foreign or domestic threat tends to unite a population. This can lead to the oppression of other nationalities and ethnic minorities and even engender hostility toward neighboring states. The persecution of minorities by newly independent nations may also be a form of aggressive compensation for their own prior oppression, whether at the hands of this or some other nation. It can also be an indication of political immaturity or oversensitivity, sometimes based on exaggerated fears of domination, absorption, or extinction.

The growth of national consciousness among one group tends to breed nationalism and a search for self-identity among neighboring groups for purposes of protection and self-enhancement. Recently revived nationalism can be vibrant and confident without necessarily being chauvinistic, or it may be insecure and breed paranoia and aggravate ethnic, cultural, or religious divisions. More aggressive nationalisms are often characteristic among groups with larger, territorially compact, and potentially more threatening minorities, especially where there is competition over scarce resources and where there are deep rooted historical conflicts and seemingly irreconcilable cultural differences.

Nationalism can be manipulated by governments and political movements for defensive or offensive purposes, and it can hold up progress toward international integration by fostering isolationist currents and preventing the voluntary surrender of some components of national sovereignty. Moreover, if political life is organized primarily according to ethnic criteria, with distinct and exclusivist ethnic parties, then power may become polarized with little opportunity for compromise or the alteration of political elites and with a restricted input of minority parties in government decision making. However, ethnic-based parties in a well-balanced democracy, depending on their size and the country's electoral laws, may receive adequate representation in national parliaments and local administrations to influence government decisions and even help to resolve domestic nationality conflicts. On the other hand, nationalist organizations in an undeveloped democracy may claim growing official repression and discrimination. This, in turn, can have a major impact on foreign policy by increasing tensions with traditionally antagonistic neighbors, particularly where oppressed ethnic minorities appeal for some outside assistance and protection.

On the international arena, exclusivist and short-sighted nationalism may prevent the formation of valuable alliances between neighboring states. During the inter-war period, as Nazi Germany and Soviet Russia revived their strength, eastern Europe lacked dependable regional alliances and found itself fragmented and vulnerable to outside pressures. The region failed to achieve any degree of solidarity or mutual assistance and was beset by multiple rivalries. For instance, the Balkan Entente between Romania, Yugoslavia, Turkey, and Greece, or the Little Entente between Czechoslovakia, Romania, and Yugoslavia did not generate lasting cooperation or long-term commitments, and did not contribute to east European unity. Each state, therefore, became susceptible to outside manipulation, political influence, and eventual domination.

Some nationalist movements have tried to transcend ethnic, cultural, or linguistic borders, and claimed leadership in various pan-Slavic or pan-Germanic movements, either because they felt too weak to act alone or needed a seemingly legitimate pretext for expansion. Some nations expressed claims to an "historic mission," whether as bastions of Christianity versus Islam or Catholicism versus Orthodoxy (or vice versa), or as representatives of Western civilization against "barbarian" domination (Turk, Mongol, Russian), or as the "chosen" or "martyred" nation, in order to stir national passions and international sympathy. Nationalism may also be manipulated by outside powers to obtain influence and advantage over a country or parts of its territories. Some governments have deliberately fanned inter-ethnic cleavages to gain political and economic benefits and to justify political or military intervention, while claiming that they are simply seeking to prevent or resolve conflicts. In general, democratic and freely elected governments do not go to war with each other and do not engage in aggression against their neighbors. Nonetheless, even a democratically elected administration facing internal unrest may employ chauvinistic nationalism and exploit popular fears or prejudices against an internal or external enemy to distract attention from its growing domestic problems. In addition, an authoritarian regime can provoke inter-state conflicts even though its neighbors may be democratic and non-expansionist.

Religion has proved to be both an integrative and a divisive factor in eastern Europe. Although the region escaped some of the worst excesses of the west European Reformation and Counter-Reformation, religious differences added to the diversity and complexity of the region and invariably served to widen ethnic and national rifts. Eastern Europe is divided between a Catholic and Protestant north and west and an Orthodox Christian south and east. In addition, pockets of Islamic populations have existed in the Balkans for centuries, as well as Jewish communities scattered throughout the region. East European nationalisms have often been closely bound up with Christian denominations and in some cases, national governments have been interwoven with religious hierarchies. National-based Churches played an important role in transforming ethnic groups into national communities, by codifying language scripts and national histories and even providing long-term community leadership. In some countries, the Church became a primary source of ethnic self-identity, cultural defense, and a virtual surrogate governmental authority against occupying powers: for example, this was the case in Catholic Poland against Protestant Prussia and Orthodox Russia, and in Orthodox Bulgaria against Islamic Turkey.

Various Churches became closely intertwined with national identity and helped to foster a group's ethnic and cultural distinctiveness. The Serbian Orthodox Church was founded in the 12th century and became virtually synonymous with the Serbian nation in opposition to Muslim Turks and Catholic Austrians. The Hussite Protestant reform movement in the 16th century developed a close identification with Bohemian-Czech nationality against the Catholic Habsburgs. Religion has, in fact, endowed nationalism and ethnic peculiarity with additional sources of divine and non-secular legitimacy, particularly where an acephalous Church became associated with a specific nation in contra-distinction to neighbors of another faith. National Churches could buttress the position of a central government, but they could also seriously undermine the stability of multi-ethnic empires where they supported the aspirations of various ethnic minorities.

A Church or religious denomination may have both a national and international dimension. The latter may endow national aspirations with wider sources of legitimacy and rally neighboring nations confessing the same faith against alien religious entities. As with ethnic nationalism, religious nationalism can have both positive and negative qualities. On the positive side, Churches can ensure cultural and linguistic survival and strengthen an ethnic renaissance. They can buttress calls for national self-determination and help transcend national peculiarities through a stress on an international community of believers. Religious leaders have, in some instances, been at the forefront of major educational, literary, and cultural activities, and some charismatic clergymen have also stepped into national leadership roles in absence of a coherent national intelligentsia and a viable political elite.

On the negative side, there remains the potential of religiously sanctioned ethnocentrism and intolerance against other religious communities or against atheists. Religious belief may raise national destiny to an exalted and infallible concept, engaged in a life or death struggle with other nationalities and faiths. National religious messianism and fundamentalism may be exhibited where a particular nation is believed to possess a God-given mission to proselyte and expand, whether by persuasion or outright coercion. There is an equal danger of too close an identification of Church and state, in which prolonged clerical interference in governmental affairs results in the manipulation of state policy to promote Church interests and discriminate against non-believers. The employment of religious beliefs, symbols, and institutions by the state may be useful in ethnically and religiously homogeneous countries to gain credibility and legitimacy for the government. But in a multi-ethnic, multi-religious state, the favoring of one denomination over another through political, social, economic, educational, and religious discrimination may incite serious social and ethnic conflicts.

The defeat of the imperial Central Powers at the close of World War One liberated numerous nationalities, altered national boundaries, and effected inter-ethnic relations throughout eastern Europe. In several instances, as new states were established, there were widescale population transfers and border shifts. Some countries became ethnically fairly homogeneous, others emerged as extremely heterogenous entities, while some peoples failed to obtain full political recognition through independent statehood.[17] Many former minority groups in the old empires now assumed majority status, while large segments of some majority groups were divided and separated and became sizable minorities within the new nation states.[18] Of the approximately 115 million "liberated peoples," about 24 million became national minorities within the new countries. Redrawn frontiers placed some large minorities under foreign rule. It was virtually impossible to draw up ethnically uniform states that would be simultaneously economically viable and strategically protectable. Some areas were so complex and ethnically mixed, that only a policy of massive and intricate population adjustments would have sufficiently adjusted the balance. But this would have severely disrupted economic and social life and proved highly costly and ultimately impractical. The complexity was compounded by the fact that in many territories two or more groups had equally valid historical claims to indigenous status.

After the fall of the empires in 1918, several previously suppressed nationalities regained their statehood (Poles, Czechs), or combined to form new states (Yugoslavia, Czechoslovakia), while others became minorities in the new states (Macedonians, Belarusans, Ukrainians) and began to suffer from discrimination and the chauvinism of dominant groups. Some nationalities like the Ukrainians in Poland or the Hungarians in Romania were denied political autonomy or were considered unripe for self-government and independent statehood. During the inter-war period, the League of Nations sought to strengthen and insure minority protection in eastern Europe by obliging all the re-created states to sign treaties or make declarations guaranteeing the protection of minority rights, such as religious freedom, equal treatment under law, and the use of language in schools. While this seemed fair in principle, it created a great deal of local resentment because the western powers, including Germany, were not obliged to comply with such provisions. Moreover, some states exploited and aggravated nationality grievances to undermine neighboring governments and question their borders.

Political, territorial, and demographic changes after World War One were also accompanied by major socio-economic transformations. Leaders of the majority groups used their newly acquired power to redistribute economic assets and educational opportunities to their advantage, and often to the disadvantage of minority groups. Moreover, all states entered the post-War era with serious economic problems and, in some cases widespread social unrest verging on revolution. The wartime destruction added to years of neglect and the lack of economic modernization, particularly in the ex-Ottoman and ex-Russian areas. Poor material conditions were magnified by a lack of industrialization, by tremendous population pressures through the growth of a surplus peasantry and insufficient non-rural employment, by the lack of capital and investment, and by unsatisfactory land reforms. The internal integration of new states, and even of specific ethnic groups which had previously been divided between the old empires, proved problematic as inter-regional rivalries came to the fore. Such problems were intensified where states encompassed large minorities with a history of inter-group and ethnic rivalry.

Minority nationalism may be a critical ingredient of domestic politics, as well as a tool of foreign policy manipulated by hostile governments. Eastern Europe has a history of autonomist, secessionist, and irredentist movements. Such movements can be fomented by antagonistic states to promote instability on route to possible annexation. Even manifestations of non-separatist ethnic aspirations among minorities, especially when backed by outside powers or international pressures, can be perceived as subversive by an unstable government and the local majority population. If left unchecked these developments could result in the curtailment of central controls over a minority region or even the disintegration of the state. The existence of ethnic or cultural minorities resisting assimilationist trends may be a serious obstacle to national integration, especially if they claim some form of cultural or political autonomy that the government is pressurized to grant. This can, in turn, fuel inter-communal conflict and spark protests against government policy.[19] Such manifestations of popular opposition may result in greater discrimination or repression against the minority population.

South east Europe, in particular, possesses an uneven record in protecting minority rights. Such shortcomings have been exploited by outside powers to press for territorial revisions and annexations. This is partly where the term "Balkanization" originates, as a negative description of persistent ethnic clashes and a dangerous manifestation of international instability.[20] Minorities could, in theory, have a positive role to play as a bridge between neighboring states in furthering cooperation and mutual understanding. Unfortunately, such a role has invariably been submerged in the region's multifarious domestic and regional conflicts.

Demands for minority rights can be divided into two broad kinds and they may be mutually conflictive. First, is the right to fully equal opportunities in education, economic life, culture, and political participation, as well as non-discrimination based on ethnicity, culture, or creed. Second, is the right to special protection, preferential access to certain resources, and positive discrimination or "affirmative action" for minority members, reinforced by government funding to preserve and promote minority cultures. The application of the second principle could lead to profound resentments among the majority population or among other minorities whose interests are not favored and promoted by government policies.

Nationalism among a minority ethnic group may be a valuable lever for community mobilization and for gaining political influence in the state.[21] Conversely, the withholding of concessions and resources to minority leaders could increase anti-centralist feelings, undermine the legitimacy of the government, and lead to more radical demands for autonomy or even secession.[22] In such instances, demands for ethnic autonomy may become more than just a means for protecting the cultural identity of distinct population groups. Autonomism itself may be divided into two general types: cultural and political. Cultural autonomy implies control by local ethnic leaders over all aspects of education, the mass media, and a variety of cultural activities. Political autonomy is potentially more far-reaching and covers every aspect of social, economic, and administrative life, short of national defense and foreign affairs.[23] In practice, autonomism covers a spectrum of ethnic "self-determination," from modest demands for linguistic rights to calls for outright self-rule within a federal or confederal structure.

Under the Communist systems, various social and cultural organizations were established for recognized minority nationalities. But its leaders were either co-opted and directly served the interests of the government among the minority population, or they remained neutral and focused on innocuous cultural, social, educational, and folkloristic activities. Nonetheless, some minority leaders were able to gain a degree of independence and successfully pressed for various concessions from the state to help preserve or strengthen a group's distinct identity. In most cases, however, there were clear limits to the development of ethnic rights, while national distinctiveness was periodically under direct attack from a centralizing and all-encompassing state. Clear prohibitions were placed on organizing separate political parties or independent organizations based on ethnic principles. Likewise, restrictions were upheld on any campaigns for meaningful territorial autonomy and self-administration in minority areas.

After the 1989 democratic revolutions in eastern Europe and the evaporation of the one-party state, the floodgates were opened for national self-assertion and the revival of ethnic consciousness.[24] A plethora of ethnic-based national organizations quickly sprung to life in each country, representing both the majority and minority populations. While some remained predominantly focused on cultural, linguistic, educational, and religious rejuvenation, others pressed for more wide-ranging political and economic concessions. While some organizations were more easily accommodated in the emerging system of political pluralism, others were viewed with suspicion and distrust by influential elements of the majority population. In the midst of a destabilizing and uncertain period of capitalist and democratic restoration, ethnic politics began to occupy an important role not only for minority groupings seeking greater self-determination, but also for some majority populations fearful of losing their influence and access to resources.

The unravelling of the Soviet bloc and the disintegration of Communist controls has released previously submerged national ambitions. It has stimulated the formulation of new foreign policies among all the east European states. Emerging nationalisms in the post-Communist period are unlikely to replicate the often destructive historical disputes. Nevertheless, some domestic and international conflicts may have the potential of escalating into political crises, military threats, and even low-intensity armed clashes. Political leaders searching for popular support in the midst of often severe social and economic disruption could capitalize on nationalist feelings and exploit the presence of minority scapegoats. Extremist groups may also attempt to take advantage of public disorientation during the destabilizing reform process. In order to gain public influence, assorted populists and militant nationalists, sometimes in league with the remnants of the ex-Communist apparatus, may launch attacks on various domestic minorities and historical foreign adversaries. Perceived internal and external threats could, in turn, act as a catalyst for the emergence of authoritarian regimes demanding "national unity" and displaying intolerance toward domestic criticism and political diversity. Such developments could slow down progress toward the institutionalization of political pluralism and the emergence of productive market economies in some parts of eastern Europe.

Notes

1. For a valuable early history of the Central European region consult J. P. Malbry *In Search of the Indo-Europeans: Language, Archaeology and Myth* (New York: Thames and Hudson, 1989).

2. See Francis Owen, *The Germanic People: Their Origin, Expansion, and Culture* (New York: Dorset Press, 1960).

3. Check Francis Dvornik, *The Slavs in European History and Civilization* (New Brunswick: Rutgers University Press, 1962).

4. See George Ostrogorsky, *History of the Byzantine State* (New Brunswick: Rutgers University Press, 1969).

5. See Robert A. Kann, *A History of the Habsburg Empire, 1526-1918* (Berkeley: University of California Press, 1974); and Robert A. Kann and Zdenek V. David, *The Peoples of the Eastern Habsburg Lands, 1526-1918* (Seattle: University of Washington Press, 1984).

6. Consult Halil Inalcik, *The Ottoman Empire: The Classical Age, 1300-1600* (New York: Praeger, 1973).

7. See Charles and Barbara Jelavich, *The Establishment of the Balkan National States, 1804-1920, A History of East Central Europe, Vol. VIII* (Seattle: University of Washington Press, 1986); and Barbara Jelavich, *History of the Balkans: Eighteenth and Nineteenth Centuries, Volume 1* (Cambridge: Cambridge University Press, 1989).

8. See H. W. Koch, *A History of Prussia* (New York: Dorset Press, 1978).

9. Consult Edward C. Thaden, *Russia's Western Borderlands, 1710-1870* (Princeton, New Jersey: Princeton University Press, 1984).

10. For background read Daniel Chirot (Ed), *The Origins of Backwardness in Eastern Europe: Economics and Politics From the Middle Ages Until the Early 20th Century* (Berkeley: University of California Press, 1989).

11. For essential reading see Joseph Rothschild, *East Central Europe Between the Two World Wars, A History of East Central Europe, Vol. IX* (Seattle: University of Washington Press, 1974); Barbara Jelavich, *History of the Balkans: Twentieth Century, Vol. 2* (Cambridge: Cambridge University Press, 1989); and Hugh Seton-Watson, *Eastern Europe Between the Wars, 1918-1941* (New York: Harper Torchbooks, 1967).

12. For valuable histories of Communist eastern Europe see J. F. Brown *Eastern Europe and Communist Rule* (Durham: Duke University Press, 1988); and Zbigniew Brzezinski, *The Soviet Bloc: Unity and Conflict* (Cambridge, MA: Harvard University Press, 1967).

13. A useful discussion can be found in Woodrow J. Kuhns, "Political Nationalism in Contemporary Eastern Europe," in Jeffrey Simon and Trond Gilberg (Eds.), *Security Implications of Nationalism in Eastern Europe* (Boulder: Westview Press, 1986), pp. 81-107.

14. For a valuable evaluation of the significance of ethnicity in the modern world see Cynthia H. Enloe, *Ethnic Conflict and Political Development* (Lanham: New York University Press of America, 1986).

15. See Peter F. Sugar, "External and Domestic Roots of East European Nationalism," in Peter F. Sugar and Ivo J. Lederer (Eds.), *Nationalism in Eastern Europe* (Seattle: University of Washington Press, 1969), pp. 3-54.

16. Gregory Gleason, "Nationalism in Our Time," *Current World Leaders,* Vol. 34, No. 2, April 1991, International Academy at Santa Barbara, California.

17. For a trenchant analysis of minority and nationality problems see Trond Gilberg, "State Policy, Ethnic Persistence and Nationality Formation in Eastern Europe," in Peter F. Sugar (Ed.), *Ethnic Diversity and Conflict in Eastern Europe* (Santa Barbara, CA.: ABC-CLIO, 1980), pp. 185-235.

18. Consult Stephan M. Horak, *East European National Minorities, 1919-1980: A Handbook* (Littleton, Colorado: Libraries Unlimited Inc., 1985).

19. A valuable evaluation of state formation is contained in Anthony M. Birch, *Nationalism and National Integration* (London: Unwin Hyman, 1989).

20. As Brass points out, the term "Balkanization" gained negative connotations this century because of the persistent ethnic conflicts in the region before World War Two. It continues to be employed as a pretext for opposing minority demands and supporting the integration of existing multi-national states. See Paul R. Brass, "Ethnic Groups and Nationalities," in Peter F. Sugar (Ed.), *Ethnic Diversity and Conflict in Eastern Europe* (Santa Barbara, CA.: ABC-CLIO, 1980), p. 61.

21. See John Breuilly, *Nationalism and the State* (New York: St. Martin's Press, 1982).

22. For an invaluable analysis of autonomist and separatist movements see Colin H. Williams (Ed.), *National Separatism* (Vancouver: University of British Columbia Press, 1982).

23. See Anthony D. Smith, *The Ethnic Revival* (Cambridge: Cambridge University Press, 1981), pp. 8-25.

24. Useful accounts of the collapse of Communist rule in eastern Europe can be found in J. F. Brown, *Surge to Freedom: The End of Communist Rule in Eastern Europe* (Durham: Duke University Press, 1991); and Judy Batt, *East Central Europe From Reform to Transformation* (New York: Council on Foreign Relations Press, 1991).

2

Post-Soviet Enmities

The collapse of the Soviet bloc drastically altered relations between Moscow and all the east European capitals. While there were rapid formal improvements at the inter-governmental level, some anxieties persisted that a conservative Communist backlash in the Kremlin could again imperil relations and even derail the region's democratic reform programs. Some states were also embroiled in several unresolved disputes with Moscow, revolving around questions of military security and the withdrawal of Red Army troops stationed on their territories. The attempted hard-line Soviet coup in the summer of 1991 highlighted the persistent fears in the region over a sudden Kremlin reversal. Although the coup failure reassured the new democratic governments that there was no imminent danger of a forceful restoration of Soviet domination, it also served to emphasize a series of additional threats to east European stability. In particular, the accelerating disintegration of the political, economic, and military structures of the USSR greatly raised the specter of a major spillover resulting from a comprehensive economic collapse and widening social unrest. Moreover, growing national independence among the post-Soviet republics also increased prospects for both regional cooperation and for new sources of conflict between the east European states and the new republican governments. In exploring the most contentious international issues, it is useful in each case to briefly consider the historical background to the current manifestations of discord.

Poland and the Commonwealth

Although Polish-Russian antagonisms can be traced back to the Middle Ages, more intensive conflicts began in the 17th century, particularly over the vast intermediate territories claimed by both protagonists. During the 18th century, absolutist Muscovite Russia expanded at the expense of the eroding Polish Commonwealth, and after the three partitions of 1772, 1793, and 1795, Poland was divided between Russia, Austria, and Prussia. The Russian portion, with its administrative center in Warsaw, came to be known as the

Congress Kingdom. During the 19th century, the Poles staged several failed uprisings against Russian rule. But the aftermath of each insurrection brought severe repression and the banishment of insurgent political and military leaders. Poland regained its independence in 1918, after the defeat of Germany and Austria and the withdrawal of Russia from the World War One battlefields in the wake of the Bolshevik takeover.[1] Warsaw and Moscow then fought a two year war over disputed territories in Ukraine and Belarus. The new Polish state sought to regain its pre-partition lands, while the Russian Communists endeavored to push their revolution westward. After a stalemate was reached in the hostilities, the 1921 Treaty of Riga demarcated a new border acceptable to both sides.

During the inter-war period, Poland was embroiled in numerous disputes with its eastern neighbors, including the newly independent Lithuania and the Soviet Union, whose Belarusan and Ukrainian republics bordered on Poland. The dispute with Lithuania centered on the city of Vilnius (Wilno in Polish) and surrounding areas that were predominantly Polish but historically Lithuanian. After Polish forces captured the city in 1920, diplomatic relations between the two states were severed and contacts remained strained as Lithuania resisted Warsaw's overtures for a new confederal arrangement. A considerable Lithuanian population in north eastern Poland was also subject to a campaign of polonization which bred further inter-state resentments. After World War Two, Lithuania regained the Vilnius region but was, in turn, annexed by the USSR and transformed into a new Soviet republic. Despite subsequent population transfers, sizable Polish and Lithuanian minorities were left on both sides of the frontier.

The disputed Belarusan area was divided between Poland and the USSR under the Treaty of Riga, and a large Belarusan minority remained within Polish borders. It underwent a campaign of assimilation but had no independent Belarusan state to campaign for its rights. Ukraine was also divided between Warsaw and Moscow after achieving a brief period of independence in the wake of World War One. Polish-Ukrainian relations were soured because initial promises of autonomy were not fulfilled for the several million strong Ukrainian minority in southeastern Poland.

Following the signing of the Ribbentrop-Molotov pact of August 1939, German and Soviet forces invaded Poland and partitioned the country. Polish grievances against Moscow accumulated during the Second World War: over 1.5 million Polish citizens were deported to Siberia, the Arctic, and Central Asia, of whom several hundred thousand perished; about 15,000 Polish officers and intellectuals were massacred by Soviet security forces; an unpopular Communist regime was installed in Warsaw under Russian supervision; the non-Communist Polish Home Army was liquidated; and the USSR annexed one-third of Poland's pre-war territories, assigning them to the Lithuanian, Belarusan, and Ukrainian Soviet republics. Substantial minorities were also left on both sides of the border. Forty five years of Communist rule further aggravated Polish-Russian hostilities: from the repressive Stalinist years, through the crushing of several workers' rebellions in the 1950s and 1970s, to the imposition of martial law under Soviet supervision in 1981 in an attempt to eradicate the independent Solidarity labor movement.

Relations between Moscow and Warsaw markedly improved with the removal of Soviet military, political, and economic controls over eastern Europe after the 1989 democratic revolutions. During the past three years, more equitable relations have been established and fears of renewed Russian domination have largely subsided in Poland. But despite these visible improvements, relations could, once again, become severely strained in three critical areas: through the likelihood of massive instability on the territories of the former Soviet Union; in the handling of a potential mass exodus of refugees from the western post-Soviet republics; and over Poland's developing contacts with the newly independent republican governments. The contentious question of Soviet troop withdrawals through and from Polish territories has also soured contacts between Warsaw and Moscow.

Poland's politicians remain fearful about the prospects and consequences of economic breakdown, political turmoil, and social unrest in the former USSR, renamed as the Commonwealth of Independent States in December 1991. Economic collapse would result in major interruptions or even a complete cut-off in vital energy supplies (primarily oil and gas) and a further damaging disruption of important trading networks. Moreover, Warsaw is concerned that any major attempt to forcibly restore central authority in Moscow could halt or reverse the reform process that has thus far proved largely advantageous for Poland. Such a crackdown could reverberate throughout eastern Europe by cooling relations between the new democratic governments and any harder-line Russian or Commonwealth leadership. These potentially regressive developments may undermine Poland's political progress, by narrowing Russian government tolerance of the emerging democratic system, calling into question the looser security arrangements between Moscow and Warsaw, and even resuscitating fears of renewed Russian expansionism with or without a Leninist ideological facade. Although the use of military force to reverse the Polish reform process appears highly unlikely, the Kremlin retains substantial leverage to influence or even destabilize the incumbent Warsaw administration.

Polish spokesmen also harbor misgivings that civil disorder, ethnic conflict, inter-republican rivalries, and economic breakdown in the Commonwealth states could spill over their eastern border. Social unrest and economic hardship could trigger the mass exodus of refugees, and this, in turn, would strain Poland's meager resources. It is probable that the bulk of refugees would seek to migrate to western Europe, merely using Poland as a transit point. But Warsaw is also worried that the Western countries will place tight restrictions on the numbers of migrants permitted to enter. Without substantial international assistance and a commitment to accept Commonwealth émigrés, a wave of refugees could severely exacerbate Poland's already precarious economic conditions.

From the outset, Warsaw has supported democratic reforms in the USSR. The government calculated that the introduction of a multi-party system and increasing republican sovereignty would decrease the likelihood of a future Red Army threat and enhance peaceful progress throughout the region. To encourage this process, the Warsaw administration endeavored to establish amicable relations with the neighboring republics. But Polish moves also raised Moscow's concerns about foreign interference in internal Soviet affairs, particularly in support of nationalist forces, democratic parties, and free labor unions that opposed central Communist rule. The development of Poland's direct relations with the republics, which have increasingly bypassed the Kremlin, could still complicate future relations between Warsaw and Moscow. Before the failed hard-line coup in August 1991, it was feared that an internal crackdown by the Soviet regime against any of the new republican administrations would place the Polish authorities in an awkward position. Warsaw feared that even in a decentralizing or disintegrating USSR, the central government could grow fearful of expanding bilateral relations and regional alliances between Poland and the neighboring republics. Soviet authorities, as well as the new Russian republican government, could also attempt to exploit historical inter-ethnic antagonisms in the region in order to intercede as a dominant mediator.

Tensions between Warsaw and Moscow increased somewhat during 1990. Polish officials remained anxious about internal Soviet developments and especially over what impact the ongoing struggle between conservatives and reformers, or any hardening in Moscow's domestic policies, would have on the Kremlin's foreign affairs. A major point of conflict involved the timetable and conditions for the withdrawal of Soviet military divisions from Poland, as well as the projected passage through Polish territory of over half a million soldiers and dependents stationed in eastern Germany, together with substantial quantities of military hardware.

After the 1989 revolutions, Warsaw, unlike Bonn, Prague, and Budapest, did not sign an agreement with Moscow with regard to a Red Army evacuation from its territories.[2] The newly installed democratic government of Tadeusz Mazowiecki initially calculated that a continuing Soviet presence would act as a deterrent to potential German claims on western Poland. Whatever the merits of these estimations, once the German issue appeared to be settled in late 1990, difficulties began to surface with the Kremlin. The Mazowiecki position toward a Soviet pullout proved to be less consequential than the attitude adopted by Hungary and Czechoslovakia. Both states reached accords in early 1990 for the speedy departure of all Soviet military divisions. The

Soviet presence in Poland was relatively small; it consisted of under 50,000 troops situated near the German frontier and mostly acting as logistical and communications support for Red Army forces in eastern Germany. The prevarications of Chancellor Kohl's German government in settling the border question with Poland caused Warsaw to delay its requests for a swift Soviet military departure. This stirred some controversy between Prime Minister Mazowiecki and Solidarity leader Lech Walesa who publicly commented that Russian troops should leave the country as quickly as possible. Bonn's ambiguous position also played into the hands of Soviet military leaders who opposed quickly abandoning their strategic positions in both Poland and Germany.

Demands for a Soviet pullout intensified after the Oder-Neisse border question between Poland and Germany was virtually settled in the fall of 1990. Initial talks between Moscow and Warsaw proved inconclusive, as Soviet delegates opposed the Polish position of a complete withdrawal by the end of 1991 and non-linkage with the removal of troops from Germany. Moscow complained that it was experiencing severe difficulties in housing soldiers returning from eastern Europe and its transports could not handle any increased load. Polish suspicions mounted over Moscow's intentions and in the early part of 1991, the new government of Prime Minister Krzysztof Bielecki accused the Kremlin of unnecessary delays in signing an accord.[3] Polish border guards began to refuse access to Soviet troop trains intending to pass through Poland from Germany but lacking prior agreement as to timing, numbers, and the separation of soldiers from their weaponry.

The Soviet position toward Warsaw appeared to stiffen, particularly after the partial crackdown by Interior Ministry forces in Lithuania in January 1991 and with the growing influence of conservative forces in the Kremlin. A series of talks on troop movements failed to resolve the critical issue of timing. The Poles wanted the Soviets to complete their evacuation by the end of 1991 and to find alternative routes for their contingents leaving Germany. Moscow was intent on leaving most of its forces in Poland until the bulk of its divisions had vacated German soil by early 1993. Statements by General Viktor Dubynin, the commander of Soviet forces in Poland, further exacerbated Polish concerns. Dubynin asserted that the Red Army would unilaterally decide on the phases of its withdrawal and would not be treated as an occupation force by being secluded from its weapons. Despite the rift, talks continued at the highest levels and Premier Bielecki visited Moscow in April 1991 in preparation for a future visit by President Lech Walesa. In the aftermath of the collapsed August coup and with the victory of reformist forces in Russia, the troop issue lost some of its urgency. A compromise solution materialized by October 1991 when Moscow agreed to vacate the bulk of its forces by the end of 1992, leaving only support units to be withdrawn from Poland by the close of 1993. Nevertheless, the drawn out dispute over Red Army troops perpetuated the legacy of mutual suspicion and distrust.

Negotiations were also concluded in October 1991 on a comprehensive treaty of cooperation between the Warsaw and Soviet governments, and the agreement was initialled in December 1991. The Kremlin finally withdrew clauses in the agreement that would have empowered Russia to interfere in Poland's security alliances and its relations with individual Soviet republics.[4] Nonetheless, problems persisted between the two sides over mutual financial compensations for the Red Army withdrawal and for the environmental damage caused in and around military bases on Polish soil. Furthermore, at the close of 1991 questions remained over the long-term authority of the Soviet regime and on whether its current foreign commitments would be respected by any future post-Soviet central administration. Even the ratification of the cooperation treaty with Poland would prove time consuming because it needed approval by both republican and central authorities.

Unreliable economic relations between Poland and the USSR have also concerned Warsaw since the unravelling of the Council for Mutual Economic Assistance (CMEA) trading system. Warsaw initially feared that the Kremlin could apply strong economic pressures to influence Polish foreign policy. Cutbacks in vital Soviet energy supplies during the course of 1990, whether deliberate or caused by domestic production and distribution problems, appeared to confirm these fears. In fact, Soviet gas and oil deliveries to practically all the east European countries declined by about 40% in 1990 and continued to drop throughout 1991. However, the region-wide switch from barter deals to hard currency trading at the start of 1991 encouraged Poland and other states to try and diversify their energy suppliers, partly to avoid the pitfalls of prolonged delays and the opportunity for economic blackmail by Moscow. Despite these initiatives, the full redirection of Polish trade away from the USSR will be a long-term process, leaving the country prone to short-term disruptions of important supplies and markets.

Continuing political turmoil and the disintegration of the Soviet Union has presented serious economic and security headaches for Poland along its eastern borders. The most immediate problem is a large-scale exodus of refugees from the former USSR seeking shelter in Poland or trying to emigrate to the West. The Warsaw authorities are unable to effectively patrol the entire frontier area, especially if Commonwealth border guards were to loosen their controls and Moscow were to implement its liberal emigration bill, scheduled to take effect in January 1993.[5] Polish frontier guards could find themselves in a difficult predicament of having to forcefully turn back waves of refugees. This could develop into a major dilemma if the bulk of refugees were ethnic Poles escaping economic hardships or civic unrest in the neighboring republics. Some sources estimate that about 1.5 million Poles live in the USSR and the majority are located in the western republics. Warsaw also faces a quandary over whether to impose visa requirements on Commonwealth citizens at a time when it is seeking visa-free travel for Poles to Western countries. Such a move could expose the government to charges of inconsistency and hypocrisy.

The danger of a large influx of refugees increased during the winter of 1990-1991 as economic conditions sharply deteriorated. At the same time, the Kremlin's position appeared to harden with the likelihood of a sustained military crackdown in several rebellious republics. Uncertainty about the future was compounded by an evident breakdown in authority and growing public disorientation throughout the USSR. In December 1990, Poland's refugee commissioner revealed that Warsaw was preparing for a possible worst case scenario and had established a refugee office in the Interior Ministry. He warned somewhat dramatically that if millions of refugees were to pour across the porous border, the Polish state could rapidly disintegrate.[6] Since late 1990, the Warsaw authorities have strengthened their troop levels in preparation for a possible refugee flight and drawn up contingency plans to mobilize special units to stem a large influx of refugees in case of massive unrest in the Soviet Union. But Poland has an 1100 kilometer long frontier with the Commonwealth states and Lithuania that it cannot completely safeguard.

Some sources estimate that the east European states could face between six and ten million post-Soviet émigrés during the next decade and that Poland would be confronted with the bulk of them. The majority will claim refugee status if civil conflict were to escalate or if martial law was declared in areas of the Commonwealth bordering on Poland.[7] In such a scenario, Western governments are likely to impose strict quota restrictions on immigrants. Poland would then require urgent relief supplies from international organizations and foreign governments if the refugees were to be properly accommodated. Otherwise, the drain on Poland's limited resources could prove staggering and may even provoke widescale economic breakdown and social disruption.

Fears have been expressed that a refugee crisis could trigger confrontations on Poland's eastern borders and even military engagements by frontier troops. The general chaos may be perceived as threatening Poland's territorial integrity and raise questions over border delineations. An influx of refugees could also aggravate inter-ethnic tensions and anti-foreigner sentiments in Poland as unemployment swells and competition for work and resources is dramatically heightened. The growing number of workers from the former USSR willing to work for much lower wages than their Polish counterparts in various menial jobs has certainly aggravated local hostilities against foreigners. Ethnic strife would in turn impair the country's relations with neighboring republican governments. Before the reformist victory in August 1991, observers feared that Moscow could seek to exploit the refugee flow to exacerbate nationality conflicts between Poland and the resurgent western republics. Such developments would have presumably promoted Soviet interests by pressuring the Warsaw government to make various political concessions. Other commentators suspected that the refugee threat had been deliberately exaggerated by Moscow as a lever against the wayward east European governments and primarily as a scare tactic, in order to gain precious Western aid for the Soviet economy. With the collapse of central authority amid attempts to implement far-reaching and disruptive market reforms in Russia, Ukraine, and Belarus, the refugee threat continued to hover over Poland throughout 1992.

Poland and the Republics

Poland borders on four post-Soviet republics—Lithuania, Belarus, Ukraine, and the Russian *oblast* of Kaliningrad. The Warsaw administration has tried to establish and expand good relations with these emerging states and avoid resuscitating any dormant historical conflicts. Lithuanian, Belarusan, and Ukrainian leaders have, in turn, sought cooperation with Warsaw, realizing that Poland was a potential political and economic gateway westward that could even serve as a model of democratization and marketization. But contacts have not been devoid of latent tensions, particularly over territorial and minority issues and over future security arrangements in the post-USSR. Moreover, the development of Polish-republican relations closely interest the Russian government. Moscow may be supportive if such relations bring economic benefits but it could also prove hostile if they further estrange the republics from Russia.

With regard to territorial questions, the Polish authorities have no outstanding border claims on any of the four republics, even though final frontier agreements and peace treaties have still to be concluded. Since 1989, Poland's Foreign Minister Krzysztof Skubiszewski has periodically declared that Warsaw harbors no demands on its former eastern territories or on former Polish cities such as Vilnius or Lviv. The Polish parliament has adopted resolutions affirming the permanency of all the country's borders, thus discounting any claims to regions in the Commonwealth inhabited by substantial Polish minorities. The operative notion has been that any questioning of the eastern boundaries could destabilize the region and resuscitate disputes over Poland's western frontiers with Germany.

The new republican authorities have also formally discounted any ambitions toward Polish territories inhabited by Lithuanian, Belarusan, or Ukrainian communities. However, minorities on both sides of the border remain a lingering source of friction, especially if discrimination were to increase or if any government was perceived to be interfering in a neighbor's internal affairs by vehemently promoting the rights of its co-ethnics. Some Polish spokesmen also fear that radical forces in neighboring republics could, in the future, try to divert attention from domestic problems by lodging claims to Polish territories. A similar charge could of course be levelled against ultra-nationalist organizations recently reactivated in Poland.

After the formation of the independent Lithuanian government in March 1990, Prime Minister Kazimiera Prunskiene confirmed that Vilnius held no border claims on Poland. The Polish authorities simultaneously issued similar statements. Warsaw was quick to express its support for Lithuanian sovereignty. But, it did not overtly recognize the country's independence for fear of antagonizing Moscow before Lithuania's status was formally binding under international law. But the Poles took a more forthright position than many other states and Polish senators were among the first foreign guests to visit the independent Lithuanian parliament. The Polish government came under some domestic criticism for not adopting a more forthright "Eastern policy" by recognizing the Baltic states before the Soviet coup attempt in August 1991. Its evident caution may indeed have diminished Warsaw's influence and good will in Vilnius and other republican capitals.

Serious discords between Poland and Lithuania did not appear at governmental level before Lithuania was permitted to secede from the USSR in August 1991. But some apprehensions were voiced in Vilnius about the activities and aspirations of the Polish minority which comprises some 350,000 people, or over 8% of the population, located primarily in south eastern Lithuania. Soon after Lithuania's initial declaration of independence in March 1990, a split appeared in the Polish community in its stance toward Vilnius. A faction within the Union of Poles in Lithuania (UPL) came under pronounced Communist influence and aligned itself with the conservative Russian dominated *Edinstvo* organization, which vehemently opposed Lithuanian sovereignty. It declared the Salcininkai and Vilnius *raions,* areas with large compact Polish populations, as a "National Autonomous District." Some activists also campaigned for a referendum on the creation of an eastern Polish republic to remain part of the Soviet Union or to join the Belarusan Soviet republic. These moves were reportedly inspired by hard-liners in Moscow and by the local *nomenklatura* who endeavored to destabilize the independent Lithuanian administration.

In May 1990, the Lithuanian parliament overruled the proclamation of an autonomous Polish district, arguing that it threatened the country's unity and ultimately served Moscow's objectives. Warsaw also distanced itself from the pro-Soviet Polish factions and thereby helped to undermine their impact. The UPL leadership seemed to be gradually wrested away from the pro-Moscow activists, and the Union gradually adopted a clearer pro-Lithuanian stance. This was reinforced after the partial crackdown in January 1991, when Polish deputies to the Vilnius legislature condemned the violence perpetrated by Soviet security forces against unarmed civilians.

Dissatisfaction continued to be voiced over the material conditions of the Polish minority in Lithuania, even though its cultural, educational, and linguistic rights have been recognized in various legal guarantees. Polish activists also expressed apprehensions over the rise of Lithuanian nationalism and particularly about the openly anti-Polish stance of militant nationalist organizations such as the "Vilnija" group. On the Lithuanian side, there were fears that some nationalist-revanchist groups in Poland were seeking to separate and eventually annex portions of Lithuanian territory, even though such parties have remained marginal and uninfluential in Warsaw. Some government officials also questioned the long-term loyalty of the Polish minority to the Lithuanian state. Others retained qualms that Polish aspirations could be exploited by Moscow to destabilize the country and claim minority protection as a pretext for intervention.

In May 1991, the local authorities in the Polish areas of eastern Lithuania once again declared the region a "Polish Autonomous District." Even though they did not openly seek to secede from Lithuania, they established a local parliament as the highest point of political authority in the area.[8] Lithuanian President Vitautis Landsbergis warned about the dangers of separatism but offered no tangible new initiatives to improve ethnic relations. Shortly after Lithuanian independence was formally recognized by Moscow and the international community in early September 1991, the government decided to impose direct rule over the Vilnius and Salcininkai regions, which encompassed the rebellious Polish district. It dismissed the local councils, charging them with supporting the failed Soviet coup, and appointed special state administrators for the region. The government did not set a date for new regional elections, thus sparking a boycott by Poles in the Lithuanian parliament.[9]

While the Lithuanian authorities charged that local councils in Polish areas were dominated by old guard Communists opposing the country's independence, some Polish leaders feared that Vilnius would rescind its promise to establish a single administrative district embracing all Polish regions. Such a move would deprive Poles of a significant measure of self-government. Suspicions were also heightened that some Lithuanian nationalist deputies were planning to gerrymander the territory by dividing up and parcelling out Polish-majority districts and settling more Lithuanian families in the region. Such a policy would seriously dilute Polish and Russian political rights, as the two populations would become minorities in the new districts.

Warsaw has been careful in expressing any direct support for the Polish minority in Lithuania, fearing that overt involvement would play into Soviet hands and sour relations with its new neighbor. However, government officials voiced concern over the allegedly deteriorating position of the Polish minority as Vilnius reasserted its independence following the foiled Soviet putsch.[10] In mid-September 1991, Polish Foreign Minister Krzysztof Skubiszewski postponed his visit to Vilnius despite Poland's recognition of Lithuania's independence. Talks on bilateral relations were interrupted over the question of Polish minority rights.[11] The two sides failed to reach agreement on national minority schooling and on the question whether Poles in the Vilnius region had to declare loyalty to the Lithuanian state before acquiring Lithuanian citizenship. President Walesa publicly declared his concerns over the purported curtailment of Polish minority rights; his statements were strongly criticized by President Landsbergis. The Lithuanian leader defended the decision to dissolve Polish regional councils on the grounds that they were controlled by Communists who opposed the country's independence and were spoiling inter-ethnic relations. He also promised that new local elections were to be held within six months.[12] In the light of these assurances, a wide-ranging declaration of friendship and a consular convention were signed by Vilnius and Warsaw in mid-January 1992.

Vilnius itself has sought Polish government guarantees for the 30,000 Lithuanians resident in north eastern Poland, primarily located in the Suwalki voivodship. Since Lithuania's declaration of independence, this minority has become more active by establishing separate cultural and educational associations. However, unlike their Polish counterparts in Lithuania, the leadership has not expressed any aspirations toward political or territorial autonomy.[13]

In July 1990, the Belarusan declaration of sovereignty was recognized in a Polish Senate resolution, while the Warsaw government announced plans to develop inter-state cooperation in various spheres. The Belarusan legislature's declaration of independence in August 1991, after the Soviet coup fiasco, was welcomed by the Polish parliament. Even though no overt territorial demands have been voiced by either side, Polish-Belarusan relations have not been trouble free. This was evident during Skubiszewski's visit to Belarus in October 1990, which failed to produce a joint declaration on cooperation. The Minsk government objected to any reference to the Polish-Soviet state border agreement of August 1945 at which Belarusan representatives were absent, although it evidently accepted the inviolability of the post-war boundaries. After months of negotiations, in October 1991 the Polish and Belarusan Prime Ministers signed a declaration on good-neighborly relations as a first step toward the conclusion of a full treaty and the restoration of diplomatic relations between the two states.

The minority issue has also created some controversies between Warsaw and Minsk. The Belarusan government wanted the Bialystok area of eastern Poland, where approximately 250,000 co-nationals reside, to be declared an ethnically Belarusan region. Warsaw opposed granting such a status to the area, fearful that this would undermine the country's territorial cohesiveness. Warsaw was also perturbed over suggestions about frontier changes published in some of the national Belarusan press. A growing ethnic consciousness has been visible among the Belarusan minority in Poland. Several new organizations have been established, including the Social Committee *Hramada* and the Belarusan Democratic Assembly (BDA), which stood as a political party in Poland's local and parliamentary elections. They have campaigned for the official use of the Belarusan language and the introduction of bilingual schooling, and managed to elect some Belarusan deputies to local government bodies in Bialystok during the May 1990 balloting. They have also striven to expand cross-border contacts with the Belarus republic, without advocating secession from Poland.[14] One consistent source of tension has been over religious issues, as Poles are primarily Roman Catholic and Belarusans mostly Eastern Orthodox. Disputes have focused on such questions as the use of churches for Orthodox services, the language employed during masses, the allegedly anti-Belarusan and missionary attitude of the Polish clergy, and accusations of Polish discrimination in local education and employment.

Belarus also contains a substantial Polish minority, numbering somewhere between 400,000 and 500,000, and residing primarily in the western part of the republic. With the loosening of central Communist controls, in June 1990 activists established an independent Union of Poles in Belarus (UPB) with chapters in several major cities and a membership of some 15,000.[15] It pressed for the implementation of educational, linguistic, and cultural rights, but has not been involved in any major disputes with the Belarusan authorities. Unlike the UPL in Lithuania, the UPB has not demanded autonomous status for the Polish community. Nonetheless, nationality problems could materialize in parts of the republic if economic conditions were to further decline and autonomist demands were to spiral through the intervention of outside actors, whether Polish or Russian. This could revive fears of Polish separatism and annexation among the Belarusan majority.

In May 1990, both the Ukrainian and Polish governments confirmed the absence of any outstanding mutual territorial claims. The July 1990 declaration of Ukrainian sovereignty was followed by expressions of support from the Warsaw government. In October 1990, Polish Foreign Minister Skubiszewski visited Ukraine and signed a declaration of friendship and cooperation with Kiev.[16] It fell short of a formal treaty, but was part of Warsaw's effort to establish direct diplomatic and trading relations with several post-Soviet republics. The declaration recognized the territorial integrity and existing borders of both states, thereby serving to reduce the possibility of frontier disputes. Following the Ukrainian parliament's declaration of independence in August 1991, in the wake of the failed Soviet coup, the Polish authorities decided to establish direct diplomatic relations with Ukraine.

Indeed, Poland became the first country to recognize the Ukrainian state after the overwhelming vote for independence in the December 1991 referendum. Despite these formalities, Warsaw grew concerned over Ukraine's increasingly independent military posture and the prospect that major conventional force imbalances could emerge in the region. Shortly after gaining independence, Ukrainian authorities embarked on the creation of a separate military structure. Numbers ranging from 150,000 to 450,000 have been floated by the government in Kiev; the latter figure would constitute twice the size of the Polish military. Uncertainty over the eventual dimensions of the Ukrainian forces continues to trouble officials in Warsaw. Furthermore, substantial quantities of war material remain on the western territories of the former Soviet Union, with little prospect for a rapid destruction or conversion to civilian uses. The equipment constitutes a significant source of instability, particularly as it could be used to rapidly recreate disbanded military units. Such developments could further erode Poland's sense of security and leave the country susceptible to military pressures as well as continuing instability on its eastern borders.

Relations between Warsaw and the pro-independence *Rukh* movement, which gained in stature after Ukraine's independence declaration, have, in general, developed positively. *Rukh* pledged that it would grant full nationality rights for all minorities, including the approximately 250,000 strong Polish community in the western *oblasts* where *Rukh* won the 1990 republican elections. In fact, the first congress of Polish organizations in Ukraine was allowed to be held in May 1990, and was attended by over 400 delegates. However, some *Rukh* spokesmen have expressed anxiety over lingering Polish claims for a special status for the city of Lvov (Lviv in Ukrainian) and the surrounding areas. Conversely, some Polish activists have complained that Ukrainian authorities have not done enough to satisfy the minority's cultural and educational aspirations. Others have voiced fears that full Ukrainian independence could actually worsen conditions among Poles, especially in the face of allegedly mounting Ukrainian nationalism.[17] These concerns were heightened in December 1991 when the Ukraine's State Independence Organization (USIO), a self-proclaimed successor to the war-time Organization of Ukrainian Nationalists, held a conference in Lviv and claimed that ethnic Ukrainian lands included territories that are currently part of Poland, Moldova, Belarus, and Russia.[18]

The Ukrainian minority in Poland, comprising about 300,000 people scattered in the western and south eastern regions of the country, could also become an ingredient in any future inter-state disputes. In February 1990, the Union of Ukrainians in Poland (UUP) was established to defend minority rights in culture, education, language, and religion. These activities won approval among officials in Warsaw, who argued that they would help in forging cooperative links with the Ukrainian republic. But more contentious issues also materialized, including calls for the return of Ukrainians to the Bieszczady mountains, from where many had been deported after World War Two on charges of collaboration with anti-Communist guerrillas, and the return of property seized by the state in the late 1940s. The latter includes over 250 churches confiscated from the Greek-Catholic (Uniate) church in 1947. The implementation of such proposals could aggravate frictions with the local Polish population, as was evident during the prolonged dispute over the Carmelite Cathedral of St. Theresa in Przemysl during the spring and summer of 1991.[19]

An additional complication has arisen between Poles and Ukrainians, in that some of the expelled people consider themselves to be Lemko Ruthenians who do not accept the appellation "Ukrainian." Some Lemko leaders have established citizens circles and other organizations in Poland to press for their rights as a distinct ethnic and cultural minority. They stressed that they did not want to become a bargaining chip in Polish-Ukrainian negotiations.[20] Conflicts have arisen over the ethnic identity of the Lemko Ruthenians and whether they form a separate nationality or are actually part of the Ukrainian nation. Some of the younger Polish Lemkos have adopted more militant, non-Ukrainian positions, refusing to cooperate with the Union of Ukrainians or even the official Lemko Union (LU). The Lemko organizations are not separatists and implicitly support Poland's territorial integrity. Their objectives are the restoration of Lemko Ruthenian cultural and educational rights, with the possibility of returning some of their communities to their ancestral mountain areas in south eastern Poland.

The Kaliningrad *oblast* of the Russian federation, situated on Poland's northern border, has the potential of provoking a three-way regional conflict, between Russia, Poland, and Germany, and it could also embroil the new Lithuanian state.[21] The area was cut off from surrounding countries at the close of World War Two, and has been populated largely by Russian settlers and Soviet military units. During the past decade, the *oblast* has lost some of its significance as a "special military zone," and in recent years, some discussions have been held to convert Kaliningrad into an economically important enclave. Polish officials have voiced concerns that Moscow may be willing to allow for substantial German investments in the area, alongside a mass resettlement of Germans from Kazakhstan and the Volga area. This could culminate in the emergence of a German-controlled free trade zone. More intensive German-Russian cooperation to develop the area may disregard Polish strategic and economic interests and leave open the question of Kaliningrad's future affiliation. The specter of a revived East Prussian enclave on Poland's northern border has provoked some nervousness in Warsaw.

To counter prospective German ambitions, Warsaw has lodged proposals for buttressing Polish trade, tourism, and investment in Kaliningrad, as this could also invigorate the country's neglected north east regions. But compared to Germany, Poland is at a clear disadvantage because it possesses only limited foreign investment potential. Officials in Moscow have assured Warsaw that the Kaliningrad area would not be opened up for major resettlement and could develop economic ties with adjacent Polish voivodships. Despite these assurances, several thousand Soviet Germans from Central Asia were reportedly settled in the zone during 1990, and again raised Polish fears. German organizations have also sprung up in the region, including the Eintracht Society for German Culture (ESGC), promoting the resuscitation of German identity and self-organization. The Kaliningrad dispute subsided somewhat as German reunification accelerated and Bonn became preoccupied with its internal problems. Moreover, there has been no recent evidence of large scale German resettlement, while Moscow has vowed that it has no intention of germanizing the area. But the question remains open whether in the long term Germany will be interested in regaining economic control of the region, with a view to potential political annexation in the event that the Russian federation decentralizes or disintegrates. The Poles will be watching these developments very closely.[22]

Poland also displayed concern about the control of post-Soviet strategic and tactical nuclear weapons and their division between the four nuclear republics. Warsaw would prefer some form of centralized management over strategic arms, for fear that either a future authoritarian government in Russia, Ukraine, or Belarus could threaten Poland or that nuclear weapons could fall into the hands of a hard-line military clique or irregular detachments near Poland's borders. Indeed, continuing uncertainty over the nuclear issue may encourage Poland to develop or purchase its own nuclear, chemical, or biological capabilities as protection against potential nuclear blackmail. Indeed, this was an element of the campaign platform of the populist politician Stanislaw Tyminski, who finished in second place to Lech Walesa in the 1990 presidential elections. If Poland's political life undergoes further radicalization, the nuclear issue could gain renewed prominence. Furthermore, Poland possess a nuclear capability, both in terms of trained personnel and equipment, that may be useful to potential proliferators. Such developments could lead to unregulated and mismanaged nuclear proliferation, especially where the cost of modernizing conventional forces would prove prohibitive.

The specter of massive unrest in the Commonwealth states continues to haunt Poland as it would have a major impact on the country's security. The optimal result of the ongoing turmoil would be far-reaching but peaceful decentralization and democratization, in which the republics gain complete political and economic independence. Warsaw has encouraged such a process by establishing cooperative relations with its eastern neighbors and laying the groundwork for a future system of alliances. But pronounced uncertainty remains about internal Commonwealth developments even after the recent revolutionary changes. Economic collapse and another conservative or authoritarian backlash in Russia or in other neighboring republics could seriously destabilize the region.

Various scenarios of instability have been considered by the Polish government on its eastern borders, including: economic collapse and social chaos; large scale demonstrations and rioting; military crackdowns; hard-line coup attempts; provocations by local elites losing their privileges; the rise of militant nationalism; ethnic conflicts and clashes; the formation of irregular detachments; lack of central control over military units in the republics; and armed clashes between republican and renegade forces. Violent conflict could, in turn, have a spill-over effect on Polish territory. This could take the form of hot pursuit incursions by military formations seeking to outgun guerrilla units or the use of Polish territory by rebel forces. Moreover, Moscow could still apply military or economic blackmail against Poland in efforts to influence Warsaw's eastern policies. In a much longer time frame, the Russian government may endeavor to recreate a more coherent "sphere of influence" in parts of eastern Europe. Poland would, of course, figure as a key link in any projected security chain. It seems unlikely, however, that any administration in Warsaw would easily succumb to such pressures and any attempted re-satellization of Poland would, undoubtedly, spark intensive conflicts in the years ahead.

Czechoslovakia, Ukraine, and Ruthenia

The Czechs and Slovaks did not share a frontier with the Russians until after World War Two, and few significant disputes materialized between Prague and Moscow in the pre-war period. In 1919, under the Treaty of St. Germain, the new Czechoslovak state gained Subcarpathian Ruthenia as its easternmost province but the area did not border with the USSR.[23] After the creation of the Soviet Ukrainian republic, the Bolshevik regime claimed that the Ruthenians were simply western Ukrainians, thus indicating plans for the eventual integration of Carpatho-Ruthenia into the USSR. Although the Prague government was reasonably benevolent toward its Ruthenian and Ukrainian minority, it built a centralized state rather than a looser federal system and despatched Czech administrators and teachers into its largely agrarian eastern domains. Such policies created some resentments among the local population, amid charges of patronizing colonialism by Prague.

After the liberation of Czechoslovakia by Soviet troops in 1945, Ruthenia was annexed by the USSR and merged with the Ukrainian republic. Some demographic movements were permitted as Czechs and Slovaks in Ruthenia-Ukraine were given the choice of Soviet or Czechoslovak citizenship. Under Communist rule, the Ukrainians-Ruthenians in eastern Slovakia were provided with legal rights to their own schools, newspapers, and cultural associations, although many of these concessions were not actually implemented. At the height of the Stalinist tyranny in the late 1940s and during the 1950s, the Ukrainian Uniate Church, similarly to other Christian denominations, was subjected to vigorous persecution. The 1968 Prague Spring resulted in some liberalization in the government's minorities policies, and prospects for Ukrainian autonomy in Slovakia were discussed. But following the armed Soviet intervention and the "normalization" of Communist rule, Ukrainian-Ruthenian autonomy plans were shelved.

In the post-World War Two period, popular attitudes in Czechoslovakia toward the Soviet regime grew increasingly negative as a result of bitter historical experiences. Under Moscow's direction, the Communist Party forcefully seized power in 1948 and initiated a campaign of Stalinist terror and intimidation. The Prague Spring reformist experiment was crushed by Soviet tanks, and the popular reform-Communist government was overturned and a new dictatorship imposed under Kremlin supervision. Moreover, Moscow maintained a dogmatic anti-reformist regime in power in Prague for the next twenty years.

Since the collapse of Communist rule in Czechoslovakia, and the termination of Soviet military, political, and police controls, relations between Prague and Moscow have been placed on a more equal footing. Although no critical territorial or minority issues currently require resolution between the two states, some historical tensions could resurface. For example, the fate of Transcarpathian Ruthenian, once under Czechoslovak administration, may be raised by a more independent and self-confident Czech or Slovak government. This could provoke disputes with the independent Ukrainian authorities. Two other potential problems loom ahead: the refugee threat coupled with economic disruption, and the developing relations between Czechoslovakia and the newly independent post-Soviet republics.

Similarly to Poland, the Czech and Slovak authorities fear a mass influx of refugees in the event of major economic and social turmoil, a military crackdown, or inter-republican struggles in the Commonwealth. Czechoslovak resources would be insufficient to handle any substantial human wave across its border, and the country would require extensive assistance from international agencies and a commitment from Western governments to accept large numbers of refugees. The authorities in Prague, as well as in Warsaw and Budapest, have also grown alarmed by the precipitous decline in trade with the USSR during the past two years. They have criticized proposed western aid to Moscow that may not only negatively effect the volume of assistance to eastern Europe, but could further undercut their exports to the former Soviet Union. At an international conference in June 1991, Czechoslovak Foreign Minister Jiri Dienstbier, together with high-ranking Polish and Hungarian officials, urged the West to grant aid that would be used to purchase east European goods and would require Moscow to honor its supply contracts. Without such stipulations, it was feared that the central European economies would seriously suffer from the closure of traditional markets while the Commonwealth states redirected their trade westward.

The expansion of ties between Czechoslovakia and the republics that extricated themselves from Soviet tutelage, could also provoke some international tensions. This scenario may become especially conflictive if Moscow attempts to freeze or reverse the process of republican independence. Prague and Bratislava, like other east European capitals, would then be placed in a difficult predicament, as to whether they should support the new republics in their struggles with Russia.

During the past two years, the Ukrainian authorities have made a concerted effort to establish good relations with their western neighbors. In July 1991, Kiev concluded an agreement with the federal government in Prague; it also signed separate agreements with the Czech and Slovak republics. The Ukrainian administration also pursued bilateral relations with territorial sub-units of larger federal states; these included Slovakia, Croatia, and Bavaria. In March 1991, Slovak Prime Minister Vladimir Meciar visited Kiev to sign an "international communique" that promised to strengthen cooperation between Bratislava and Kiev.[24] But despite the progress achieved, the Ruthenian-Ukrainian minority question has recently reappeared and it could increasingly complicate relations between Prague, Bratislava, Kiev, and Moscow.

About 100,000 to 150,000 Ruthenians and Ukrainians live in eastern Slovakia. Their official organization, the Union of Ukrainians and Ruthenians in Czechoslovakia (UURCS), which changed its name from the Cultural Association of Ukrainian Workers soon after the November 1989 revolution, has supported the preservation of a federal Czech and Slovak state. The UURCS has also complained about efforts by some Slovak parties to create an independent Slovak republic. It fears that in such a scenario, the rights of various minorities would be denied while Prague would lack the leverage to protect their distinct interests.

In the 1991 Czechoslovak census, a Ruthenian nationality was registered for the first time without parentheses, and almost half of those who had previously declared themselves as Ukrainian opted for Ruthenian nationality. During the last two years, Slovak Ruthenians have become more active through the social-cultural organization Ruthenian Revival (RR) and the magazine *Rusin,* whose leaders consider the population a separate ethno-linguistic group. The RR organized the First World Congress of Ruthenians in March 1991 in eastern Slovakia. Congress participants pressed for the recognition of Ruthenian cultural and educational organizations in Ukraine.[25] In the meantime, the Ruthenian language is in the process of codification, to distinguish it from both Slovak and Ukrainian, and Ruthenian cultural traditions are being cultivated to help develop a distinct self-identity among the population. Activists have asserted that the process of slovakization and ukrainianization, visible since the close of the World War Two, needs to be reversed. This has led to deep rifts within the minority population as to their precise ethnic and cultural identity.

With the rise of national consciousness throughout the former USSR, Ruthenians in the western part of Ukraine have also been energized. According to the 1989 Soviet census, out of a Transcarpathian population of 1.25 million, 977,000 were registered as Ukrainians, of whom 600,000 were estimated to be Ruthenians. Since the mid-1940s, Ruthenians have not been officially recognized as a separate nationality. They were classified as Ukrainians, and subject to a policy of russification. In February 1989, a Society of Carpathian Ruthenians (SCR) was formed in Ukraine to campaign for specifically Ruthenian interests. The SCR wants the Ruthenians to be recognized as a separate nation. Some reports indicate that a few of the newly formed Ruthenian organizations have espoused the return of Ruthenia to Czechoslovakia.[26] Others have as their goal the establishment of a sovereign republic of Ruthenians in the Subcarpathian region.[27] During the vote on Ukrainian independence in December 1991, the population of the Transcarpathian *oblast* also voted in favor of a "special self-governing administrative status" for the region within Ukraine. Some groups have demanded a referendum on full territorial autonomy for the region and the restoration of the autonomous status of the *oblast* granted by Prague in 1938. According to some participants at the First World Congress of Ruthenians, Ruthenian identity is subjected to the threat of Ukrainian nationalism and to alleged extremist plans to establish a more centralized Greater Ukraine.[28] The unity achieved between Ruthenia and pro-independence Ukrainian forces against Communist and Soviet rule began to unravel once independence was attained. Ukrainian authorities have been opposed to Ruthenian territorial and political autonomy and the staging of any referendums on the issue, regarding this as an encroachment on the country's sovereignty and a first step towards secession. The question of Ruthenian self-determination has therefore remained unresolved and uncodified in Ukrainian law.

Although the Czech and Slovak governments have lodged no formal claims to the Subcarpathian region, and the federal authorities have renounced any European border revisions, some newly formed radical parties in Czechoslovakia have taken aboard the Ruthenian cause. The nationalist Prague-based Republican Party-Association for the Republic (RP-AR) has asserted that the annexation of Ruthenia by the Soviet Union was unconstitutional and illegal, and that the future of the territory has to be decided by the newly elected governments and brought to the attention of international bodies. The Republican Party platform has stressed eventual reunification with Ruthenia, while PR-AR leader Miroslav Sladek has travelled to Mukachevo in Ukrainian

Ruthenia where on one occasion he publicly hoisted the Czechoslovak flag. Sladek called for a referendum in the region, evidently confident that the majority of Ruthenians wished to rejoin Czechoslovakia and benefit from its economic progress.[29] Prague would also avowedly stand to gain from such reabsorption, in that Ruthenia contains substantial oil and gas deposits. Interestingly enough, the Republicans registered significant growth during 1991 and according to public opinion polls were the fifth most popular party in the Czech republic by mid-year. The Republican Party has been planning to organize its own World Ruthenian Congress, so that the Ruthenian delegates could freely decide in what state they want to reside in the future. The RP-AR itself favors reincorporating the area in an expanded Czech-Slovak federation. Other groupings have also been formed in Czechoslovakia to promote the Ruthenian cause and bring the regions closer together. The most notable is the Society of Friends of Subcarpathian Ruthenia (SFSR), a successor to a similar pre-World War Two Organization based in Bohemia.

According to a Czechoslovak Foreign Ministry spokesman, although Prague harbors no claims on Soviet or Ukrainian territory, if the inhabitants of Subcarpathian Ruthenia "expressed interest in joining Czechoslovakia, with the consent of the Soviet and Ukrainian governments, we would naturally not reject them."[30] The Czech-Slovak authorities intend to improve cultural and trade ties with the region, but emphasize that any decision to hold a referendum in Ruthenia has to be made by the governments in Kiev and Moscow. They have also expressed some fears that in the event of a break up of Czechoslovakia, Ruthenia itself could become a magnet drawing Slovakia closer toward Ukraine.

Conversely, some Ukrainian nationalists have raised claims to the eastern Slovak borderlands inhabited by Ruthenian minorities, whom they consider to be western Ukrainians. Although nationalist-revisionist groups in both countries are currently only marginal phenomena, they may prey on growing disquiet among the minority groups to press for autonomy status and eventual border changes. Hence, the aspirations of resurgent ethnic groups need to be treated carefully by any future Czech, Slovak, or Ukrainian administrations. As elsewhere in eastern Europe, minorities will tend to be attracted to those states that offer them the most tangible economic benefits and political liberties.

The potential influx of refugees from the post-Soviet Union could also foment difficulties for Czechoslovakia. Although the country's border with the Commonwealth is under 100 kilometers long, the authorities have steadily reinforced their frontier guards. In December 1990, Deputy Interior Minister Jan Ruml announced that the government planned to channel any possible flood of refugees to transit camps and would place severe restrictions on Soviet tourism. Fears persist that many of the 15,000 Czechs and Slovaks, as well as tens of thousands of Ruthenians in western Ukraine, could seek repatriation and refugee status in Czechoslovakia. A growing number of illegal border crossings have been reported during the last two years, but the real test will come when Moscow and Kiev relax their travel and emigration restrictions. Any large inflow would of course damage the Czech-Slovak economy and could provoke social unrest in the most disrupted regions of the country.

Prague's relations with the independent post-Soviet republics will also affect its relations with Moscow. President Havel and other government leaders spoke out early on in defense of Baltic sovereignty and criticized the Kremlin's denial of Lithuanian, Latvian, and Estonian independence. The federal government established good relations with the western republics, but stopped short of formally recognizing their independence until the Baltic states were allowed to secede from the USSR, largely to avoid antagonizing Moscow. If economic decline and political conflict were to escalate in the Commonwealth, or if a new authoritarian regime were to capture power in Moscow or Kiev, Czechoslovakia would have to reassess its relations with the nearby republics, especially if conflicts between Russia and Ukraine were to sharpen. It could then be caught in a complex dilemma: whether to support the Ukrainian or Russian position, or maintain a studiously neutral stance while ensuring that the dispute does not contribute to further de-stabilizing the Czech-Slovak relationship.

Hungary and Ukraine

Throughout the period of Habsburg domination, Hungary did not share a common border with Russia and no major points of dispute were evident. Hungarian animosity toward the Russians can be traced back to 1848-1849, when Tsarist forces intervened on the side of Vienna to help suppress a nationalist Magyar uprising against Austrian rule. The Russian and Austrian regimes wanted to maintain the international *status quo* and feared their positions were threatened by the nationalist upsurge. After Austro-Hungary was transformed into a "dual monarchy" in 1867, Budapest gained greater control over territories that included sizable Ukrainian and Ruthenian minorities in Subcarpathian Ruthenia. Hungary's policy of magyarization bred antagonisms between the two ethnic groups, until the outbreak of World War One when the Habsburg empire began to unravel. After the creation of Czechoslovakia in 1918, Budapest lost Ruthenia but briefly regained the territory after aligning itself with Hitler during World War Two. It thereby obtained a border with the USSR, which had annexed the neighboring Ukrainian inhabited territories of eastern Poland.

At the close of World War Two, Ruthenia was incorporated into the Ukrainian Soviet Republic and a more durable Hungarian-Soviet border was established. A Communist regime was imposed in Budapest by Moscow and the Stalinist terror campaign eliminated thousands of Hungarian nationalists and democrats. The crushing of the 1956 Hungarian revolution by the Red Army, in which several thousand people perished and about 200,000 people fled to the West, deepened Magyar bitterness against the Russian occupation and Communist rule. This resentment was only partially mitigated by the economic reforms and political liberalization introduced by the regime of Janos Kadar between the late 1960s and the late 1980s.

Post-Communist relations between Budapest and Moscow have not been marked by any significant antagonisms. Minority issues or territorial settlements have not figured highly on the political agendas of either state, even though Hungary has sought closer cultural and economic ties with the Magyar minority in Ukraine. Agreements on Soviet troop withdrawals were arranged fairly smoothly in the past three years, and despite some frictions over financial compensation for environmental damage their departure has not been hindered or interrupted. But as with its northern neighbors, two issues may increasingly preoccupy Hungarian-Commonwealth relations. First, the prospects for social turmoil and violent conflict in the nearby post-Soviet republics would adversely affect energy supplies and trading arrangements with Budapest and increase the chances of refugees fleeing to Hungary and overburdening its fragile economy. Second, although the Budapest authorities adopted a cautious approach toward Soviet disintegration, they also sought to establish cooperative relations with the pro-independence government in neighboring Ukraine. In the event of a serious political crisis in Ukraine, or a major conflict between Ukraine and Russia, Hungary could find itself drawn into the turmoil. Budapest would naturally remain particularly concerned to safeguard the position of the Magyar minority in Ukraine.

Approximately 170,000 Hungarians reside in western Ukraine, in a section of Transcarpathian Ruthenia, a region that formed part of upper Hungary for several hundred years until 1919. According to Hungarian statistics, the actual number of residents may exceed 200,000, thus making Magyars the second largest nationality in the region. After the democratic changes in both states, Hungarian commentators became more outspoken on the minority issue and criticized the continuing deprivation of Magyar national rights in the USSR.[31] Under the Gorbachev regime and the increasingly sovereign government in Kiev, greater tolerance has been shown for the Magyar minority and a Hungarian Cultural Association of Subcarpathia (HCAS) was established in Uzhgorod in February 1989. It promoted Hungarian identity, culture, language, and education.[32] Its membership reached some 30,000 by late 1991. A Hungarian Youth Association of Subcarpathia (HYAS) was also founded in November 1990, which promptly established contacts with Magyar organizations in Transylvania and Slovakia. The HCAS proved very successful in the 1990 local elections, returning eighteen deputies to the

Transcarpathian *oblast* council, as well as deputies to village *raion*, and city councils. It has also supported the right of Ruthenia to autonomy and self-determination, provided that Magyar ethnic autonomy within the republic were to be guaranteed. In October 1991, a Hungarian Democratic Alliance of Ukraine (HDAU) was established to help coordinate the activities of all Magyar organizations in the republic.

In September 1990, Hungarian President Arpad Goncz visited Kiev and Uzhgorod and met with representatives of the Magyar minority. Steps were taken to establish diplomatic ties with the Ukrainian republic, and to help guarantee full cultural rights for the Hungarian population. Ukrainian President Leonid Kravchuk agreed to grant "cultural autonomy" to the Magyars and to draft a joint "national minority charter" with Hungary. Budapest also established consular ties with Ukraine as a first step toward full diplomatic relations. Hungarian consulates were opened in both Kiev and Uzhgorod even before the declaration of Ukrainian independence in August 1991.[33] After the Ukrainian referendum on independence in December 1991, the consulate in Kiev was upgraded to an embassy and Budapest became one of the first capitals to afford diplomatic recognition to Ukraine. In the same month, Hungary signed a treaty with the Russian government and became the first country to afford diplomatic recognition to Russia.

In the December 1991 Ukrainian referendum, the population of Beregszasz region within the Transcarpathian *oblast,* where almost half of Ruthenia's Hungarian population reside, voted overwhelmingly for the creation of a Magyar "national district" in the *raion*. Hungarian leaders also proposed expanding the district by incorporating neighboring Magyar settlements. Although relations between Budapest and Kiev have developed relatively smoothly, they could become clouded by the Subcarpathian issue, especially if Magyars in the region press for autonomy and closer links with Hungary, or if Kiev adopts a more nationalistic anti-minority stance.

Closer Hungarian-Ukrainian ties are unlikely to antagonize the reformist Russian government at this stage. The development of such relations depends partly on the structure, content, and longevity of the Commonwealth between Ukraine, Russia, and Belarus, and on how much political and economic sovereignty the western republics will be able to maintain in the difficult years ahead. Budapest also remains concerned about a potential flow of refugees from Ukraine in the event of widespread unrest in the Commonwealth. Most of the migrants could in fact be ethnic Hungarians and may be welcomed in the country, but they could also strain the country's economic capacity and provoke social unrest.

One remaining point of dispute with the former Soviet Union revolves around the question of compensation for Red Army damages to the Hungarian environment.[34] This controversy has also arisen in Poland and Czechoslovakia. Moscow in turn has claimed reimbursement for the construction work it completed in Hungary since the 1950s, as well as payment for the immovable assets it has left behind in the country. A compromise agreement will probably be reached through a zero balance assessment, where costs and benefits may be calculated to have roughly balanced out for both sides.

Romania, Ukraine, and Moldova

With the weakening of Ottoman rule during the 18th and 19th centuries, Romanian-Russian conflicts surfaced over the territories north of the Black Sea. The Russians pressed south toward the Balkans and seized Bessarabia, or eastern Moldavia (Moldova), in 1812 and embarked on a policy of russification. Modern Romania was created in 1859, with the unification of Wallachia and western Moldavia. The 1856 Treaty of Paris returned Bessarabia to Romanian control, but when Romania obtained full international recognition in 1878 after the Russo-Turkish war, the Russians annexed Bessarabia once again as payment for their defeat of the Ottoman Turkish armies. The other source of territorial conflict between Russia and Romania was the province of Bukovina, which contained a substantial Romanian and Ukrainian population. Austria annexed Bukovina at the end of the 18th century and incorporated the area into Galicia until the 1840s, when it became an autonomous province of the Habsburg empire. In 1920, after the fall of Austro-Hungary and the revolutionary upheaval in Russia, Romanian leaders in Bukovina proclaimed the union of Bukovina with Romania. That same year, the whole of Bessarabia was also reincorporated into the Romanian state.

During the early part of World War Two, Nazi Germany pressurized Bucharest to cede Bessarabia and northern Bukovina to the Soviets to honor the Hitler-Stalin pact. But resentment mounted over Moscow's claims that the Moldavians (in Bessarabia) were not ethnically Romanian, and over the imposition of the cyrillic alphabet in the province. When Bucharest allied with Germany, Hitler promised to return Bessarabia to Romania after the defeat of Soviet forces. The area was occupied by Romanian troops as Bucharest contributed substantially to the German war effort against Moscow. At the end of World War Two, after Russian forces occupied Romania, Stalin incorporated northern Bukovina and parts of southern Bessarabia (the Herta district) into the Ukrainian Soviet Republic, annexed the rest of Bessarabia to create the Moldavian Soviet Republic, and occupied Romania's Serpents Island off the Black Sea coast. Resentment over the loss of these territories was muffled by overwhelming Soviet power and Moscow's acquiescence to a degree of Romanian independence in return for the shelving of any land claims.[35]

As Bucharest achieved some measure of autonomy from Moscow during the late 1950s, Soviet troops were withdrawn from the country and Romania stopped participating in Warsaw Pact military exercises. In 1964, the Romanian Communist Party issued a "declaration of independence" stressing the integrity of small nations. This document encapsulated Bucharest's distinctive approach to foreign policy within the Soviet "sphere of influence." Romania refused to participate in the 1968 Warsaw Pact invasion of Czechoslovakia, and President Nicolae Ceausescu explicitly rejected the "Brezhnev Doctrine" of limited sovereignty for Communist states. Although the Kremlin tolerated Bucharest's maverick stance, especially as its domestic policies were not veering away from hard-line Leninism, it applied occasional pressures on Ceausescu and used proxies such as Hungary to criticize certain Romanian policies. Bucharest remained concerned that Hungarian grievances over Transylvania could one day be used as a pretext for Warsaw Pact intervention if the Kremlin grew overly alarmed by Bucharest's independent stance. As a protective measure, the Romanian leadership adjusted its military strategy during the 1970s toward a system of comprehensive national defense and began to improve its relations with Western states.

Relations between Bucharest and Moscow improved substantially after the violent overthrow of the Ceausescu regime in December 1989. The Soviet regime expressed full support for the National Salvation Front (NSF), which seized power in Romania and subsequently won the first general elections in May 1990. However, the Moldovan issue in particular placed some strains on inter-state contacts. The declaration of sovereignty by the new government of the Soviet Moldavian (or Moldovan) republic put the Romanian regime in a difficult position. On the one hand, Bucharest supported the aspirations of Moldovans to national independence and could not ignore growing calls in the republic for reunification with Romania. On the other hand, it wanted to avoid a dangerous rift with the Kremlin by directly supporting the Moldovan independence movement. Moreover, as various nationalist and pro-unification groups become more active in Romania itself, the NSF government came under increasing pressure to openly back the Moldovan authorities.

The Moldovan question will also have an impact on Bucharest's relations with the independent Ukrainian authorities. Controversies could easily escalate over Romanian territories that were incorporated in Soviet Ukraine after World War Two, including northern Bukovina, parts of northern Moldova, and some Danubian districts of southern Moldova. Such territorial disputes could also embroil Moscow, particularly if a future Russian government engages in fostering divisions and disputes between neighboring republics in an effort to prevent the emergence of a united front against Moscow's influence. Since Ceausescu's fall, a growing interest has been visible in both Romania and Moldova in moving closer together. The initial focus was on furthering family contacts, expanding cultural ties, stressing the common ethnic, linguistic, and cultural heritage of both peoples, and pressing for an open border.[36] But as Moldova aspired to greater political independence, the question of reunification has increasingly preoccupied both states.

About 3.2 million Romanians live in Soviet Moldova, constituting nearly three-quarters of the republic's population, and another 800,000 live in the Bukovina area and the southern Danubian districts of Ukraine. Since its inception, the independent, non-Communist Moldovan Popular Front (MPF) has been extremely active in establishing contacts with Romania and in pressing for the restoration of the Romanian language, Latin alphabet, and national flag. During the Romanian revolution, the MPF staged demonstrations in solidarity with their co-ethnics and calls for reunification were also heard among the Moldovan crowds. In May 1990, thousands of people gathered on both sides of the Prut River frontier to express their desire for closer links and open borders. The rallies were organized by the MPF, other pro-sovereignty groups in Moldova, and a number of Romanian-based organizations. With their election victory in the summer of 1990, the MPF proclaimed the republic of Moldova a sovereign state and further expanded contacts with Romania.

Moldovan political groups have questioned the permanence of the present border with Romania: the possibility of territorial adjustments with Ukraine has also been raised in the local press. According to some reports, support for reunification with Romania grew markedly among the younger generation, as it became increasingly frustrated with life in the USSR. Pro-Romanian feelings have also been spurred by various demands for territorial autonomy among Ukrainian, Russian, and Gagauz Turkish minorities within Moldova that made up about 25% of the population and threatened to fracture the republic. The authorities in Kishinev (Chisinau in Romanian) have been highly critical of the Soviet failure to control separatist tendencies among ethnic Russians and Gagauz Turks, who declared autonomous regions within Moldova in late 1990. Indeed, the Moldovan authorities suspected that Moscow was encouraging separatist forces in order to apply pressure on the republican government and then pose as a viable mediator and protector.

In late December 1990, with the ascendancy of hard-liners in Moscow, the Soviet regime turned up the heat on various independence movements in the USSR, including the Moldovans, in order to maintain the union and discourage separatist trends. But instead of cowering Moldova to abide by Soviet laws, Moscow's conservative swing stiffened resistance and even radicalized former supporters of gradualism in their drive for national independence.[37] The partial crackdown also motivated Kishinev to canvass support from other countries, including Romania, for Moldovan sovereignty. In March 1991, the republican authorities opposed the holding of a Soviet referendum on preserving the USSR. The vast majority of ethnic Moldovans boycotted the balloting, although a moderate turnout was reported among the Russian, Ukrainian, and Gagauz minorities who opposed Moldovan secession. Moldova was also one of the six republics that refused to sign the April

1991 agreement to forge a new union treaty. It pressed instead for outright independence from the Soviet Union.

Conservative Soviet forces continued to voice disquiet over developments in Moldova and over Bucharest's alleged ambitions in the republic. They charged that "right wing forces" in Romania were cultivating anti-Soviet feelings and even lodging territorial claims on the USSR.[38] Romania's National Peasant Party (NPP) was singled out for vehement criticism because it demanded the return of Soviet Moldova, northern Bukovina, and the Zmeina islands off the Black Sea coast. In late 1990, such accusations began to emanate from high levels of the Soviet government. For example, in December 1990 the Ministry of Foreign Affairs issued a strongly worded statement criticizing Romanian "interference in Soviet domestic affairs" and explicitly attacked comments by Prime Minister Petre Roman supporting Moldova's struggle for independence.[39] During early 1991, unsubstantiated reports appeared in the central Soviet media alleging that Romania had been supplying arms to Moldovan separatists. The charge was strenuously denied by the Bucharest government, at a time when Moscow was trying to reassert its control over the renegade republics and appeared to be looking for pretexts for intervention. The USSR's Foreign Affairs Ministry warned "extremist elements" in Romania against demanding the return of Moldovan lands, and declared that any "acts of provocation" would be adamantly opposed and all Soviet territories resolutely defended.[40]

Romania's ruling National Salvation Front initially did not overtly or publicly support Moldovan reunification, but it has endeavored to steadily improve relations with the republic. Although the Bucharest government asserted that the annexation of Bessarabia and Bukovina in 1941 was an "historical injustice," it did not press for any border revisions. Instead, throughout 1990 and 1991 efforts were made to develop humanitarian, economic, cultural, and political ties with Moldova at various levels.

In February 1991, Moldova's President Mircea Snegur visited Bucharest and met with Romania's president Ion Iliescu, finalizing a series of bilateral economic and cultural agreements. The possibility of opening up consulates in Iasi (in Romania) and Kishinev was also discussed, and work was begun on new inter-state treaties.[41] Even though the visit was relatively low key, Snegur's statements contained various references to national unity and thus implicitly questioned Soviet contentions that Romanians and Moldovans were different peoples. He also asserted that Moldova sought to protect the Romanian population in those counties of southern Bessarabia and northern Bukovina that were allocated to Soviet Ukraine after the war, again implying that their recovery could become a future goal. Snegur advanced the concept of a "cultural confederation" between Romania and Moldova that could also be extended to other fields, and he laid the groundwork for an inter-governmental treaty between Kishinev and Bucharest. In March 1991, during a trip to Latin America, Romanian Premier Petre Roman went much further than

Snegur, by acknowledging that Romania eventually expected to regain Moldova from the Soviet Union.[42]

During the course of 1991, Bucharest came under increasing pressure to recognize Moldova from domestic public opinion and as a result of Kishinev's accelerating progress toward sovereignty. In June 1991, the Romanian parliament condemned the Soviet annexation of Bessarabia and northern Bukovina, and urged a strategy of "small steps" toward the integration of Romania and Moldova.[43] But it stopped short of making direct territorial demands on the USSR. After Moldova's declaration of independence in August 1991, Bucharest and Kishinev agreed to exchange ambassadors and Romania officially recognized the independence of Moldova and called for international acceptance of the new state. President Iliescu also stated that reunification was eventually inevitable, but underscored a cautious, gradualist approach toward such an objective.[44]

In many respects, some of the non-Communist Romanian opposition parties have been more outspoken than the Bucharest regime on the Moldovan issue. Unlike the NSF government, they did not have to balance their support for Moldovan independence with any fears of antagonizing the Kremlin. In December 1990, the extra-parliamentary opposition group, the Civic Alliance Movement (CAM), publicly professed its support for Moldovan sovereignty. Some CAM spokesmen called upon the government to grant Romanian citizenship rights to all Moldovans. The Alliance criticized the Bucharest government for signing a treaty of cooperation and friendship with Moscow in early 1991, because it did not declare null and void the Molotov-Ribbentrop Pact which assigned Moldova and Bukovina to the USSR. Alliance leaders considered that any ratification of the treaty would be equivalent to an act of national treason, by abandoning the Romanians in the Soviet Union.[45] The Assembly of the Moldovan Popular Front also condemned the treaty for its content and timing, which purportedly undermined Romanian national interests.

Throughout 1990 and 1991, ultra-nationalist Romanian political groups such as *Vatra Romaneasca* criticized the ongoing Soviet occupation and the continuing threats against the Moldovan population. In March 1991, a number of Romanian parties, including the National Liberals, Social Democrats, and National Peasants, issued a declaration condemning the Soviet referendum as an aggressive act by an occupying power and at variance with the norms of international law.[46] This statement mirrored the condemnations made public by Iurie Rosca, President of the Moldovan Popular Front. He insisted that the Moldovan authorities would be prepared to organize a referendum throughout the entire "ethnic Romanian territory" so that all Romanians would have the opportunity to express their allegiances. Rosca also asserted that Moldovans were legitimate citizens of the Romanian state "temporarily under Soviet occupation."[47] A month later, Rosca endorsed

Romania's democratic opposition and pledged that the MPF would work toward the democratization of the country. He also underscored that only a democratic system in Romania would prove attractive to the Moldovan public.[48]

Several nationalist Romanian organizations have actively campaigned for closer ties with Moldova, as well as the return of provinces lost to Ukraine after World War Two. The Pro-Bessarabia and Bukovina Association (PBBA), a nominally socio-cultural organization, has staged rallies and demonstrations to demand full border openings and closer links with Moldova and Bukovina at every level.[49] They have supported the nationalist revival in Moldova and formed contacts with some MPF factions in the republic. The Iasi-based Romanian Popular Front (RPF) has gone even further by demanding immediate reunification. Romanian nationalist groups have increasingly pointed to German reunification as a precedent for Romanian-Moldovan unity, if the majority of Moldovans so desired.

There were signs of growing impatience in Romania with the pace of political progress in the Soviet Union, as well as anger at Moscow's attempts to bring Kishinev into line. In October 1990, protests were held in several Romanian cities against what were perceived as separatist provocations by Russian and Gagauz minorities in the Trans-Dniestr region of Moldova, allegedly backed by Communist Party leaders in Moscow. Further rallies in support of Moldovan independence were organized in Romania by *Vatra* nationalists, non-Communist political parties, and some Romanian student groups. At the same time, the Romanian parliament, under visible pressure from public opinion, adopted a position of support for the leaders of the Moldovan republic in a show of solidarity with the beleaguered aspiring state.

Before and during the August 1991 Soviet coup attempt, Romania's political leaders displayed some nervousness about a potential internal crackdown by the Kremlin and a dramatic reversal in the decentralization process. This also raised concerns about a potential flood of Moldovan refugees fleeing into Romania as internal conditions deteriorated in the USSR. Either Moscow could encourage such a population exodus to deflate pressures for independence, or widespread political chaos and economic collapse would stimulate Moldovans to seek refugee status across the border. Such developments could contribute to further destabilizing Romania, which already confronts serious domestic economic problems.

The Moldovan parliament declared the republic's independence in late August 1991, and proceeded to dismantle its political ties to the Soviet Union while maintaining some economic links with Moscow. Kishinev sought international recognition as an independent state but did not place reunification with Romania on its immediate agenda. Bucharest in turn recognized Moldova's independence but did not press forward on reunification. In fact, a split developed between leaders of the MPF and President Snegur and a majority of parliamentary deputies over the question of unification. While the Front sought an early union, the government placed emphasis on Moldovan statehood and an indefinite postponement of reunification.[50] Snegur's position was reinforced during the single-candidate direct presidential elections in December 1991, in which he obtained 98% of the vote.

It appeared that as Moldova neared the achievement of national statehood, aspirations for reunification receded, particularly as Romania had little to offer the republic on the economic front, in terms of trade, resources, and markets, and continued to be racked by its own economic and political problems. Indeed, many Moldovan activists contended that democracy in the republic was actually further advanced than in Romania. Moreover, leaders of the non-Moldovan minorities clearly favored separate Moldovan statehood over reunification with Romania. Nonetheless, some Moldovan leaders calculated that continuing international isolation, coupled with persistent territorial demands and lingering opposition to Moldovan independence among substantial segments of the Ukrainian, Russian, and Gagauz minorities, could eventually push the republic toward closer association with Romania even if the minority territories were to secede.[51]

Moldova also faces looming territorial disputes with an increasingly self-assertive and independent Ukraine; a conflict into which Romania could easily be drawn. The MPF, one of the dominant forces in the republic, has spoken out for the "re-integration of historical Moldovan lands." This would presumably signify the re-unification of Moldova with the three Bessarabian counties attached to Ukraine after World War Two, as well as the north Bukovina region in south western Ukraine. In this regard, some political circles in Kishinev began to raise the "Greater Moldova" question, envisaging the reconstitution of the Moldovan state in its historical dimensions.[52] This would involve the annexation of territories currently held by both Ukraine and Romania; a position that is extremely controversial and vehemently rejected by proponents of immediate reunification with Romania.

After Ukraine's declaration of independence, it remained unclear whether any territorial issues could be amicably resolved between Kishinev and Kiev. Tentative proposals have been floated about some mutual and peaceful border readjustments, assigning areas with large concentrations of Romanians to Moldova and zones with Ukrainian majorities to Ukraine.[53] Bucharest itself could also become actively engaged in this process, but it must be careful not to antagonize Kiev by claiming unilateral territorial changes. For instance, condemnations of the Molotov-Ribbentrop pact by the Romanian parliament have caused some consternations in the Ukrainian Supreme Soviet that Bucharest was supporting major border revisions.

Although the Bukovina issue has been less visible in Romania than the Moldovan problem, the Romanian community in the region (part of the Chernovtsy *oblast*), which comprises over 20% of the population, has begun to organize during the past two years. In October 1990, the first national assembly of Bukovinian Romanians was held in Chernovtsy and delegates demanded various cultural and political concessions from Kiev.

Romanian activists in Bukovina established the Mihai Eminescu Society for Romanian Culture (MESRC) in order to "defend the history and culture" of northern Bukovina and the Herta district in southern Bessarabia. They also complained about being neglected by Bucharest during the latter's negotiations with Moscow and Kiev over the status of former Romanian territories.[54] According to the MESRC leadership, Ukrainian authorities have actually intensified the republic's de-romanianization program in Bukovina during the past years.[55] Meanwhile, the pro-Bukovina organizations in Romania have called upon Romanians in northern Bukovina to apply for Moldovan citizenship. For these groupings, future links with Romania are projected through closer association between Bukovina and a sovereign Moldova. Some disputes have also arisen with regard to the rights of the 50,000 strong Romanian population in Transcarpathian Ruthenia, and over the position of the 70,000 Ukrainians in northern Romania.

Both positive and negative trends have been visible in Ukrainian-Moldovan relations. On the positive side, both the Ukrainian and Moldovan authorities have agreed to promote the language, education, and culture of their respective ethnic minorities. Indeed, Kishinev has probably offered more than Bucharest would countenance in a reunified Romania by considering some form of territorial autonomy for the compact Russian, Ukrainian, and Gagauz populations. On the negative side, the danger exists that radical nationalist Ukrainian groups will oppose any political or territorial compromises with either Moldova or Romania. They may refuse to offer far-reaching concessions to Romanian minorities within the republic, and could campaign for the secession of Ukrainian-populated districts from Moldova. Moreover, Moscow could either seek to arbitrate or exploit the Ukrainian-Moldovan dispute to its advantage in order to preserve Russian influence over both republics. The stance of Bucharest in such circumstances could prove crucial in either exacerbating or muting potential conflicts.

The reformist National Salvation Front government has tried to avoid major controversies with its northern neighbors. But it may be irresistibly drawn into the fray, and it could in turn seek to capitalize on a foreign policy issue to garner domestic credibility. With the disintegration of the Soviet Union, the NSF has placed increasing stress on reunification and demanded the return to Romania of territory seized by the USSR. A future Romanian government, following the next general elections, may be less inclined to remain circumspect over Moldova—a position that has helped Bucharest curry favor with the Kremlin in the past. The specter of a four-way confrontation over Moldova and northern Bukovina, between Bucharest, Kishinev, Moscow, and Kiev, could then become a reality.

Notes

1. For background on Polish history consult Norman Davies, *God's Playground: A History of Poland, Vol. 1, The Origins to 1795* and *Vol. 2, 1795 to Present* (Oxford: Clarendon Press, 1981).

2. Some background on the conflict can be found in Roman Stefanowski, "Soviet Troops in Poland," Radio Free Europe, *Report on Eastern Europe*, Vol. 1, No. 9, 2 March 1990.

3. For a review of Soviet-Polish negotiations over the troop issue see Louise Vinton, "Soviet Union Begins Withdrawing Troops—But On Its Own Terms," Radio Free Europe, *Report on Eastern Europe*, Vol. 2, No. 17, 26 April 1991.

4. Check Jan B. de Weydenthal, "Policy Toward the Eastern Neighbors" Radio Free Europe, *Report on Eastern Europe*, Vol. 2, No. 47, 22 November 1991.

5. For a useful summary of the potential refugee problem see Christopher Wellisz, "Soviet Coup Renews Fears of Exodus," Radio Free Europe, *Report on Eastern Europe*, Vol. 2, No. 37, 13 September 1991. See also Klaus Segbers, "Migration and Refugee Movements from the USSR: Causes and Prospects," Radio Liberty, *Report on the USSR*, Vol. 3, No. 46, 15 November 1991.

6. See Vladimir Kusin, "Refugees in Central and Eastern Europe: Problem or Threat?" Radio Free Europe, *Report on Eastern Europe*, Vol. 2, No. 3, 18 January 1991.

7. For a valuable perspective see Halina Sterczynska, "Before the Migration of Peoples," *Zycie Gospodarcze*, Warsaw, 27 January 1991.

8. See the statute of the "Polish Vilno National Territorial Land," *Magazyn Wilenski*, Vilnius, 1-15 June 1991.

9. *The Economist*, London, 14 September 1991. Also see Jan B. de Weydenthal, "The Polish-Lithuanian Dispute," Radio Free Europe, *Report on Eastern Europe*, Vol. 2, No. 41, 11 October 1991.

10. See Radio Free Europe/ Radio Liberty, *Daily Report*, No. 177, 17 September 1991. For some analysis check Richard J. Krickus, "Lithuania's Polish Question," Radio Liberty, *Report on the USSR*, Vol. 3, No. 48, 29 November 1991.

11. *PAP*, Warsaw, in English, 13 September 1991.

12. See *PAP*, Warsaw, in English, 17 September 1991, and the interview with President Landsbergis in Warsaw on 15 September 1991, on *Radio Warszawa Network*, in Polish, 16 September 1991, in *FBIS-EEU*-91-180, 17 September 1991.

13. See "Lithuanians and Poles," in *Kontrasty*, Warsaw, July 1990.

14. For some background see Agnieszka Magdziak-Miszewska, "Understanding Belarus," *Zycie Warszawy*, Warsaw, 16 October 1990; and Stanislaw Brzeg-Wielunski, "The Belarusn Democratic Union," *Lad*, Warsaw, 7 October 1990.

15. Interview with Tadeusz Gawin, president of the Union of Poles in Belarus, in *Rzeczpospolita*, Warsaw, 31 October-1 November 1991.

16. See Anna Sabbat-Swidlicka, "Friendship Declarations Signed With Ukraine and Russia," Radio Free Europe, *Report on Eastern Europe*, Vol. 1, No. 44, 2 November 1990.

17. For example, see the interview with Stanislaw Szalacki, Chairman of the Polish Cultural Association in Ukraine, in *Tygodnik Gdanski*, Gdansk, 27 January 1991.

18. *PAP*, Warsaw, 27 December 1991, in *FBIS-EEU*-91-250, 30 December 1991.

19. See Grzegorz Polak, "Dispute Over the Cathedral," *Gazeta Wyborcza,* Warsaw, 6 March 1991.

20. From the interview with Pawel Stefanowski, head of the Lemko Citizens Circle, by Zaneta Semprich, "We Don't Want to be a Bargaining Card," *Rzeczpospolita,* Warsaw, 30 October 1990.

21. For a useful article on the Kaliningrad area see Stanislaw Kulawiec, "Within a Hand's Reach: To Get a Start on the Germans in Kaliningrad," *Polityka,* Warsaw, 21 April 1990.

22. See Bartlomiej Lesniewski, "Tantar for the Brave," *Wprost,* Warsaw, No. 46, 17 November 1991.

23. Background on the Ruthenians can be found in Alexander Bonkalo, *The Rusyns,* East European Monographs (New York: Columbia University Press, 1990).

24. See Natalie Melnyczuk, "Ukraine Develops an Independent Foreign Policy: The First Year," Radio Liberty, *Report on the USSR,* Vol. 3, No. 43, 25 October 1991.

25. See the interview with Paul Robert Magocsi, "Ruthenians Are No Longer in Parentheses," *Smena,* Bratislava, 29 March 1991.

26. See Jaromir Horec, "Subject: Ruthenia," *Lidove Noviny,* Prague, 21 September 1990.

27. See Peter Juscak, "Ruthenian Renaissance," *Hlas Demokracie,* Kosice, Slovakia, No. 7, 1991.

28. See "The Fate of the State and the Country," *Lidova Demokracie,* Prague, 19 June 1991.

29. See Jiri Pehe, "The Emergence of Right-Wing Extremism," Radio Free Europe, *Report on Eastern Europe,* Vol. 2, No. 26, 28 June 1991.

30. *CSTK,* Prague, 23 October 1991, in *FBIS-EEU*-91-206, 24 October 1991.

31. See "Real Change Instead of a Semblance of Rights: Debate Over the Situation of Hungarians in the Lower Carpathian Region," *Nepszava,* Budapest, 13 January 1990.

32. For details on the Hungarian population in Ruthenia see Alfred A. Reisch, "Transcarpathia's Hungarian Minority and the Autonomy Issue," *RFE/RL Research Report,* Vol. 1, No. 6, 7 February 1992.

33. For background see Alfred Reisch, "Hungary and Ukraine Agree to Upgrade Bilateral Relations," Radio Free Europe, *Report on Eastern Europe,* Vol. 1, No. 44, 2 November 1990.

34. For background see Zoltan D. Barany, "Not a Smooth Ride: Soviet Troop Withdrawals from Hungary," Radio Free Europe, *Report on Eastern Europe,* Vol. 1, No. 24, 15 June 1990, and Alfred E. Reisch, "Free of Soviet Military Forces After Forty-Six Years," Radio Free Europe, *Report on Eastern Europe,* Vol. 2, No. 30, 26 July 1991.

35. For background see N. Dima, *Bessarabia and Bukovina: The Soviet-Romanian Territorial Dispute* (New York: Columbia University Press, 1982).

36. For information see Mihai Carp, "Cultural Ties Between Romania and Soviet Moldova," Radio Free Europe, *Report on Eastern Europe,* Vol. 1, No. 30, 27 July 1990.

37. See Vladimir Socor, "Moldova Resists Pressure and Boycotts Union Referendum," Radio Liberty, *Report on the USSR,* Vol. 3, No. 13, 29 March 1991.

38. For example, see Lt. Col. W. Manin, "What is Romania's Right Wing Achieving?" *Krasnaya Zvezda,* Moscow, 20 August 1990.

39. Check "Who's Actually Destabilizing?" *Romania Libera,* Bucharest, 5 December 1990.

40. See "The Foreign Policy and Diplomatic Activity of the USSR (November 1989-November 1990)," A Survey Prepared by the USSR Ministry of Foreign Affairs, *International Affairs,* No. 4, April 1991, Moscow, p. 102.

41. Vladimir Socor, "Moldovan President Breaks New Ground in Romania," Radio Liberty, *Report on the USSR,* Vol. 3, No. 8, 22 February 1991.

42. See *Tanjug,* Belgrade, in English, 8 March 1991, in *FBIS-EEU*-91-047, 11 March 1991.

43. Vladimir Socor, "Annexation of Bessarabia and Northern Bukovina Condemned by Romania," Radio Liberty, *Report on the USSR,* Vol. 3, No. 29, 19 July 1991.

44. Radio Free Europe/ Radio Liberty, *Daily Report,* 29 August 1991, No. 164.

45. Appeal by the Civic Alliance Movement to the Romanian parliament, "Bessarabia: A Teardrop of My Nation," in *Romania Liberia,* Bucharest, 26 April 1991.

46. See *Dreptatea,* Bucharest, 13 March 1991, in *FBIS-EEU*-91-054, 20 March 1991.

47. In an interview with Iurie Rosca in *Romania Libera,* Bucharest, 12 March 1991, *FBIS-EEU*-91-052, 18 March 1991.

48. Radio Free Europe/ Radio Liberty, *Daily Report,* No. 73, 16 April 1991.

49. For some information on the PBBA check *Rompres,* Bucharest, in English, 28 November 1990 in *FBIS-EEU*-90-230, 29 November 1990.

50. Vladimir Socor, "Moldavia Builds a New State," *RFE-RL Research Report,* Vol. 1, No. 1, 3 January 1992.

51. Vladimir Socor, "Moldova Proclaims Independence, Commences Secession from USSR," Radio Liberty, *Report on the USSR,* Vol. 3, No. 42, 18 October 1991.

52. Vladimir Socor, "Why Moldova Does Not Seek Reunification with Romania," *RFE-RL Research Report,* Vol. 1, No. 5, 31 January 1992.

53. For a useful analysis see Vladimir Socor, "Moldovan Lands Between Romania and Ukraine: The Historical and Political Geography," Radio Liberty, *Report on the USSR,* Vol. 2, No. 46, 16 November 1990.

54. Check the interview with Vasile Tariteanu, "The Drama of Bukovina: A Forced March Toward National Oblivion," *Romania Libera,* Bucharest, 19 June 1991.

55. See the interview with Vasile Tariteanu, Secretary of the Mihai Eminescu Society for Romanian Culture, in *Romania Libera,* Bucharest, 31 July 1991.

3

Central European Disputes

After the collapse of Communist rule in central Europe in 1989, four former Soviet satellites veered away from Moscow's orbit. During the following year, the German Democratic Republic (GDR) moved rapidly toward economic, political, and military integration with the German Federal Republic, while Poland, Czechoslovakia, and Hungary achieved their sovereignty and national independence. The new democratically elected governments in all three states embarked on far-reaching programs of domestic reform. The objective in each case was the creation of a pluralistic political system and a competitive market economy that would facilitate beneficial association with the Western democracies and the expanding pan-European institutions. But the disintegration of Communist structures and the difficult transition to democratic capitalism also unleashed new domestic tensions. These have revolved around the competition for scarce economic and political resources, and have been exacerbated by the absence of entrenched and stable democratic institutions.

The post-Communist transformations also exposed long dormant ethnic and national tensions, both within state borders and in the foreign relations of the newly liberated countries. Although in central Europe these enmities did not seriously jeopardize the direction of the reform process, in some instances they have contributed to complicating the evolving system of international relations. German unification and Soviet disintegration have also created new sources of inter-state discord that will need to be settled if a stable post-Cold War European order is to develop. Not all international disputes in the region are of the same order of magnitude: indeed some appear benign and can be resolved peacefully between responsible democratic governments. Others, however, appear more problematic and could even escalate into more menacing conflicts. This chapter provides some historical context to current conditions in central Europe, describes and evaluates the more important points of national friction, and considers some likely scenarios in the development of inter-ethnic and international relations in the region.

Czechs, Slovaks, Moravians, and Silesians

The closely related western Slav groups, the Czechs and Slovaks, maintained a loose association in the great Moravian Empire but underwent separate development after the 11th century. The Czechs came under stronger Germanic influence and adopted a variant of Protestantism, but were absorbed by the Austrian Habsburg empire by the 17th century and subjected to forcible conversions to Catholicism. The Slovak areas were annexed by the Hungarian crown in the 11th century, and the largely Catholic population underwent a prolonged process of Magyar assimilation. The two regions also experienced differing forms of economic development. The Czech areas of Bohemia and Moravia began to industrialize during the 19th century and a sizable middle class and proletariat emerged. Slovakia remained predominantly rural and semi-feudal and its population was mostly peasant.

After the collapse of the Austro-Hungarian empire at the close of World War One, the new state of Czechoslovakia was formed to help protect the Slav peoples against foreign domination.[1] The country consisted of the Czech lands of Bohemia, Moravia, parts of formerly Austrian Silesia, and the ex-Hungarian provinces of Slovakia and Subcarpathian-Ruthenia. Although both Czech and Slovak leaders agreed on this essentially voluntary union, problems soon arose over the structure of the state and on relations between the two major nationalities. A key bone of contention revolved around the definition of the new state: whether it was the common property of two nations (Czech and Slovak) or of one nation (Czechoslovak). Czech leaders favored "Czechoslovakism," with a unitary government structure and the gradual blending of separate ethnic identities. Some Slovak leaders became anxious that such an arrangement would dilute and eventually extinguish their national distinctiveness and Catholic faith. The Slovaks also complained that the country's economic strength was concentrated in the Czech lands and that Slovakia would remain an exploitable appendage to Prague. Although in the inter-war period, the major Slovak parties favored a single state structure, a growing sense of grievance was expressed by autonomist and nationalist groupings.

The Czechoslovak state was dismembered by Germany in 1938. Bohemia and Moravia were transformed into Nazi protectorates, Slovakia became a semi-independent German protectorate ruled by a Fascist regime, and Ruthenia was annexed by Hitler's ally, Hungary, in 1939. Following the German defeat and the liberation by Soviet forces at the close of World War Two, the Czechoslovak state was re-established, initially under a multi-party coalition government. But in 1948, the Communists staged a political *coup d'etat* and began to centralize the political and economic systems along Stalinist lines. In the 1950s and early 1960s, Czechoslovakia remained a staunchly pro-Soviet Communist state, with little sign of political dissent, government reform, or regional autonomy. During the extensive but short-lived Prague Spring liberalization in 1968, Slovakia attained some measure of political autonomy. This arrangement survived the Soviet invasion and the subsequent Communist "normalization" that extinguished the embryonic democracy. In 1969, Czechoslovakia was declared a federal socialist state consisting of two republics (Czech and Slovak) with nominally equal rights in the federation. In practice, the federal arrangement was emasculated by the Communist Party's monopolistic control over the country's political, economic, and cultural life.

Following the 1989 "velvet revolution" and the abrupt termination of Communist control, Czechoslovakia began to build a pluralistic and democratic political system. At the same time, pressures began to build in Slovakia for far-reaching political and economic sovereignty. Several new Slovak parties placed regional demands on the national agenda, even though they differed on the timetable and content of Slovak autonomy. The pro-autonomist Slovak Christian Democrats and the separatist Slovak National Party scored well in the country's first multi-party elections in 1990. Their influence, together with that of a pro-independence wing of the governing coalition, Public Against Violence, increased over the following months. Several unresolved issues began to sour relations between Prague and Bratislava, especially with regard to the content of the new republican and federal constitutions, the degree of economic decentralization, and the foreign relations of the Slovak republic.

As Slovak politicians became more assertive, the country appeared threatened by a major political rupture. President Vaclav Havel requested emergency powers to deal with the crisis and called for a referendum to settle the issue of Slovak secessionism. But with economic conditions declining as extensive market reforms began to be implemented, the potential for Slovak radicalism grew substantially. The shape and content of political and economic relations between the two republics in a democratic setting has still to be determined. Meanwhile, increasing numbers of Czech and Slovak politicians and commentators have expressed dissatisfaction with each others' performance and raised serious doubts about the survival of the federation.

During the past two years, a new source of discord emerged between the federal government and increasingly assertive political groups in the Moravian and Silesian part of the Czech republic. Moravian autonomist parties performed well in the June 1990 elections, and began to speak openly about their demands for a tripartite federation between Bohemia, Moravia-Silesia, and Slovakia. This presented Prague with a novel set of constitutional, political, and economic headaches, and further complicated inter-ethnic and inter-republican relations in the country.

After the crushing of the Prague Spring in 1968, the Czechoslovak Communists made some concessions to mute persistent Slovak grievances against excessive centralization in the federal arrangement. The republic obtained greater economic investments and a measure of administrative decentralization, but the latter proved to be of limited practical value because the Communist apparatus dominated all regional affairs and thwarted independent political life. Since the peaceful revolution of November 1989, Slovaks in various newly formed political parties became more outspoken on the issue of self-determination for the region. Slovak deputies remained resentful over Czech discrimination in an unbalanced federation, and in early 1990 they successfully pressured the Federal Assembly into changing the country's name to the Czech and Slovak Federal Republic. This move formally assigned equal status to the two republics. But this was merely a symbolic measure which revealed the deep-seated mistrust between representatives of the two nationalities, and it served to further stimulate Slovak aspirations.

A range of approaches has been adopted by the new political forces toward Slovak sovereignty and toward Slovak relations with the Czech republic and the federal government. Liberal democratic movements such as the Public Against Violence (PAV), which won the majority of seats in the Slovak National Council in June 1990, proposed a looser federal structure. The Christian Democratic Movement (CDM), which finished in second place in the ballot, initially adopted a similar stance but began to seek more far-reaching decentralization of various ministries and increasing decision-making powers for the Slovak republican government. Nationalist groupings, including the Slovak National Party (SNP) and the Slovak Heritage Foundation (SHF), went even further and demanded full independence for the republic and a speedy separation from Prague. While the major parties differed on the content and timetable for achieving self-determination through legalistic means, the nationalist groupings were prepared to capitalize on popular frustrations to boost their cause in street rallies and other protest actions.

During 1990, public support for the nationalists began to climb; by late summer sympathy for the SNP had reportedly grown from 14%, at the time of the general elections, to over 20%. This figure later dropped during the November 1990 local elections, partly because of internal party conflicts, because of competition with other nationalist groups, and because the Christian Democrats and even some PAV deputies had taken aboard nationalist issues and more actively campaigned for Slovak "national interests." The SNP rallied a mere 3% of the November vote, but the CDM gained 27% after recasting its program in a more nationalist direction; it thus became the strongest political force in the republic at local level.

During 1990, several even more radical nationalist organizations were formed, calling for rapid moves toward a fully independent Slovakia. For example, in July 1990 the militant Movement for an Independent Slovakia

(MIS) was established, and a National Salvation Movement (NSM) was inaugurated in October 1990 to press more forcefully for Slovak separation. Other openly separatist groups created during the past two years included the Slovak People's Party (SPP) and the Party for National Prosperity (PNP).[2] Although these militant groups were not very influential, they raised a number of important issues with a wide enough resonance to effect the deliberations and decisions of the Slovak republican administration.

In September 1990, a Ministry for International Relations was established in Bratislava. It gave some credence to Slovak demands for international recognition, even though it did not have the foreign policy prerogatives of the federal foreign ministry in Prague. Slovak authorities also pressed for substantial decentralization in economic planning and sought to establish another separate ministry in Bratislava dealing with foreign economic relations. These moves evidently took the Czech authorities by surprise and contributed to further spoiling relations between the two capitals.

Prague and Bratislava further diverged by adopting different approaches toward economic reform. Slovak leaders indicated that they planned to retain a greater share of the state sector and the welfare system. They contended that the Slovak economy was more fragile than the Czech, and the republic's population would suffer disproportionately from the closure of large factories and the disruption of trading networks with the Soviet Union. Bratislava also suspected that the Czechs would unfairly benefit from Western economic ties, as most of the outside assistance and foreign investment continued to be channelled through Prague. President Vaclav Havel calculated that administrative devolution and a far-reaching division of powers between the two republics would help mute separatist sympathies, undercut local grievances, and satisfy Slovak aspirations.[3] But it remained uncertain whether decentralization would actually prove a deterrent or an incentive to demands for national independence.

During the fall of 1990, Slovak nationalist groupings mounted several campaigns to promote the republic's sovereignty and to re-assert Slovak ethnic identity. They focused on the language issue, or the proposed exclusive use of Slovak in the republic's internal affairs.[4] Media and street campaigns were launched to gain popular support for these measures and to apply pressure on the republican government to pass the appropriate legislation. A version of the language law was approved by the Slovak National Council in October 1990, but it was not as radical as the SNP and other nationalist groups had demanded. It confined the use of non-Slovak minority languages, including Hungarian, Ukrainian-Ruthenian, and Czech, to communities where 20% or more of the population was non-Slovak. Prior to this legislation, minority languages could be employed in all official dealings in areas where compact ethnic minorities resided. The contentious law angered Hungarian leaders who saw it as an act of blatant discrimination that curtailed the Magyars' existing liberties. By contrast, most of the Slovak leaders depicted the law as a progressive development and a valuable demonstration of national self-determination. The issue placed further strains on relations between Slovaks and Hungarians both at communal and international levels.

Nationalist groupings continued to raise the language question in their struggles with Prague, and used it to purportedly test the patriotism of republican deputies and Slovak government leaders. They claimed that the Slovak population still experienced administrative discrimination in parts of the republic, especially in the southern areas of Slovakia that contained a large Hungarian minority. Conversely, political commentators in Prague warned the Slovak nationalists that without Czech and federal government protection, an independent Slovakia would become prone to Hungarian demands, while Slovakia's southern borders could come under dispute with Budapest. Some Slovak leaders in turn accused the Czechs of exploiting real and potential disagreements with Hungary to maintain their dominance over Bratislava.

The inter-republican crisis deepened in early December 1990, when President Havel announced that the country faced a potential breakup. He simultaneously pressed for expanded powers in case of a major governmental crisis, including prerogatives to declare states of emergency and to hold a national referendum on the future of the federation. Havel wanted to retain such powers until a new federal constitution was approved and enacted. Slovak leaders had protested against draft amendments to the Czechoslovak constitution, seeking instead the passage of republican constitutions on the basis of which a federal constitution could be drawn up. The constitutional crisis was temporarily resolved in mid-December 1990, when an amendment on power-sharing between republican and federal jurisdictions was passed. It gave broad economic powers to the Czech and Slovak republics, while the federal authorities were to maintain control over national defense, foreign affairs, and important macro-economic policies.

Slovak deputies attacked Havel's propositions for assuming emergency powers as another example of Prague-centrism that subverted Slovak national interests. Although both governments supported a significant devolution of powers to the republics, they continued to differ on the speed, extent, and precise content of administrative decentralization. Slovak leaders sought greater leeway for republican independence and no absolute prohibitions against separation. Some deputies asserted that if constitutional changes failed to fulfill their expectations then they would declare that Slovak republican laws took precedence over federal legislation. In early 1991, Slovak nationalists produced a draft "Declaration of Slovak Sovereignty," emphasizing that laws promulgated by the Slovak National Council took supremacy over federal laws. They also proposed the formation of separate and independent Slovak police and military forces. The Czech authorities became especially perturbed over Slovak demand for separate military formations, as such a move would seriously undermine the country's security and defense capabilities.

In March 1991, new controversies arose between republican leaders. Pro-federalist Czechs and Slovaks claimed that a conspiracy was being hatched by a combination of Slovak nationalists and reform Communists. The alleged plan envisaged severing the federation and forming a closer link with the Soviet Union in the wake of a political *coup d'etat* in Bratislava. The conspiracy theory was repeated by presidential spokesman Michal Zantovsky, who declared that a dangerous new "red-brown coalition" was being formed in Slovakia between Communists and separatists.[5] These statements may have been issued in good faith and were conceivably based on some credible information. But in the midst of the escalating Czech-Slovak dispute, such accusations appeared to be a deliberate scare tactic designed to arouse anxiety and decrease demands for Slovak independence.

In March 1991, the ruling PAV split into pro-federalist and pro-sovereignty wings. The latter moved closer to the CDM and SNP positions on autonomy, leading to additional Prague accusations of a leftist-nationalist conspiracy against the federation.[6] The pro-federalist faction renamed itself the Civic Democratic Union–Public Against Violence (CDU-PAV) in October 1991, to be organized as a distinct political party. Slovakia was also shaken by a major governmental crisis in April 1991. Prime Minister Vladimir Meciar, who led the breakaway PAV faction, Movement For A Democratic Slovakia (MDS), was replaced by the Christian Democratic leader Jan Carnogursky. Meciar was accused by Prague and some of his former PAV colleagues of populism and of adopting extremist positions in seeking greater autonomy for the republic. Pro-Meciar demonstrations were staged in Bratislava, amidst allegations that Prague had actually engineered the coup against him in order to mute Slovakia's drive for autonomy. But the government shakeup seemed to have the opposite effect, by accelerating the rift in the federation.

The Christian Democratic leadership subsequently proposed a confederal system based on a "state treaty" between Czechs and Slovaks, while the MDS also favored a looser confederal arrangement, based on separate republican constitutions and a new inter-state agreement. Meciar himself retained a high degree of popular support and indicated that he was considering teaming up with some nationalist organizations prior to the next general elections. Carnogursky on the other hand experienced persistent problems in keeping the CDM united on the question of Slovak autonomy. In March 1992, the party split into two; the pro-independence wing led by Jan Klepac established the Slovak Christian Democrats (SCD) and called for the declaration of Slovak sovereignty.

In July 1991, the Deputy Chairman of the Slovak National Council proposed establishing an armed Slovak home guard. Even though the notion was defeated by the Slovak legislature, about one-third of the Council actually supported the proposal as did the Slovak Interior Minister Ladislav Pittner. The purported objective of the home guard was to provide greater security for citizens in case of some natural disaster or a destabilizing social upheaval in the republic. But it created dismay among the pro-federalist Slovaks and among Czech leaders, who envisioned the proposition as another attempted step toward separation.[7]

It appeared likely that some kind of referendum would be held in Czechoslovakia to ascertain whether the majority of citizens favored retaining the federation or severing the two republics. But the exact wording of the plebiscite has proved extremely difficult to decide, particularly as a simple yes-no response would leave open the question of what kind of federal arrangement would be pursued and how much power would devolve to the two republican governments.[8] MDS leader Meciar and various Slovak nationalist politicians opposed President Havel's call for an early referendum, fearing majority support for preserving the federation in line with the results of several recent public opinion polls. Instead, Meciar advocated further political debate between elected representatives leading to a new confederal agreement with Prague. In September 1991, MDS leaders signed a document entitled the "Initiative for a Sovereign Slovakia" and pressed for the approval of a new Slovak constitution.[9]

The growing frustration of the Czech authorities became evident in November 1991. President Havel publicly appealed to the population to support his calls for a referendum without the consent of the Federal Assembly, where an impasse on the issue proved difficult to overcome.[10] Although a breakthrough appeared imminent in early 1992, in negotiations over a "state treaty" between Prague and Bratislava, in February 1992 the Slovak parliamentary presidium narrowly rejected the draft treaty contending that negotiators had offered too many concessions to the Czechs. The draft specified that either republic had the right to secede from the federation on the basis of a referendum.

Other points of Czech-Slovak disagreement are likely to materialize before the next general elections, scheduled for the summer of 1992. Although Czechoslovakia has speeded up its progress toward a market economy and a pluralistic political system during the past year, ethnic regionalization is not subsiding. The danger remains that as economic conditions degenerate, under the marketization and privatization programs, Slovaks will remain susceptible to populist, nationalist, and separatist appeals. The Czechs in turn may grow impatient with persistent Slovak demands and could plausibly support the process of separation, even though most government leaders have maintained that Slovak disengagement will slow down the country's integration into the European Community.

Some Czech politicians and commentators have suggested that a full separation between the two republics may actually prove advantageous, because the current conflicts are simply delaying economic progress and paralyzing federal institutions. They cite various reasons that might favor Czech independence, including: economic benefits for Prague once it terminates its financial support for the Slovak economy; the end of political bickering at the federal level that has hindered legislative and economic progress; the creation of a Slovak buffer zone between the Czech lands and an unstable post-Soviet Union; the avoidance of potential tensions between Prague and Budapest over the minority issue in Slovakia; and the possibility of faster European integration for the Czech republic as a more compact, market-oriented, and democratic state.[11] Demands for Czech separatism could gain popularity in response to the continuing Slovak controversy and worsening economic conditions. Indeed, in September 1991, the Czech National Council adopted a resolution confirming that the declaration of full sovereignty by Slovakia would be unconstitutional and would push the Czech republic toward asserting its own independence.

During the past two years, the question of Moravian-Silesian autonomy has also surfaced in the country. In January 1991, several newly formed Moravian groupings signed a "Charter for Moravia and Silesia" in the Moravian capital of Brno. It called for the establishment of a Moravian-Silesian government and parliament, the redrawing of the region's historic boundaries and electoral districts, and the re-allocation of resources from Prague so that the region could control its own economic affairs. In the June 1990 elections, the Movement for Self-Government–Society for Moravia and Silesia (MSG-SMS) scored well in the region, claiming over 10% of the vote and 22 seats in the Czech National Council. It began to place demands for regional autonomy on the republic's political agenda. In the March 1991 census, about 1,400,000 out of 3,000,000 inhabitants of Moravia-Silesia openly declared their nationality as Moravian or Silesian for the first time in the country's recent history.[12] In February 1991, deputies from an assortment of political parties and movements in Moravia-Silesia gathered to discuss proposals for a new territorial set-up in the country. They resolved that the federal authorities must work out a constitutional variant for a tri-partite federation between Czech-Bohemia, Moravia-Silesia, and Slovakia, and proposed the drafting of a separate Moravian constitution. Czechoslovakia's federal prime minister Marian Calfa disagreed with the idea of creating a tri-state, but conceded that the question should be further reviewed.

Slovak developments have also had an impact in Moravia, by encouraging some activists to demand extensive political and economic decentralization. Moravian leaders began preparations for a draft Moravian-Silesian constitution while seeking tripartite roundtable talks with the Czech and Slovak governments. According to some public opinion polls, popular support for Moravian self-determination and republican status has also increased during the past two years; this trend is being closely watched in Prague. Street rallies have been organized in several large Moravian and Silesian cities, including Brno, Ostrava, and Olomouc, protesting against alleged political and economic discrimination by Prague.

The MSG-SMS has demanded autonomy for the region as a transitory stage toward a tri-partite republican federation. Other activists have proposed creating two autonomous regions within the Czech republic—Bohemia and Moravia-Silesia—rather than granting Moravia full republican status. In March 1991, a roundtable session with representatives from 25 political parties and movements in Moravia rejected a presidential resolution on the federal constitution, because it did not provide the region with the status of an equal and constituent federal subject. At a founding meeting in November 1991, the newly formed Moravian-Silesian Council (MSC), comprised of 13 parties and movements, called for an equal and independent status for Moravia and Silesia in the Czechoslovak federation.[13]

Some small militant groups have also become active of late, including the illegal and unregistered Radical Moravian Nationalist Party (RMNP), which is seeking full Moravian sovereignty and a remodelled relationship with the Czech and federal governments. Prague accused the group of being a front organization, designed as a political provocation by unrepentant local Communists who wanted to cling to their privileges. Moves toward autonomy in Moravia-Silesia will also effect relations between the Czechs and Slovaks. Slovak leaders faced a serious dilemma. Although they may support Moravian self-government in principle, they also harbored fears about the potential dilution of the Slovak position in a three-way federation. Con- versely, the creation of an independent Slovakia could actually energize demands for sovereignty in Moravia-Silesia. The Moravian issue was heated up again in late October 1991, when MDS chairman Meciar asserted that a union between Slovakia and Moravia was possible if the Slovak and Czech republics failed to reach agreement on a state treaty.[14] Such prospective developments could in turn stiffen Prague's opposition to both Slovak secession and Moravian self-administration.

Czechoslovakia and Hungary

Slav-Hungarian conflicts date back to the 9th century, when Magyar tribes completed their migration from Central Asia into the Danube plain and occupied a wide swath of territory separating the western and southern Slavs. In the 11th century, the Hungarian kingdom absorbed the Slovak areas south of the Carpathians—a region that Budapest held until the close of World War One. The Magyars dominated this territory as land-owning nobles, while the

Slovaks remained predominantly peasants and serfs. Budapest did not allow the development of a distinct Slovak nation and pursued a policy of gradual linguistic and cultural assimilation. This program would probably have extinguished Slovak identity, if not for the revivalist intellectual movements in the 19th century led by Protestant and Catholic clergymen that culminated in the creation of a Czechoslovak republic in 1918.

With the collapse of the Austro-Hungarian empire and the subsequent Treaty of Trianon in 1920, Hungary was carved up and Slovakia was incorporated in the newly formed Czechoslovak state.[15] Budapest was even denied the southern portions of Slovakia, an area that contained a predominantly Magyar population. The Hungarian government claimed that this arrangement violated the principles of national self-determination that the victorious Allied powers were supposedly applying throughout eastern Europe. Budapest opposed any expatriation of Magyars from Slovakia, fearing that those territories would then become irrevocably lost to Hungary. The secession of Slovakia created profound resentment in inter-war Hungary among a diversity of political groups, and it bred irredentist sentiments to regain lost territories and populations. In fact, Hungary's main revisionist campaigns in the inter-war period were directed against Czechoslovakia. Budapest increasingly allied itself with Nazi Germany and Fascist Italy which appeared to be the most promising patrons for regaining its former lands. Between 1938 and 1941, Hungary obtained parts of southern Slovakia and Subcarpathian Ruthenia as the Germans carved up the Czechoslovak republic. These lands were lost again after World War Two as the price of the Axis defeat. But a large Magyar minority was again left in Slovakia; by the late 1980s, it numbered over 600,000 people, or almost 10% of the population in the Slovak republic.

The post-war government in Prague planned to expel the entire Hungarian minority. But it desisted under Allied pressure, and citizenship rights were restored to the Magyars. The demographic strength and potential political influence of the Hungarian minority was diminished through the reorganization and merger of Slovak counties in 1960. The Magyars retained a majority in only two of the enlarged county administrations. However, as a result of Soviet domination in the region, the potential for major conflicts between Prague and Budapest over the minority issue remained somewhat dwarfed. The 1968 Prague Spring reforms loosened restrictions on the Hungarian population by improving its cultural and educational facilities and employment opportunities, and allowing for the creation of separate political parties. After the Soviet invasion, the federated Slovak republic dismantled some of the guarantees for minorities in its pursuit of ethnic assimilation. This campaign was vehemently opposed by local Hungarian leaders and the Budapest regime occasionally spoke out on behalf of its compatriots, specifically on the issue of their threatened linguistic and cultural liberties.

Following the freeze in Czechoslovak-Hungarian contacts during the last stages of the anti-reformist Milos Jakes regime in Prague, relations visibly improved after the democratic turnarounds in both states during 1989. No significant or outstanding disputes have been visible between Budapest and the Czech republican or the Czechoslovak federal governments. However, contacts with the Slovak authorities in Bratislava have remained markedly strained. The chief bone of contention has remained the position of the large Hungarian minority in southern Slovakia, that Magyar activists contended continued to suffer from official discrimination and public hostility. By contrast, Slovak spokesmen complained that some Hungarians were seeking to separate the southern Slovak territories in order to link them with the Hungarian republic. Slovak groups have also charged Budapest with discriminating against the small Slovak minority in northern Hungary.

The Czech authorities also became embroiled in the Slovak-Magyar controversy. Some Prague commentators have warned that the granting of full sovereignty to Slovakia could encourage the Hungarian population to demand autonomy in southern Slovakia, while Slovak separation would leave the smaller republic vulnerable to pressures from Budapest. On the other hand, Hungarian activists feared that a more independent government in Bratislava may prove less understanding toward minority issues by imposing more onerous restrictions. The Magyar population would then have little or no recourse to the Prague authorities to mediate or settle nationality disputes. As in the rest of eastern Europe, there was also a lingering fear that economic deterioration could exacerbate social unrest and nationality tensions. This would leave Slovakia prone to ethnic conflict, with the possibility that the Hungarian minority will seek protection from Budapest against possible Slovak repression.

Relations between Hungary and the increasingly assertive Slovak republic have been marred by problems during the past three years. They revolve primarily around the position of the Magyar minority in Slovakia, which numbers in excess of 600,000 people, or about 10% of the Slovak population, with a further 25,000 resident in the Czech lands.[16] In some southern Slovak counties, Hungarians comprise about half of the inhabitants. After the democratic revolutions in November 1989, Hungarian activists began to organize openly and to campaign for minority rights. Three main associations were established early on: the Independent Hungarian Initiative (IHI), which joined the PAV umbrella, the Hungarian Christian Democratic Movement (HCDM), and the Forum of Hungarians in Czechoslovakia (FHC), which maintained some links with the existing Cultural Association of Hungarian Working People in Czechoslovakia. In early 1990, the Forum renamed itself as *Egyutteles* (Coexistence), and although focusing on the Hungarian population, it also endeavored to involve other minorities (including Poles, Ruthenians, and Ukrainians) in a common front to promote minority interests.[17]

Whereas the IHI gauged that campaigns for minority rights should not take precedence over the wider democratization process, particularly in the early post-Communist phase, *Egyutteles* viewed the nationality issue as paramount and resolvable alongside the democratization program. As a result of its stance, *Egyutteles* came under criticism from the PAV for being too radical and nationalistic. This did not deter its leadership, who denied that they were seeking any kind of territorial autonomy or secession from Slovakia. Their main programmatic planks consisted of equitable representation for Hungarians and other nationalities in state institutions, and the protection of their cultural, educational, religious, and linguistic activities. *Egyutteles* stood as a separate political party in the June 1990 general elections and won 14% of the vote in Slovakia, thereby gaining 14 seats in the Slovak National Council.

Both *Egyutteles* and the Hungarian government have consistently demanded an end to various forms of official discrimination against the Magyar population, in addition to minority participation in the republican and federal governments. They protested the Slovak government decision in the summer of 1991 to cut subsidies to ethnic minority cultural organizations. They have also called for the expansion of Hungarian language, educational, publishing, and media activities, including the establishment of a Hungarian university in the southern Slovak city of Komarno. Furthermore, *Egyutteles* proposed the creation of a Ministry of Nationalities in the federal government and has opposed the country's current 5% election minimum needed to gain seats in the Federal Assembly. In practice, such a stipulation excludes or constrains the smaller parties from representing distinct minority interests.

Hungarian groups have also insisted that the position of minorities was under threat from rising Slovak nationalism and increasing neglect and disengagement by Prague. For instance, *Egyutteles* objected to the package of language laws introduced by Bratislava that made Slovak the chief official language even in minority areas. Instead, they proposed legislation on the public use of minority languages in areas with significant minorities, and not just in districts containing 20% or more ethnic minority inhabitants. The law passed in October 1990 was received as only a partially satisfactory compromise solution. *Egyutteles* approved of the fact that at least the new legislation nullified the variant proposed by the Slovak National Party. The latter would have made Slovak the sole language in all districts regardless of minority proportions.[18] Hungarian leaders have also lodged complaints over the federal law on rehabilitation. This has set February 1948, the date when the Communists seized power in the country, as the limit for any kind of material compensation to unjustly dispossessed individuals. In fact, the Hungarian, German, and other minorities effectively lost their "collective rights" during the period from 1945 to 1948, under pressure from the Soviets and local Communists. During this time, a substantial amount of property was confiscated from the Magyar population and presumably cannot now be reclaimed.

Hungarian organizations have expressed anxieties about the incitement of ethnic frictions by ultra-nationalist forces in Slovakia. During the past three years, several incidents have been reported in which violent attacks on Magyar community activists were evidently provoked or arranged by extremist political groups. There is little indication, however, that the bulk of the Slovak population is prone to engage in violence against the Hungarian community. But as economic conditions continue to degenerate, unemployed youths could prove more susceptible to militant nationalist and racist appeals. Anti-Hungarian demonstrations have periodically been staged in some Slovak towns by radical groups who accuse Budapest and local Hungarian organizations of seeking autonomy and territorial separation. Some extremists have called for the expulsion of Hungarians and other minorities in order to create a "pure Slovak state." Conspiracy theories continue to be circulated that Budapest is again seriously questioning the post-war borders in order to destabilize Slovakia and eventually annex valuable lands adjacent to Hungary. Accusations have also been advanced that a Czech-Hungarian plan to carve up Slovakia is being secretly hatched and could be implemented if the Slovaks push toward national independence.[19]

In demanding greater recognition for the Hungarian minority in Slovakia, Budapest has been accused by some Bratislava-based parties of interfering in Slovakia's internal affairs. This was allegedly the case during the June 1990 elections, when the Hungarian media openly supported *Egyutteles* while organizations in Hungary supplied it with some campaign material. According to Slovak nationalists, such activities prove that Hungary has irredentist designs on Slovak areas where Magyars form compact communities. These initiatives apparently constitute the first steps toward territorial autonomy and secession.

The comments and actions of Hungarian statesmen are carefully monitored in Bratislava for any indications of policy changes. Statements by Prime Minister Jozsef Antall in early 1990, that he considered himself the leader and protector of all Hungarians, regardless of their country of residence, created a stir in Slovakia among a variety of political groups.[20] The more outspoken Slovak nationalists condemned it as unwarranted interference in the country's internal affairs. Antall's remarks were depicted as revisionist, designed to destabilize Slovakia, and as deliberately inciting the Magyar minority to rebellion in preparation for territorial annexation. Radical nationalist forces in Bratislava have also spread rumors that Budapest is preparing military action against Slovakia.[21] Extremist groups have charged that Hungarian parties have been smuggling arms into the republic; an accusation that was strenuously denied by *Egyutteles* chairman Miklos Duray.[22] Such allegations are clearly intended to stir nationality tensions in order to rally Slovak public opinion behind the nationalists and against the Magyar minority.

Slovak nationalists also claim that the position of Hungarians in Slovakia is actually much better than conditions among the approximately 20,000 Slovaks in northern Hungary. Complaints are frequently voiced that the Slovaks have been subjected to human rights violations and sustained assimilationist pressures. Allegations have also been made that the Slovak minority may be larger than Budapest admits because a proper population census has never been conducted while many Slovaks evidently do not reveal their true ethnic identity for fear of repercussions. Figures ranging from 100,000 to 150,000 have even been floated. Slovak nationalists object to Hungary's contention that the minority question has been settled in the country; in their opinion it has simply been suppressed.[23]

Increasing Slovak minority activism has been visible in Hungary following the establishment of the Association of Slovaks in Hungary (ASH) in November 1990. The ASH has coordinated the activities of local organizations and pressed for the introduction of Slovak language instruction at all educational levels, the official use of Slovak in minority areas, the creation of Slovak publishing houses and cultural institutes, and for Slovak representation in local councils. ASH has reportedly received some direct assistance from Slovakia for its educational, cultural, and organizational endeavors. Although the influence of Slovak nationalist groups in Bratislava on Slovak minority organizations in Hungary is difficult to measure, it could perceptibly increase as a counterweight to Hungarian influence in Slovakia.

Since the general elections of June 1990, Bratislava has pursued a more independent foreign policy, especially in economic, cultural, and regional affairs. In February 1991, Slovak Prime Minister Vladimir Meciar visited Budapest and made some progress in improving Slovak-Hungarian relations at governmental level. Theoretically, the Magyar and Slovak minorities could act as a bridge between the two states, especially if bilateral agreements are reached between Bratislava and Budapest to assist each others' minorities. But the Slovak government has been wary of engaging in substantive talks and signing bilateral agreements with Hungary on the minority question. Fearful that Budapest could gain some unilateral advantage from such an accord, Bratislava prefers that any negotiations be conducted in a wider multilateral international framework.

Prague has also become involved in the minority dispute, even though it has generally avoided taking sides. The governing Civic Forum coalition has supported the formation of a Ministry for Minority Affairs in the central government once a new federal constitution is drafted. Proposals have also been made to establish a non-governmental consultative body, empowered to monitor the position of ethnic minorities and report on the government's performance. In many respects, the Czech and federal authorities have responded more positively to Hungarian minority demands in Slovakia than has the administration in Bratislava. Czech Prime

Minister, Petr Pithart, also suggested that the Czech government could act as a mediator in the Slovak-Hungarian dispute. However, such proposals have been viewed skeptically in Slovakia and have fueled nationalist charges that Prague and Budapest are in collusion to wrest unacceptable concessions from Bratislava.

Hungarian leaders remain troubled that increasing Slovak autonomy and potential national sovereignty will have a negative impact on the position of minority groups. In October 1991, *Egyutteles* leader Miklos Duray spoke in favor of preserving the federal state and expressed his dismay at the radical political parties who were the driving force behind Slovak statehood.[24] Slovak self-assertiveness could easily be turned against the large Magyar minority, which may be depicted as threatening national interests and challenging the republic's territorial integrity. Such conflicts could escalate during a period of widespread economic dislocation when a market economy is being painstakingly constructed. Dissatisfaction and frustration among workers and youths, in particular, can be channelled by militant forces against large ethnic minorities, especially if they are seen to be inequitably benefiting from the reform process or are perceived to have claims to Slovak territory in liaison with foreign powers. Such sentiments may prove difficult to dispel during a period of severe political and economic instability.

In the long term, Slovak independence could prove to be a double-edged sword for the Hungarians. On one hand, it could result in more repressive policies by Bratislava, and curtail some of the rights already gained by the Magyar minority. The letter would in turn have little or no recourse to mediation or protection from Prague and the federal authorities. On the other hand, Slovak sovereignty could actually stimulate Hungarian activism and even fuel demands for minority self-determination as protection against Slovak domination. In time, this could draw in the Budapest government as well as various political organizations in Hungary eager to provide assistance to their co-nationals abroad. In such a scenario, a spiral of conflict can be envisaged at both the communal and inter-state levels, unless Slovak aspirations are satisfied and Hungarian minority grievances are comprehensively addressed.

With the disintegration of the Soviet Union and the achievement of independence by Ukraine, the status of Transcarpathian Ruthenia could also assume more prominence in relations between Czechoslovakia and Hungary. Commentators in Prague have evinced some disquiet over Budapest's numerous initiatives in the Transcarpathian area, in comparison to the relative passivity of the Czech-Slovak authorities.[25] The two capitals, together with Slovakia, may be expected to compete for the loyalties of the Ruthenian population, while assuring the Ukrainian authorities that they are not aiming to annex the region.

Poland and Germany

Conflicts between Poles and Germans date back to the earliest contacts between western Slavonic and Germanic tribes. Profound cultural and linguistic differences were magnified by centuries of territorial competition, mutual expansionism, and dynastic rivalries between Polish and German monarchs. From the 17th century onwards, the faltering Polish-Lithuanian Commonwealth faced the imperialist ambitions of two Germanic empires—the Austrian Habsburg and the Prussian. When the Polish Kingdom collapsed at the end of the 18th century, the two powers together with Russia partitioned the country. Aside from a brief and partial reinstatement during Napoleon's eastern campaigns in the early part of the 19th century, a sovereign Polish state disappeared from the map of Europe until the end of World War One.

During the 19th century partitions, Prussia controlled the northern and western portions of Poland and Austria held the southern regions. While the Habsburgs pursued a relatively tolerant policy toward large minorities such as the Poles, Prussian Germany grew increasingly chauvinistic and repressive. With the rise of German nationalism in the 1870s, under Bismarck's *kulturkampf,* Berlin launched a campaign of cultural assimilation and germanization of the Polish population. A Prussian colonization commission was established in the 1880s, to encourage German settlement in traditionally Polish territories. The program of administrative, economic, and cultural discrimination alienated much of the Polish population and provoked a marked increase in religious fervor, political opposition, nationalist resistance, and anti-German sentiments.

With the defeat of Germany and Austria-Hungary in World War One, Poland regained its independence, although the new state was significantly smaller than the pre-partition Commonwealth.[26] The Versailles peace treaty emasculated Germany in terms of its territory and military strength, and contributed toward creating new sources of tension with Poland. Berlin retained East Prussia, while Warsaw obtained Poznania in the west and a narrow northern strip between German territory with access to the Baltic Sea. This "Polish corridor" and the free port city of Danzig (Gdansk) became major sources of inter-state tension in the inter-war period. After inconclusive plebiscites during 1921 in the southern industrial region of Silesia, an international commission divided up the area between the two states. A large German minority was left in the western parts of Poland, whose grievances Berlin magnified and exploited in its persistent anti-Polish campaigns.

During the 1930s, Germany's Nazi regime escalated its pressures on Warsaw, barely disguising its claims on Polish territory. In August 1939, Hitler signed a pact with Stalin that contained a secret protocol to partition the country. German forces overran Poland in September 1939 and initiated a brutal six year occupation during which most of the country was eventually incorporated in the Third Reich; the remnants formed a German controlled "General-Government." Over six million Polish citizens died during the war, including three million Polish Jews; Warsaw and other major cities were levelled; and massive quantities of property were stolen or destroyed by the Nazis.

After the German defeat at the close of World War Two, Polish borders were redrawn by the Allied powers. The country lost one-third of its eastern territory to the Soviet Union but gained stretches of German territory in the west, including Pomerania, the southern portion of East Prussia, the remainder of Silesia, and all land up to the Oder and Neisse rivers. The new border continued to be a source of dispute between the Polish Communist authorities and the West German government. The latter maintained that the frontier could not be irrevocably settled until the signing of a peace treaty between Poland and a unified Germany. By contrast, the Communist East German regime under Soviet direction accepted Warsaw's position and unequivocally recognized the Oder-Neisse border. Diplomatic relations between Warsaw and Bonn were re-established in December 1970. The use of force in settling disputes was renounced and Poland's western borders were provisionally acknowledged until a final treaty could be ratified.

The position of the German minority in western Poland also remained a point of contention, even after the expulsion or flight of six million Germans in the wake of World War Two. Successive Communist governments pursued a policy of assimilation, denied full cultural liberties, and deliberately underestimated the size of the German minority. Meanwhile, some politicians in Bonn and expellee associations in the German Federal Republic claimed widescale discrimination and the systematic denial of minority rights by the Warsaw authorities. As the two German states moved closer toward political and economic unification during the course of 1990, latent and unresolved disputes with Poland again surfaced and exacerbated tensions between Bonn and Warsaw. Polish-German discords have revolved around two conflictive long-term perceptions: Polish fears of German expansionism, and Germany's sense of injustice after the post-World War Two territorial settlements.

Large sectors of the Polish population, including some of the country's political and intellectual leaders, retain lingering doubts about Germany's commitment to democracy and its renouncement of all revanchist and expansionist ambitions. Polish spokesmen recognize that West Germany has built a solid democratic system and a prosperous economy closely intertwined with the European Community. Nonetheless, worries are also periodically expressed about either the possibility of an economic downturn which could fuel political extremism and hostility toward neighboring states or the probability of irresistible and expansionist German economic power. The latter scenario could place Poland and other central European states in the position of neo-colonies, supplying cheap labor, raw materials, and other resources for the German economy. It would also facilitate the purchase and takeover of Polish industries and real estate, encourage German settlement in former German territories, and place the Polish authorities in a politically subordinate role.

In the security sphere, concerns persist in Warsaw that Germany stands to benefit from any U.S. troop pullout from Europe and from the diminution or disappearance of the NATO alliance. As a result, the Polish government has expressed strong reservations about any form of German military neutrality. A number of Polish politicians have remained apprehensive about the combination of German economic power and military autonomy, as well as the possible growth of militant nationalism in a united Germany.

An additional source of Polish disquiet revolves around prospects for German-Russian agreements that disregard Warsaw; such fears are based on tragic historical precedents. Poles of various political persuasions argue that a close German-Russian relationship has never benefited Polish interests and could seriously jeopardize them in the future. Improved political and economic ties between Moscow and Bonn-Berlin have therefore been treated with a degree of suspicion. Polish activists fear several potentially negative scenarios, including the provision of German economic benefits to the Commonwealth states that would deprive Poland of essential aid and investment; steps toward some new security arrangement in which Poland would occupy a subsidiary position; and mutual long-term territorial designs on Poland. Mistrust between the two traditionally antagonistic neighbors are unlikely to completely evaporate, even while inter-state relations steadily improve and economic, cultural, and social links are steadily expanded.

Two major issues have occupied the center of the Polish-German conflict: the border question and the position of the German minority in Poland. Disputes over the Oder-Neisse frontier line were revived in the wake of the 1989 revolutions, when ambiguous signals were sent by Bonn over the final acceptance of the post-war borders.[27] Chancellor Helmut Kohl's prevarications during the process of reunification, at a time when Poland was anxious to conclude a treaty with its powerful western neighbor, distressed various sectors of Polish society. In early 1990, Warsaw wanted a draft treaty to be signed simultaneously with the West German and East German parliaments and formally ratified by a united parliament after the all-German elections. Warsaw also demanded inclusion in the "four plus two talks" (involving the four occupying powers) on German unification, particularly in meetings dealing with border questions and security issues. After substantial international lobbying, the Polish side was included in some of the discussions, and the two German parliaments passed resolutions confirming Poland's western borders.

Following the "four plus two" conference in Paris in July 1990, Bonn assured Warsaw that a bilateral agreement would be signed and ratified shortly after German unification. The Polish government wanted the treaty concluded beforehand and signed on the day of unification, when the rights and duties of the four occupying powers vis-á-vis Germany officially expired. Kohl opposed this timetable and maintained that only a fully sovereign and united Germany would initial any border accords. Suspicions were also voiced in Poland that Kohl may have delayed signing a treaty for domestic political reasons, in order to win the upcoming elections and to guarantee the vote of the West German expellee organizations. A compromise formula was eventually arranged between Warsaw and Bonn, in which a joint text would be ready before unification but would only be signed afterward. A provisional border treaty was formally signed in November 1990, in which Poland's western frontiers were recognized as inviolable by both governments; but German parliamentary ratification was left until a later date.[28]

Final ratification of the treaty experienced delays over one main stumbling block, the position of the German minority in Poland. Bonn government spokesmen asked for national minority status for ethnic Germans and for Warsaw's acceptance of Germany's protection over its minorities in Poland. This stance was severely criticized in Poland as unwarranted interference in the country's internal affairs that could provide the German population with some special status under Bonn's supervision. Several German leaders have also raised the issue of compensation to former residents of Poland's western territories who were dispossessed and expelled at the end of World War Two. To counter these new demands, Warsaw raised sensitive questions about restitution payments from Germany for the Polish laborers and their families who suffered in slave labor camps under the Third Reich. Commentators pointed out that Bonn made such payments to the West European states in the 1960s. But as a result of Communist obstruction Poland failed to receive its just share of war reparations. Some Poles have estimated that the sum could run into several billion dollars, while German credits, charity, and compensation payments since the 1940s have certainly not covered the losses sustained by the Polish economy and by millions of its citizens as a result of German policy during the war.

In June 1991, Germany and Poland finally signed a comprehensive treaty of inter-state friendship and cooperation.[29] It contained pledges to abstain from the use of force and guarantees to respect the cultural rights of the German minority. But the minority issue may continue to sour relations between the two states in the years ahead. Disputes exist even over the question of numbers: various Polish sources give low estimates of under 200,000 while German calculations range from 500,000 to over one million, located primarily in the Opole and Katowice regions of Silesia. Warsaw contends that Bonn's policy of making it easy for Polish émigrés claiming some German ancestry to obtain German citizenship has produced split loyalties among a large number of people seeking to emigrate largely for economic reasons. The policy also purportedly undermines Polish sovereignty, by inflating the number of German residents and thus heightening the pretext for outside interference.

Under the Communist regime, the German minority was not officially recognized and many Germans disguised their identities, intermarried, assimilated, or emigrated to the West. The Communists also refused to register distinct German social, cultural, or political organizations, and prohibited German language classes in state schools. These repressive conditions eased substantially with the collapse of the Communist system, and a rapid growth in the number of schools offering German courses was registered in the Opole area. A chief feature of Bonn's diplomacy in Poland has been to assure linguistic, cultural, and religious rights for the German minority with a view to opening a consulate in Silesia. However, some local German leaders in Poland have complained about Bonn's accommodating stance on the border issue. In expressing support for the Federal Republic's League of Expellees, they have indicated that they do not consider the frontier agreement as final or binding.

Warsaw has permitted German associations to function in the country, and several social-cultural organizations have been registered during the past two years. These include German Friendship Circles (GFC) and the Social-Cultural Association of the German Minority in Silesia-Opole (SCAGMSO). They have initiated publishing, educational, and artistic ventures in the German language, promoted regional business initiatives in Silesia, and campaigned for dual citizenship for German ethnics. By the end of 1990, about 300,000 people were reportedly registered in the Circles and other German organizations, as part of the "ethnic German population."[30] The Central Council of Germans (CCG), the umbrella organization of the GFCs, estimated its membership in the first quarter of 1991 to be over 220,000, with 150,000 in the Opole voivodship, 40,000 in Katowice, and 30,000 in the Czestochowa area.[31] Because of the schisms within the Solidarity movement, SCAGMSO became the strongest political grouping in the Opole voivodship. In the local elections of May 1990, deputies representing the German minority gained seats on local councils in 35 out of 61 townships or municipalities, with an absolute majority in 26 of them.[32]

Polish spokesmen have expressed some uneasiness that the German population in Silesia is vulnerable to expellee propaganda, including promises about eventual Silesian union with Germany. On this basis, a German fifth column could allegedly be created in the country whose activities would seriously jeopardize Polish-German cooperation.[33] Some extremist although marginal German groupings have also been formed in Poland; these include the Movement for Silesian Autonomy (MSA), claiming 8,000 members and with links to expellee organizations in Germany. Polish activists fear that strong German associations may increasingly link up with revisionist circles in Germany that do not accept the permanency of the current border and may press for some form of German autonomy status in Poland. German radicalism will also trigger the formation of radical Polish groups; one such organization, the National Rebirth of Poland (NRP), has been active in the Opole region and has engaged in various anti-German manifestations.

Leaders of the West German Expellee Union have continued to raise questions about the future status of Silesia. Hartmut Koschyk, a Bundestag deputy and Secretary-General of the Union, has reportedly visited Poland regularly to meet with German minority leaders and to assure them that Polish control over Silesia was only temporary.[34] He also publicly claimed to have the support of leading Bonn politicians, including Chancellor Kohl himself. Koschyk has proposed a "third way" to "Polish-German unification," consisting of the creation of a new territory along the Oder-Neisse rivers with a joint administration, parliament, and government. In this scenario, the city of Szczecin would become a free port, and free city status would be given to towns currently divided between the two countries, including Zgorzelec-Goerlitz. According to Polish critics, the Expellee Union seeks to detach Silesia and link it with a united Germany through the transitional autonomous status, thus effectively terminating Warsaw's control over the region.[35]

The question of Silesian regionalism has gained more prominence in Polish politics in recent years. Some Polish Silesian organizations have pressed for administrative decentralization and greater autonomy in economic, cultural, and political affairs, claiming economic exploitation and discrimination by Warsaw. Groups such as the Upper Silesian Union (USU) and the Movement for the Autonomy of Silesia (MAS), which gained seven seats to the Sejm (lower house) and one seat to the Senate (upper house) during the October 1991 national elections, seek to strengthen regional and local self-government. Some of these groupings calculate that Silesian autonomy would result in a substantial inflow of German capital into the region. By contrast, many local Polish activists fear that such autonomist groupings could be courted and manipulated by radical German organizations in pursuit of their territorial and separatist ambitions. The latter evidently include the Chief Council of the Germans of Upper Silesia (CCGUS), with purported links to German expellee associations.[36]

Members of Germany's Expellee Union have engaged in political agitation among the Silesian population. They claim that the Silesians are a separate ethnic group, and have campaigned for a general referendum among the region's current and former residents in order to determine its future status. In the interim, the Union has suggested creating a "Silesian land" in former East German territories that would act as a magnet for Polish Silesia before unification with Germany. Expellee activists have provided material aid and disseminated propaganda texts among the German minority. They have also advised people to claim German citizenship and to remain in their birthplaces in preparation for future reunification. Although the influence of the Expellee Union on German foreign policy is not substantial, its impact among radicalized young sectors of the population, especially those from the GDR who are experiencing profound economic dislocation, should not be underestimated. Periodic attacks by right-wing extremists and skinheads on Polish tourists crossing into eastern Germany and on Polish workers in west Germany appears to be symptomatic of deep-rooted anti-Polish and anti-foreigner prejudices. These could be reinforced by competition over jobs between German workers and Polish migrants, and exploited by revanchist groupings for their political objectives.

Some observers speculate that German and Polish minorities can bring the two countries closer together. But, a great deal of work needs to be accomplished to eliminate mutual racial stereotypes and remove numerous "blank spots" in the two countries' history. Silesians could theoretically play a positive role as a cultural bridge, stressing positive German influences and achievements in the region, developing educational, economic, and humanitarian activities, demythologizing German-Polish relations, and defusing the enmities that once served Soviet and Communist interests. Unfortunately, greater Silesian activism could also breed Polish resentment and suspicion about German intentions in the region.[37]

German and regionalist activism has also been reported in the Warmia-Mazuria area in north eastern Poland, a region that formerly belonged to East Prussia. Two main organizations have been active during the past year: the Olsztyn Association of the German Minority (OAGM) and the Association of Polish Citizens of German Nationality (APCGN). Some frictions have been visible between the two groups, as members of the former consider themselves German while leaders of the latter affirm that they are Poles of German origin. Some smaller and more radical groupings have also become active of late: the "Roots" organization has demanded German autonomy in the Mazuria region, while the East Prussian Wolves (EPW) has sought to restore the north east corner of Poland to a greater Germany. However, these appear to be marginal associations with an extremely slender potential social base in comparison to the Silesian German organizations.

If amicable relations between Warsaw and Bonn are to be assured, the Polish government will be expected to offer full protection to the German minority and grant it comprehensive cultural, educational, and other collective rights. However, any material benefits for German communities emanating either from Warsaw or Bonn-Berlin could aggravate inter-ethnic relations in Silesia by spurring indignation among the Polish majority. The Polish authorities have tried to avoid communal polarization and the ethnicization of politics in the Opole region and other areas with compact

German minorities. They remain concerned about selective aid and investment to German villages, because economic differentiation based on ethnicity at a time of general material hardship could provoke serious communal conflicts. Preferential treatment and growing economic clout could also raise public aspirations and encourage German minority leaders to press for various political concessions from Warsaw. This, in turn, could launch them on a collision course with the Polish government, particularly as the minority question has still to be fully resolved and regulated in bilateral agreements between Warsaw and Bonn-Berlin.

Three other issues may also raise tensions between Poland and Germany in the years ahead: economic domination, refugee movements, and security arrangements. Various Polish political circles predict a likelihood of German economic exploitation of Polish assets once the country fully digests the former GDR. The takeover of Polish industries and real estate, coupled with access to a cheap labor pool and raw materials, could lead to increasing economic domination. Poland has made strenuous efforts to avoid such a scenario by seeking to diversify foreign investments, but the degree of non-German involvement in the country's economic development has thus far proved disappointing. Although German economic investment will clearly benefit Poland's transition to a market system, some Polish spokesmen remain particularly concerned about German interests in Berlin's pre-war territories. They are anxious that economic domination in regions such as Silesia, Pomerania, and Mazuria could eventually lead to more brazen political and territorial demands.

The projected influx of refugees from the Commonwealth States into Poland could also negatively effect Polish-German relations. If refugees were to pour through a porous Polish border, Germany could use the refugee threat to seal off its own eastern frontiers and even to remilitarize the border region. Such measures would seriously undermine any improvements in inter-governmental relations. Emerging German security arrangements have also provoked a great deal of debate in Poland. From the outset, Warsaw has opposed any moves toward German neutrality and supported continuing German membership of NATO, where it would remain firmly rooted in the American-European security structure. The new Polish government wants to ensure a strong military posture following the dissolution of the Warsaw Pact, in order to deter potential aggressors and cushion against Poland's numerical and technological inferiority.[38] Like its neighbors in central Europe, Poland is eager to embark on the creation of a pan-European security system or even a wider NATO umbrella. Warsaw believes that this would provide invaluable protection and mitigate against possible Russian and German threats to the country's sovereignty and territorial integrity.

Poland and Czechoslovakia

Relations between Poles and Czechs and Slovaks did not lead to any major or long-term conflicts while the three peoples were absorbed by expansionist neighbors. But soon after Czechoslovakia and Poland regained independence at the end of World War One, hostilities erupted over some sensitive border questions. Although the Carpathian mountains constitute a fairly clear-cut dividing line between the two states, three border zones have proved to be key points of contention—the Cieszyn, Spisz, and Orawa areas.

During the post-war settlements, Spisz was divided between the two countries and Poland received one village in the Orawa district according to a 1932 League of Nations decision. The most contentious problem was the Cieszyn (Teschen) area of southern Silesia. It had belonged to Bohemia since the 14th century and was strategically important to Prague, but it also contained a sizable Polish population. While Warsaw was preoccupied with repulsing the Bolshevik invasion in 1920, Teschen was occupied and annexed by the Czech authorities. This move soured relations during the inter-war years and prevented the forging of any meaningful strategic alliance between the two states. Prague also opposed Polish participation in the Little Entente—the French-sponsored alliance between Czechoslovakia, Romania, and Yugoslavia—because of fears that Warsaw would shift its focus from a defense against Hungary to an anti-German alliance that would provoke Berlin. When Hitler annexed the Czech lands in 1938, Warsaw revived its claims to disputed border zones and occupied the Cieszyn area as well as Spisz and Orawa on the Polish-Slovak border, thus re-fuelling the border controversy. During World War Two, the exiled governments of Poland and Czechoslovakia discussed the possibility of a post-war confederation. But the idea was eventually abandoned because of Soviet opposition and the imposition of Communist rule in both countries following the Nazi defeat.

After World War Two, the Cieszyn-Teschen area was split between the two states and some population exchanges took place. For all practical purposes, the frontier issue ceased to be a point of dispute. Polish forces participated in the Soviet-led eradication of the liberalizing Prague Spring in August 1968. But this decision, by an illegitimate Polish Communist regime, was generally not perceived in Czechoslovakia as a sovereign act of aggression by Poland. Throughout the Communist period, relations between the two states remained formally correct although subject to Moscow's dictat, while no serious diplomatic or political conflicts surfaced. The hard-line Prague regime attacked Warsaw in 1980-1981 for its tolerant approach toward the Solidarity movement. But this was viewed in Poland as the position of a dictatorial clique acting largely on behest of neo-Stalinist forces in the Kremlin.

Not burdened by a heavy historical load, current relations between Poland and the Czech and Slovak Federal Republic are devoid of serious hostilities. For example, the border question has not been raised by any major political forces in either state, and even the question of "collective rights" for the small Polish, Czech, and Slovak minorities could be amicably settled in various bilateral arrangements. But in the post-Communist era, several issues have the possibility of complicating ties between the two countries. These include the unequal treatment of minorities, economic competition over Western investments and resources, discords stemming from cross-border environmental pollution, and incongruencies over military postures and international alliances. The growing independence of Slovakia and the potential split of the Federal Republic will also have an impact on Poland. An independent Slovakia could seek to improve ties with its northern neighbor, as a counterweight to potential pressures from both the Czech republic and from Hungary.

The position of minority populations in the border regions needs to be watched, although their limited number will probably prevent the emergence of any serious disputes. The Polish minority in the Teschen or Zaolzie Silesian area numbers about 60,000, and its activists have established several organizations to further their cultural activities, educational pursuits, and political participation.[39] Although Polish leaders complain about Prague's patronizing and bureaucratic attitude and its apparent failure to restore property seized by the Communist regime after the war, they do receive some state funding and have been able to enhance their organizational development since the 1989 "velvet revolution." The Czech minority in Poland is estimated at fewer than 5,000, resident in the Lower Silesian area near the Czech border. The Slovak minority in the southern part of Krakow province near the Slovak border numbers approximately 30,000. The Social-Cultural Association of Czechs and Slovaks (SCACS) in Poland is seeking full recognition and greater access to resources. It has been pressing for the availability of educational, religious, and cultural facilities and the use of minority languages in schools and other public institutions. Some apprehensions have been evident among local Poles about a resurgence of Slovak nationalism based on the occasional questioning of the border delineations around Spisz and Orawa. But Slovak minority leaders have denied that any border readjustments are on their political agenda.

All the east European states are attempting to reorient their economies westward while implementing structural capitalist-oriented reforms. Due to the uneven process of market reform between Poland and Czechoslovakia, some discords have been visible over their border trade. While prices were freed in Poland in 1990 and costs rose dramatically, Prague largely maintained its state subsidies for foodstuffs and consumer goods. Substantial price discrepancies encouraged thousands of Polish petty-traders to buy up relatively inexpensive Czech and Slovak goods, thus seriously depleting some local supplies. Prague subsequently tightened up its restrictions on cross-border traffic and thereby provoked complaints in Warsaw that such a policy was not conducive to furthering European economic integration. The problem was largely resolved in early 1991, when the Czech and Slovak authorities freed prices on most goods and it became less profitable for Polish traders to shop and trade across the border.

Future economic frictions may materialize between Warsaw and Prague over mutual competition for Western investments, resources, and markets. Such competition could be a positive development, especially if it results in liberal foreign investment laws, stimulates domestic production, and encourages economic efficiency. In the meantime, trade between all the east European states will continue to decline until all national currencies become fully convertible and importable goods are of sufficiently high quality. Competition for Western involvement may also have a negative component, especially if it leads to various unilateral trade restrictions, protectionist measures, and hinders regional economic cooperation. Such enmities may also have reverberations on the political plane by spoiling inter-governmental relations at a time when cooperation is important to assist the process of integration with several pan-European institutions.

Prague and Warsaw have also been embroiled in the environmental problems caused by cross-border industrial pollution. Polish Silesia and northern Bohemia are two of the most polluted regions of central Europe, and Polish spokesmen have charged the Czech authorities with exacerbating the country's ecological degradation by failing to regulate air and river emissions northward. The major complaints have centered on Czech waste products, including those from the Stonava Coke plant, spilling into the Oder and other Polish rivers. Prague's compensation payments have been deemed inadequate, and at one point Warsaw threatened to file charges with the International Court in the Hague because the Czechs had failed to clean up or close the most polluting plants.

The realm of security and regional alliance realignments could also create some disquiet between Warsaw and Prague. Soon after the 1989 revolutions, some Polish leaders expressed annoyance that President Vaclav Havel's first foreign visit was to West Germany at a time when Warsaw was experiencing problems over Bonn's acceptance of its western borders. Polish suspicions persisted over the reliability of its southern neighbor, particularly in any future confrontation with Germany or Russia. Some Prague politicians, in turn, tended to consider Poland as a volatile country with exaggerated regional ambitions, and did not want Czechoslovakia to be drawn into any conflict between Warsaw and its larger neighbors.

An additional international problem concerns the future political status of Slovakia. If Bratislava were to drift away from Prague and achieve sovereignty or complete independence, the Slovak government could look toward Poland as a valuable ally and as a counterweight to possible Hungarian and Czech pressures on the new state. The absence of irresolvable border and minority problems between Bratislava and Warsaw could help enhance such developments. However, a closer Slovak-Polish relationship may also engender some frictions between Warsaw, Prague, and Budapest, and thus complicate the progress of central European collaboration and integration with European and Atlantic institutions.

Czechoslovakia and Germany

The Czech lands of Bohemia and Moravia were incorporated into the Austrian Habsburg empire by the 17th century after a protracted period of religious and ethnic warfare. The Protestant Czechs were subjected to a campaign of religious conversion by the Catholic Habsburgs. This left a legacy of resentment and religious indifference even among many Czech converts. Czech nationalism increased during the 19th century, as did the rise of a Czech bourgeois class which experienced mounting economic and political competition with the Austrian and German middle classes. Czech national aspirations were subdued by reactionary Habsburg policies in the aftermath of the nationalist revolts throughout the Austrian empire in 1848-49. But, this policy simply kindled frustration among the new Czech intelligentsia, which increasingly sought national autonomy and eventual independence.

Following the collapse of the Central Powers during World War One, the new state of Czechoslovakia was created. It consisted of the historic lands of the Bohemian Crown (Bohemia, Moravia, and Austrian Silesia) and the formerly Hungarian provinces of Slovakia and Subcarpathian-Ruthenia. Despite the lack of historic unity or ethnic and religious homogeneity, the state proved to be reasonably stable and democratic during the inter-war period. Leaders of the large German minority in Bohemia wanted a merger with either Austria or Germany, but the Czech army occupied the German areas until the 1919 Paris peace treaty ratified the borders. About three million Germans were left in the Czechoslovak republic, mostly concentrated around the western edge of the country and in the Sudeten mountains. Prague enacted various laws to protect the minority nationalities and its policies were fairly liberal by existing east European standards. For instance, in areas where minorities such as the Sudeten Germans formed over 20% of the population, they could use their own language in schools and in administrative affairs. But, the Germans were not easily assimilable or loyal to the new government, and at times expressed outright hostility.

The minority issue provided a useful pretext for the Nazi regime to stir up conflicts with Prague and in 1938 to intervene and annex the Czech lands.

The Sudetenland was ceded to the Third Reich, Bohemia and Moravia became a German Protectorate, Slovakia became a semi-independent Nazi protectorate, and Ruthenia was awarded to the Hungarians. Although the Nazi occupation of the Czech lands was not as systematically brutal as in Poland, it nonetheless heightened local animosities toward the Germans.

After World War Two, the German population in Czechoslovakia either fled from the Red Army advance or was forcibly expelled by the new administration. By 1950, only 1% of the population was registered as German, a precipitous drop from 22% in 1930. Germans were prohibited from setting up their own schools or cultural organizations and were not recognized as an ethnic minority until the Prague Spring reforms. According to recent statistics, about 53,400 citizens currently claim German origin which constitutes only 0.3% of the country's population.[40] During the Communist period, there were no specific territorial conflicts between Prague and Bonn, but the relationship remained strained particularly as the Czech Communists, similarly to the Poles, manipulated the notion of German revanchism to gain public legitimacy for the pro-Soviet regime.

Relations between Germany and the Czech and Slovak Federal Republic have not experienced any major discords since the 1989 "velvet revolution." No outstanding issues have, thus far, hindered the rapidly developing contacts between Prague and Bonn since the acceleration of German unification. In fact, Czechoslovakia's President Vaclav Havel placed relations with Germany at the center of the country's progress toward European integration and economic recovery. One possible source of future conflict between Germany and Czechoslovakia revolves around the German minority issue. Soon after Havel's election as President, he made an important speech apologizing for Prague's forced expulsion of several million Germans in the years after World War Two.[41] His statements were well-received in Germany but created a furor in Czechoslovakia, particularly among war veterans and several Czech political groups. They saw the speech as unnecessarily appeasing the Germans and ignoring the Nazi's repressive treatment of the Czechs during the war period. Some commentators were also perturbed that such statements could raise the expectations of expelled Sudeten Germans and their offspring by increasing their demands for material compensation and eventual territorial revisions. This, in turn, could play into the hands of Czech nationalist parties seeking to revive perceptions of a German threat for their own political ambitions.

In November 1990, the Czech-Slovak Federal Assembly rejected claims by Sudeten German expellee associations for damages sustained after World War Two. Instead, some parliamentary deputies asserted that they could equally present Germany with a list of Czech claims resulting from the severe war-time destruction. In April 1991, a spokesman for the West German-based Sudeten German Association, which contains about 100,000 members, demanded that a future treaty between Germany and Czechoslovakia include a clause for the creation of a commission to investigate all property claims.[42] But officials on both sides suggested a zero solution, in which Prague would surrender its petitions for damages sustained during the Nazi occupation while the Sudeten Germans withdrew all their property claims. In August 1991, the Czech-Slovak ambassador to Germany criticized the Kohl government for purportedly backing demands by Sudeten German groups demanding compensation for their post-war expulsions and for the right to settle in the Czech republic. Bonn rejected the criticisms and claimed that it could not simply ignore the desires of millions of Sudeten expellees and their families. Although the demands of Expellee leaders in Germany for the right to resettle in Czechoslovakia has upset some Czech activists, Prague cannot deny Germans the opportunity to live and work in the country if Czechoslovakia is serious about future EC membership.

The problem of mutual compensations remains unsettled, but it is unlikely to greatly interfere with improving relations between Bonn-Berlin and Prague. The issue did not interrupt negotiations on a new treaty between the two states that was initialled in October 1991. In fact, the Treaty on Good-Neighborliness and Friendly Cooperation did not specifically deal with the problem of property confiscations or reparations for war damages. Moreover, territorial questions have not been raised in either capital and the small size of the German minority mitigates against any major dispute over their future status. The combined membership of the recently created Union of German Cultural Associations (UGCA) in Czechoslovakia does not exceed 8,000 people, and it clearly does not have the same potential impact as the much more substantial German minority in Poland or the Hungarian minority in Slovakia.

Notes

1. For useful histories of Czechoslovakia see Josef Korbel, *Twentieth Century Czechoslovakia: The Meanings of its History* (New York: Columbia University Press, 1977); and Carol Skalnik Leff, *National Conflict in Czechoslovakia: The Making and Remaking of a State, 1918-1987* (Princeton: Princeton University Press, 1988).

2. *CTK,* Prague, in English, 18 June 1991.

3. See Vladimir Kusin, "Czechs and Slovaks: The Road to the Current Debate," Radio Free Europe, *Report on Eastern Europe,* Vol. 1, No. 40, 5 October 1990.

4. Consult Jan Obrman, "Language Law Stirs Controversy in Slovakia," Radio Free Europe, *Report on Eastern Europe,* Vol. 1, No. 46, 16 November 1990.

5. *CTK,* Prague, in English, 13 March 1991, *FBIS-EEU*-91-052, 18 March 1991. See also the interview with Bohnan Dvorak, Chairman of the Club of Nonaligned Activists, *Prague Domestic Service,* in Czech, 15 March 1991.

6. Check Jiri Pehe, "Growing Slovak Demands Seen as Threat to Federation," Radio Free Europe, *Report on Eastern Europe,* Vol. 2, No. 12, 22 March 1991.

7. See Alena Melicharkova, "Will There Be A Slovak Home Guard?" *Narodna Obroda*, Bratislava, Vol. 2, No. 12, 13 July 1991.

8. Janusz Bugajski, "Czechs and Slovaks," *The Christian Science Monitor*, 13 August 1991.

9. Jiri Pehe, "Bid for Slovak Sovereignty Causes Political Upheaval," Radio Free Europe, *Report on Eastern Europe*, Vol. 2, No. 41, 11 October 1991.

10. For background consult Jiri Pehe, "Czech and Slovak Leaders Deadlocked Over Country's Future," Radio Free Europe, *Report on Eastern Europe*, Vol. 2, No. 48, 29 November 1991.

11. Oskar Krejci, "Czech Nationalism and Separatism," *Pravda*, Bratislava, 14 June 1991.

12. See the interview with Jan Krycer, Chairman of the Movement for Self-Government-Society for Moravia and Silesia, "We Are A State-Forming Movement," *Lidove Noviny*, Prague, 23 July 1991.

13. Radio Free Europe/ Radio Liberty, *Daily Report*, No. 289, 4 November 1991.

14. Radio Free Europe/ Radio Liberty, *Daily Report*, No. 287, 31 October 1991.

15. For a history of Hungary read Jorg K. Hoensch, *A History of Modern Hungary, 1867-1986* (London: Longman, 1984).

16. For background on the Hungarian minority issue see Stephen Borsody, *Czechoslovak Policy and the Hungarian Minority, 1945-1948* (New York: Columbia University Press, 1982).

17. See Edith Oltay, "Hungarian Minority in Slovakia Sets Up Independent Organizations," Radio Free Europe, *Report on Eastern Europe*, Vol. 1, No. 11, 16 March 1991.

18. Check Jan Obrman, "Language Law Stirs Controversy in Slovakia," Radio Free Europe, *Report on Eastern Europe*, Vol. 1, No. 46, 16 November 1990.

19. See the interview with Jozef Horsky, Deputy Chairman of the Slovak National Party, by Istvan Boros, "We Are Patriots," *Magyar Nemszet*, Budapest, 19 October 1990.

20. Criticisms of Antall can be found in Martin Hric, "Once Again on Visit of Goncz, President of the Hungarian Republic, to Bratislava: It Was Not Mutual Courting," *Narodna Obroda*, Bratislava, 31 July 1990.

21. For example, see "All Quiet on the Borders," *Lidove Noviny*, Prague, 14 August 1990.

22. *CTK*, Bratislava, in English, 1 August 1991.

23. See Jan Bobak, "Slovaks in Present Day Hungary," *Literarny Tyzdennik*, Bratislava, 7 July 1990.

24. From an interview with Miklos Duray in *Respekt*, Prague, No. 41, 14-20 October 1991.

25. Jaromir Horec, "Subcarpathian Ruthenia at the Crossroads," *Lidova Demokracie*, Prague, 18 December 1991.

26. For a comprehensive treatment of Poland's international relations in the inter-war period see Jan Karski, *The Great Powers and Poland, 1919-1945, From Versailles to Yalta* (Lanham: University Press of America, 1985).

27. Some background may be found in Anna Sabbat-Swidlicka, "Polish-German Relations: Turning Borders Into Bridges," Radio Free Europe, *Report on Eastern Europe*, Vol. 1, No. 20, 18 May 1990.

28. For the text of the treaty see *DPA*, Hamburg, in German, 14 November 1990. For an assessment see Anna Sabbat-Swidlicka, "The Signing of the Polish-German Border

Treaty," Radio Free Europe, *Report on Eastern Europe,* Vol. 1, No. 49, 7 December 1990.

29. Consult Jan B. de Weydenthal, "The Polish-German Reconciliation," Radio Free Europe, *Report on Eastern Europe,* Vol. 2, No. 27, 5 July 1991.

30. See the article by Thomas Kleine-Brockhoff, "The Creeping Anschluss," *Die Zeit,* 5 October 1990.

31. *Frankfurter Allgemeine Zeitung,* 26 April 1991.

32. As reported by Wlodzimierz Kalicki in "The Closet Germans: A Holiday Issue Report on the German Minority in Poland," *Gazeta Wyborcza,* Warsaw, 21 September 1991.

33. Check the interview with Polish Senator Dorota Simonides in *Rzeczpospolita Warsaw,* 10 December 1990; and articles by Tadeusz Lubiejewski, "Poles, Germans, Silesia," *Trybuna Opolska,* Opole, 2 August 1990; and Jerzy Tomaszewski, "The Tail of the Ostrich, A Few Words on Ethnic Minorities: The Germans," *Polityka,* Warsaw, 28 April 1990.

34. Miroslaw Machnacki, "League of Expellees Proposes Szczecin, Zgorzelec, and Other Free Cities," *Gazeta Wyborcza,* Warsaw, 10 July 1990.

35. Janina Hajduk-Nijakowska, "Manipulation of the German Minority in Upper Silesia," *Trybuna Opolska,* Opole, 3-4 November 1990.

36. See Halina Kowalik, "Short Cut," *Prawo i Zycie,* Warsaw, 4 May 1991; and Barbara Cieszewska, "Upper Silesia Together or Separately," *Rzeczpospolita,* Warsaw, 5 September 1991.

37. Consult Stanislaw Wilczynski, "Poland and the German National Minority," *Tygodnik Gdanski,* Gdansk, 18 August 1991.

38. See the interview with the Polish Deputy Defense Minister, Janusz Onyszkiewicz, in *Zolnierz Rzeczpospolitej,* Warsaw, 24 September 1990.

39. For useful background see *The Role of Silesian Cieszyn in Czecho-slovak-Polish Relations From 1918 to the Present,* published by ESWS Egyutteles, Bohumin, Czechoslovakia, 1991.

40. Jan Obrman, "Relations with Germany," Radio Free Europe, *Report on Eastern Europe,* Vol. 2, No. 46, 15 November 1991.

41. See Jan Obrman, "Controversy Over Postwar Expulsion of Germans," Radio Free Europe, *Report on Eastern Europe,* Vol. 1. No. 6, 9 February 1990.

42. *CTK,* Prague, in English, 25 April 1991, in *FBIS-EEU*-92-084, 1 May 1991.

4

The Yugoslav Crisis: Internal

Since the summer of 1991, the multi-national Yugoslav federation has stood on the verge of disintegration. With the erosion of centralized Communist Party rule, the first multi-party elections were held during 1990 in each of the country's six republics. They brought to power either pro-independence nationalist parties or reformed Communist forces espousing nationalist platforms. Despite months of negotiations, the leaders of the six republics failed to agree on a new power sharing arrangement or the maintenance of an integrated economic and military structure. As a result of the impasse, Slovenia and Croatia declared their independence and undertook far-reaching steps to secede from the federation. Their decision precipitated a military intervention in the two republics by the Yugoslav federal army in a desperate effort to keep the country together. The military itself came under the increasing control of the authoritarian Serbian Socialist regime, which appeared determined to preserve the state or strengthen Serbian domination in the remaining federal structure.

As the war in Croatia intensified during the fall of 1991, there was a grave danger that the armed conflict could spread to neighboring republics where a growing number of nationalities reasserted their sovereignty and demanded self-determination. Despite the ceasefire arranged through UN mediation in the winter of 1992, the truce remained fragile and a political compromise between the warring republics was far from certain. In order to understand the complexity of current political developments and evolving inter-ethnic relations in Yugoslavia, it is useful to briefly review the history of the south Slav peoples before exploring the contours of the contemporary conflicts.

The South Slavs

The present territory of Yugoslavia has been inhabited by Slavic tribes since the 7th century AD. Slovene, Croatian, and Serbian kingdoms were subsequently established in the area, but contrasting internal structures and diverse external influences enhanced the process of differentiation. While

Slovenia and Croatia were subject to strong Catholic influence, the Serbs and kindred peoples, such as the Montenegrins and Macedonians, were converted to Orthodox Christianity. In the 8th century, the Slovenes lost their independence to the advancing Germans, and in the 10th century Croatia came under Hungarian control. An independent Serbian kingdom survived until the 14th century, when the country was overrun by the Ottoman Turks. The Turks also occupied the central territory of Bosnia-Hercegovina and converted the majority of Bosnian Slavs to the Islamic faith. Over the next 500 years, differences widened between the northern and southern Slavic groups. Slovenia and Croatia developed a feudalistic socio-economic structure and a strong Catholic faith, while the Serbs, Montenegrins, and Macedonians strengthened their independent Orthodox Churches and preserved a village-centered social and economic system.

With the gradual disintegration of the Austro-Hungarian and Ottoman Turkish empires, the Slavic peoples reasserted their drive toward independence and spawned a movement for south Slav unification. At the close of World War One, the Kingdom of Serbs, Croats, and Slovenes was established under the authority of the Serbian monarchy. A few years later the name was changed to Yugoslavia, or the "land of the South Slavs."[1] The new state also incorporated the Bosnians, Montenegrins, and Macedonians. Although the objective was to form a unified state as protection against foreign pressures and invasions, the country proved to be a fragile creation with inbuilt conflicts between the constituent ethnic groups. During the 1920s, a limited form of democracy emerged as the Serbs and Croats, the two largest nationalities, vied for control of the country. Historical, religious, and cultural divisions were exacerbated by disparate economic conditions between the richer north and the poorer south. In 1929, in response to growing political chaos, Serbia's King Alexander proclaimed a monarchical dictatorship under the pretext of preserving national unity. The system survived his assassination by Croatian gunmen, but quickly unravelled with the outbreak of World War Two. The Nazis overran the country in 1941, and created further divisions by sanctioning the creation of a Fascist Croatian state that incorporated most of Bosnia-Hercegovina. Serbia and adjoining territories were overwhelmed, fractured, and placed under either German, Italian, or Bulgarian control.

War-time developments seriously aggravated the Serbian-Croatian rift. The *Ustase* regime in Croatia massacred hundreds of thousands of Serbs or forcibly converted them to Catholicism. Meanwhile, the Serbian pro-royalist *Cetnik* resistance movement clashed with Croatian groups as well as with the Communist *Partisan* detachments of Marshal Jozef Broz Tito, who took over the country at the close of the war. The Tito administration recreated the Yugoslav state, but sought to limit the powers and ambitions of all the national groupings. Six republics and two autonomous regions were established with a significant devolution of central authority. But the political system remained under the control of the League of Yugoslav Communists. Instead of resolving inter-ethnic animosities, the Titoist system simply subdued them or provided temporary relief through cultural, religious, and economic outlets. Pent up grievances and historical animosities were released again during the 1980s after Tito's death, particularly as the Croats and Slovenes attempted to bolster their political independence while the Serbs sought to ensure a dominant position in the federation.

Yugoslavia has been able to survive Communist decentralization, economic reform, and ethnic diversity as long as this did not upset the inter-republican balance precariously established by Marshal Tito. However, Serbian, Croatian, and Slovenian self-assertion in the past few years, coupled with economic decline, industrial unrest, and ethnic friction, has capsized this arrangement. The demise of the old guard Titoist *Partisans* and the rapid disintegration of the ruling League of Communists have been exploited by all three republics. The Serbian Socialist authorities managed to capture substantial popular support since late 1987 by restricting the autonomous status of Serbia's two provinces, Kosovo and Vojvodina. They justified these measures by claiming decades of anti-Serbian restrictions under the Titoist regime. Slovenia and Croatia capitalized on the political slack in the spring of 1990 by electing nationalist right-of-center governments that began to push toward confederal status or full independence from Belgrade. All these developments served to undermine the federal structure, whose continuing existence depended on the decision-making unanimity of all six republics.

One crucial source of Communist legitimacy and Yugoslav cohesiveness has been abruptly discontinued during the past few years. The perennial Soviet threat that buttressed Tito and his successors ever since the 1948 split with Stalin receded into history. Moreover, eastern Europe's democratic revolutions during 1989 helped to accelerate the process of pluralization and decentralization, as political activists in several republics began to look eastward as well as westward for inspiration. During 1990, in the first multi-party republican elections since World War Two, reformed Communist parties were only successful in Serbia and Montenegro where they espoused nationalist causes or were not faced by credible rivals for the ethnic vote. Elsewhere, the national factor proved paramount as ethnic-based and pro-sovereignty parties scored important victories in Slovenia, Croatia, Bosnia-Hercegovina, and Macedonia.

Yugoslavia has abounded with numerous conspiracy theories that elicit a wide public resonance. Mutual accusations are based on persistent fears of encirclement, domination, and extinction. For example, the Serbs perceive a looming threat of Islamic fundamentalism among the growing Albanian population in Kosovo, Macedonia, and Montenegro, and among the Muslims in Bosnia-Hercegovina and Serbia's Sandzak region. The

Croats and Slovenes fear a resurgent and aggressive Serbia that would restrict their newly acquired freedoms; their leaders have pointed to Serbian domination of prewar Yugoslavia as an unacceptable political precedent. Zagreb also remained convinced that Belgrade was exploiting the large Serbian minorities in Croatia and Bosnia-Hercegovina to whip up opposition to the newly elected governments and undermine their drive toward sovereignty. The Macedonians have been worried about potential territorial demands from neighboring states, including Albania, Greece, and Bulgaria, in addition to an expansionist "Serboslavia." If the current Yugoslav federation were to dissolve, Serbia could also seek to extend its dominions southward into Macedonia to compensate for any loss of influence in the north western republics.

Leaders of the more than one million strong Albanian community in Kosovo have also demanded their own Yugoslav republic. The Serbian authorities dissolved the Kosovo assembly and continue to dismiss all Albanian protests as the desperate acts of renegade separatists. Albanian activists accused the Serbs of establishing a police state in Kosovo under which the local media has been silenced, political organizers have been imprisoned, and an economic war of attrition has been conducted to break the backbone of Albanian resistance. With the victory of the hard-line Slobodan Milosevic in the December 1990 Serbian elections, which the Albanians effectively boycotted in protest, fears were raised over mounting repression to eliminate the avowed Albanian threat.

All the Yugoslav republics except Slovenia contain their own restless and aggrieved minorities whose loyalties remain suspect in the eyes of the majority. For example, political leaders of the over half a million Serbs in Croatia were not enamored of the new republican government in Zagreb. Activists staged their own referendums demanding regional autonomy and seeking protection from the Yugoslav or Serbian governments if Croatia were to secede from the federation. Hungarians, Croats, and other minorities in the Serbian province of Vojvodina have also become politically active and increasingly expressed their apprehensions about the Milosevic regime.

Fears persisted in Yugoslavia that partially reformed Communists or authoritarian centralists, hiding behind nationalist rhetoric and populist slogans, were intent on manipulating political conflicts and planned to provoke an inter-republican rupture to maintain their grip on power. In such a scenario, the Yugoslav People's Army (YPA), as the last bastion of "Yugo-slavism," would be used to intimidate and overwhelm wayward republics. Even before armed hostilities erupted in Slovenia and Croatia during the summer of 1991, the YPA's officer corps was heavily dominated by Serbs and Montenegrins. But the loyalties of rank and file conscripts from other nationalities to Yugoslav unity could not be taken for granted. Instead of pulling Yugoslavia together again, it seemed that an army crackdown actually speeded up the process of disintegration, triggered bitter partisan warfare, drew neighboring powers into the imbroglio, and delegitimized both the federal and Serbian governments within the international community. Any sustained military conflicts will also have disastrous consequences for the already struggling economy. While production has sagged and foreign investment has stagnated, marketization and private enterprise have only achieved a tentative toehold in the country. Yugoslavia's reformist federal Prime Minister Ante Markovic remained virtually powerless in these circumstances and resigned at the close of 1991.

Serbia and Croatia

Yugoslavia was a multinational state in which six nations had their own republic, and several nations, or "nationalities," were dispersed as minorities between one or more republics.[2] In this patchwork federation, no nationality had an absolute majority and each harbored some historical, religious, political, or economic grievances against one or more ethnic groups. The most serious conflict with the widest impact on the future of Yugoslavia, was that between the two largest nations, the Serbs and Croats. The Serbs complain that they were emasculated during Titoist rule by the Yugoslav federal arrangement. They were confined to a minimal territory with about one-third of their co-ethnics resident outside Serbia. National equality has thereby been perceived in Serbia as a form of discrimination in favor of other nations. By contrast, Croats, Slovenes, and others contend that Serbs have occupied a preponderant position in the federation and, in recent years, have pushed menacingly toward the restoration of a "Greater Serbia" at the expense of neighboring republics. "Yugoslavism" has therefore been viewed as a cloak for Serbian domination and economic exploitation. Serbian self-assertion and nationalism have therefore stimulated anti-Serbian nationalism in a spiral of rivalry between the major ethnic units.

Croatia and Serbia drifted apart politically during 1990. In the republican elections of April 1990, Croatia elected a right-of-center pro-independence government based around the Croatian Democratic Union (CDU), whose leader Franjo Tudjman became President. Serbia re-elected a reform Communist but essentially authoritarian and pro-federalist administration under the presidency of Serbian Socialist Party (SSP) leader Slobodan Milosevic. Croatia and Slovenia sought a much looser confederal association, while the Serbian authorities were determined to preserve some kind of federation in which Belgrade would maintain the central decision-making role.

The crisis between Croatia and Serbia came to an initial head in January 1991, after the Yugoslav Defense Minister asserted that no republic would be allowed to create paramilitary units outside the federal military structure.

Both the Croatian and Slovenian legislatures had approved constitutional amendments giving republican governments jurisdiction over territorial defense and foreign relations, which they refused to surrender to Yugoslav control. An armed confrontation was narrowly averted in early 1991, when Zagreb agreed to demobilize its reserve militia forces although not its main National Guard contingents. Despite this partial compromise, tensions remained high. Croatia stood accused by the Yugoslav and Serbian authorities of creating illegal armed formations, importing weapons from abroad, and allegedly planning to sabotage Yugoslav army operations.

The secession of Slovenia could be acceptable to the Serbian government, as it would strengthen Serbia's ethnic demographics and political position vis-à-vis the remaining republics and nationalities. But the separation of Croatia has proved much more problematic for Belgrade. The Milosevic regime asserted early on that Croatia could theoretically leave Yugoslavia, but it could not take with it the large Serbian minority. He thereby implied that Zagreb's secession would provoke claims to Serbian inhabited territories in Croatia and other Yugoslav republics. This in turn would either lead to the establishment of a smaller Serbian-dominated Yugoslavia or a larger Serbian state. An independent although much reduced Croatia would still remain subject to pronounced political and economic pressure from Belgrade, as Serbia would become the strongest regional power.

The loyalties, aspirations, and activities of the approximately 600,000 strong Serbian minority in Croatia created enormous tensions both within Croatia and between the Serbian, federal, and Croatian governments. Since the Croatian republican elections, leaders of Serbian political groups have been demanding their own territorial autonomy especially in areas where Serbs form compact communities. According to the April 1991 Croatian census, Serbs make up about 12.2% of the republic's population, although less than half inhabit the disputed border regions.[3] In fact, the majority of Serbs live in Zagreb and other large towns or are scattered throughout the republic. Serbs constitute a majority in only eleven municipalities (out of 115) in the republic, and even in these Croats form a sizable minority. The Zagreb administration has not opposed granting cultural autonomy to Serbian communities, but remained convinced that pressures for territorial self-administration were orchestrated by the Milosevic regime in collusion with local radicals in order to destabilize and shatter the Croatian republic.

The draft of the new Croatian constitution was opposed by leaders of the Serbian Democratic Party (SDP), who were dissatisfied with its lack of provisions for minority rights. In December 1990, the SDP dominated Serbian National Council in Croatia announced that it was adopting a statute to establish a Serbian autonomous region before Zagreb passed a new constitution. The region was to include all territories in which Serbs constituted a majority, as well as neighboring municipalities where no single group predominated. The new authorities in the autonomous region were to assume responsibilities for judicial and policing functions independently of the Croatian state. At the end of December 1990, the Serbian Autonomous Region of Krajina was proclaimed and it incorporated ten municipalities in the Knin region adjacent to northern Dalmatia.[4] Zagreb immediately annulled the decision, contending that it was contrary to the republican constitution which provided no legal basis for forming autonomous districts within Croatia.

Serbia promptly accused the Croatian government of imposing a state of siege in minority areas through the creation of its own National Guard. It also charged Zagreb with anti-Serbian discrimination and of creating an "ethnocracy" based along war-time *Ustase* lines. In fact, purges in the old Communist apparatus in Croatia displaced many Serbs who held prominent positions in the defunct system. This policy was depicted by the Yugoslav media in Belgrade as a racist policy designed to turn Serbs into second class Croatian citizens. The Croatian President himself came under severe criticism both within and outside the republic for allegedly concentrating too much power in his hands, for enacting various press restrictions, and for maintaining exclusive control over defense policies. Zagreb justified such measures as temporary but essential to preserve national unity during a war-time emergency, especially in the face of mounting threats and pressures from Belgrade.

Croatian officials asserted that Serbian extremists had formed special battalions in Krajina since mid-1990. These units received arms from outside the republic in order to engage in sabotage and terrorism against the Croatian authorities. In February 1991, as the Serb-Croat conflict escalated at the republican level, the Serbian National Council in Knin declared the independence of Krajina from Croatia. The city of Knin was named as the region's capital. But the legality of the move was not recognized by Zagreb or even by the federal authorities. In April 1991, the Krajina Executive Council adopted a declaration on separation from Croatia and on federation with Serbia. A few weeks later the decision was reportedly endorsed in a public referendum among Serbs in the region.[5] A growing number of Serb community leaders elsewhere in Croatia, including central and eastern Slavonia, Baranja, and western Syrmia (or Srem in Serbian), also sought to link up with either Krajina or with Serbia's autonomous province of Vojvodina. The federal government, which at that time was not under full Serbian control, refused to recognize these decisions. It declared the creation of new autonomous regions to be unconstitutional, particularly the secession of territory from one republic and its incorporation into another republic.[6]

The Serbian regime itself did not automatically approve the Krajina decision or accept the region as a constituent part of Serbia. Such a move could have proved counterproductive by creating damaging rifts with the federal presidency, and it would have placed the republic on a collision course with

Croatia without unequivocal army support. This decision would also have confirmed Zagreb's charges that the Milosevic regime had engineered the entire conspiracy in Krajina in order to break up Croatia.

Since early 1991, confrontations between the Croatian militia and armed units of the Serb minority have sparked violence in several parts of Croatia. The scenarios in each case have been similar. Serb militants, many of them former policemen who refused to surrender their weapons to Croatian officials and operated in the self-proclaimed autonomous districts, armed themselves and attempted to disarm Croatian militiamen and police whose authority they did not recognize. This in turn provoked the intervention of additional Croatian militia units, who tried to disarm the irregulars, as well as Yugoslav army detachments who sought to repulse the Croatian forces. The authorities in Zagreb also claimed that some of the guerrilla groups were infiltrated into Croatia by the Serbian regime, which was attempting to embitter the relatively calm ethnic relations in the republic as a pretext for aggression.

Although in the first half of 1991 the conflicts were localized and defused, they led to a loss of life on all three sides and each had the potential of escalating into wider warfare. The federal government proved unable to resolve the conflict by bringing all sides together to forge a durable cease-fire or some workable political compromise. And indeed the federal presidency remained deeply divided between a pro-Serbian bloc consisting of delegates from Serbia, Montenegro, Kosovo, and Vojvodina, and representatives of the other four republics. The political vacuum at the federal level and the problems in rotating the country's presidency deepened the rift between Zagreb and Belgrade and accelerated the breakup of the federation. Even after the appointment of the Croatian representative Stipe Mesic as President of the federal presidency in the summer of 1991, despite strong Serbian bloc opposition, the central government institutions remained paralyzed.

At the end of June 1991, Croatia, in tandem with Slovenia, declared its independence and "disassociation" from Yugoslavia. Initially, the YPA focused its attention on crushing the Slovenian rebellion, but it also ominously moved its troops and equipment to saturate Croatian territory. The bulk of the YPA forces that subsequently withdrew from Slovenia were also repositioned in various parts of Croatia. Having failed to subdue Slovenia, the army leadership put its weight behind the Serbian government program. This focused on one of two objectives: either to ensure that Zagreb remained in a centralized Yugoslavia controlled from Belgrade, or to carve away about half of Croatia's territory and establish a "Greater Serbia" or a "Community of Serbian States" stretching to the Adriatic coast. In both scenarios, the Croatian authorities would be severely weakened, and even if nominally independent the republic would remain under pronounced Serb-Yugoslav influence. In addition, Belgrade would maintain direct control over the distribution of the national income, as well as the rich agricultural lands in Slavonia and the economically important tourist resorts of Dalmatia.

The strategy for achieving these ends seemed to have been prepared well in advance of Croatia's declaration of independence. The large Serbian community along the Croatian-Bosnian border was to be used as a pretext and a supply base for guerrilla operations. These were designed to capture extensive and contiguous tracts of territory and to cut off the economically critical Slavonian and Dalmatian regions from Zagreb. Serbian guerrillas also appeared to be deliberately pushing out Croatian residents from the contested zones in order to leave the Serbs in a majority position. Rumors also surfaced that Serbs were being resettled in some captured territories from other parts of the country in order to outnumber the Croats in the contested municipalities.

The YPA leadership evidently approved a strategy of unconventional warfare that would undermine Croatia without eliciting outright international condemnation. As the conflict escalated during August and September 1991, it became clear that the military was not a neutral party that simply interceded to keep apart the two warring factions—the Croatian National Guard and the Serbian guerrillas. On the contrary, the military provided arms, logistical support, and offensive firepower to the Serb irregulars as they proceeded to capture about one-quarter of Croatia's territory, including areas lacking clear Serbian majorities. During this time, the number of Serbian guerrillas reportedly grew from some 7,000 to over 40,000.

A dozen cease-fire agreements and peace accords, often arranged under EC auspices, were invariably broken, in most cases by the YPA and the Serb guerrillas. Any lulls in the fighting simply provided respites for regrouping and served to defuse international criticisms of Belgrade and the military leadership. But no territory was surrendered by the guerrillas whose leaders opposed the presence of international observers and human rights monitors. The Croatian forces were conducting an essentially defensive holding operation, endeavoring to keep open the major roads and lines of communication and maintain control over the larger towns, even while the unprotected countryside fell into enemy hands. By late November 1991, over 5,000 deaths were reported in the fighting, countless thousands were injured by gunshot and mortar shells, and over 500,000 refugees fled the conflict zones, with some seeking shelter in neighboring Hungary.

Frustrated by their inability to dislodge the guerrillas or forestall indiscriminate YPA shelling, in late September 1991 Croatian forces began a blockade of army bases and garrisons throughout the republic. This partial offensive netted Zagreb a substantial arms cache, including tanks, personnel carriers, missiles, and automatic weapons. But despite this windfall, the 50,000 strong Croatian National Guard remained seriously outgunned by the YPA, lacking an air force, navy, tank regiments, or even sufficient heavy weaponry such as anti-tank or anti-aircraft missiles to repulse army onslaughts. In response to the growing threat of a full-scale army assault, Zagreb weighed the possibility of a general mobilization in Croatia, even though it was unable to supply sufficient arms to all military recruits.

With the expiration of the EC brokered Brioni moratorium on independence, in early October 1991, the Croatian parliament restated the republic's disassociation and negated all federal laws and Yugoslav jurisdiction in Croatia. These moves did not forestall the armed conflict or ensure international recognition for the republic. By the close of 1991, Croatian forces had lost control of several key towns in the eastern Slavonia region and remained hard pressed in other war zones. Although the Serbian government expressed agreement for an international UN peace-keeping force to enter Croatia, there was little indication that any of the captured territories would be surrendered by the Serb guerrillas or the Krajina government.

The unequal war in Croatia has also led to some radicalization on the Croatian political scene. President Tudjman was subject to severe criticism by more militant right wing parties for his willingness to compromise with the federal army and the Serbian regime, during a series of EC-sponsored peace talks, for his failure to create an effective anti-insurgency force, and for his inability to protect Croatian citizens in disputed territories throughout the republic. In the summer of 1991, some independent Croatian militia forces were formed, but were condemned by the Zagreb government for acting outside the republic's laws. Among these was a militant and quasi-fascist anti-Serbian formation, the Croatian Defense Association (CDA), linked with the right wing Croatian Party of Rights (CPR).[7] The CDA claimed to have 15,000 fighters, while the CPR stressed its commitment to establishing a "Greater Croatia" with borders stretching from Istria and Dalmatia to the outskirts of Belgrade. There were also indications that some of the Serbian guerrilla units in Croatia were acting independently of the YPA, being either under the direct control of the Serbian republican regime or tied to various radical Serbian parties outside the influence of both the YPA and the Belgrade government.

Despite its successes in Croatia, as the war dragged on the YPA experienced increasing internal ruptures. Daily desertions were reported, particularly by non-Serbian troops serving in Croatia, the response to the fall 1991 call-up was less than enthusiastic even within Serbia and Montenegro, while the morale of many front-line units was wearing extremely thin. To assure a more disciplined and motivated fighting force, a purge of non-Serb officers was reportedly undertaken, and loyalist Serbs and Montenegrins were placed in the most vital command positions. Reports also surfaced that "ethnically pure" Serbian and Montenegrin military units were being formed for front line duty in Croatia. Volunteers were also recruited by the irregular Serb formations in Krajina from other Serb-inhabited republics, including Bosnia-

Hercegovina. Some were allegedly financed, armed, and controlled by radical Serbian parties, including a resuscitated *Cetnik* movement led by the radical nationalist politician, Vojislav Seselj.

Croatia's President Tudjman has been lambasted since the start of the conflict for ignoring the Serb minority question and thus allowing the problem to be exploited by Belgrade. Although the new Croatian constitution appeared to be a reasonably democratic document, Serbian leaders charged that it was not explicit enough in recognizing and assuring the "collective rights" of the Serbian minority. While the human rights of all citizens were verbally guaranteed in the constitution, together with the cultural and educational rights of minority groups, the issue of political or territorial self-determination was not clearly enunciated. Such omissions were condemned by the Serbian authorities as a deliberate negation of specifically Serbian interests and an indication of growing Croatian repression. The Belgrade media capitalized on the situation, by launching a full-scale propaganda barrage accusing the Croatian government of genocidal *Ustase* inclinations and of preparing to expel or massacre all Serbs in the republic. This served to increase fears among the minority and cast the guerrillas in the role of patriotic national defenders. The reappearance of traditional Croatia insignia and the purge of former Communist Serbian officials fostered paranoia and aided the recruitment drive by guerrilla forces. The latter were also not averse to applying coercive measures in order to expand their numbers.

As the conflict escalated, Croatian government officials came under mounting international pressure to make some clear concessions to the Serbian population and to underscore their commitment to minority rights. In late July 1991, Zagreb offered an olive branch by agreeing to negotiate over the question of granting Serbs some form of limited political autonomy. Croatian officials proposed forming districts with a special status, in which the municipal Serbian authorities would have legislative powers and some control over the local police force, education, and culture. These were to include the areas of Kninska Krajina, Banja, Kordun, and parts of eastern Slavonia. But such proposals came too late to have any impact on the armed struggle, and the rebel government in Krajina rejected the status of an autonomous region within Croatia as a way of settling the crisis.[8]

In a display of defiance and disregard of Zagreb's authority, the Baranja area in eastern Slavonia, between the Drava and Danube rivers and the Hungarian border, was effectively annexed by the Serbs, and its municipalities were planned to be merged with Serbia's neighboring Vojvodina province. In August 1991, a new Serbian Autonomous Region of Western Slavonia was proclaimed as a separate "political-territorial unit" and an integral part of the Serbian Autonomous Region of Krajina. The land controlled by Serb and federal forces in eastern Croatia was declared as the Serbian Autonomous Region of Slavonia, Baranja, and Western Srem.[9] Krajina itself was increasingly referred to by local leaders and the Yugoslav media as Western Serbia. The Krajina authorities were evidently only prepared to weigh three possible political options: unification with Bosnian Krajina as a separate federal unit within Yugoslavia, the creation of a Krajina republic in its own right within a federal Yugoslavia, or the transformation of Krajina into a component region of an expanded Serbia. All three options were unacceptable to Zagreb, which refused to countenance any loss of territory, particularly as a result of armed actions.

In order to appease international public opinion and underscore Zagreb's commitment to minority rights, in December 1991 Croatia's parliament passed a law on minority autonomy. The legislation was meant to underscore that in the predominantly Serbian areas, the police, courts, schools, and media would be left in Serbian hands once Croatia achieved independent statehood. But these initiatives failed to reassure Serbian minority leaders or convince them to lay down their arms. That same month a Republic of Serb Krajina was proclaimed to include the "autonomous regions" of Krajina, Slavonia, Baranja, and Srem: the republic was to remain a constituent part of a federal Yugoslavia.[10]

The federal authorities found themselves increasingly powerless as the war in Croatia escalated: the collective presidency could not reach any meaningful agreements, while their decisions were patently ignored by Yugoslav army commanders. The federal Prime Minister Ante Markovic declared that a virtual military coup had taken place in the country. The armed forces had become an independent political actor and army commanders were no longer under the control of any federal authority. As the YPA expanded its operations in Croatia and refused to be bound by cease-fire agreements, Markovic demanded the resignation of YPA Army General Veljko Kadijevic, the Federal Minister for National Defense, and his deputy Admiral Stane Brovet.[11] Both commanders brazenly ignored the premier's order. Markovic charged that the military was obviously siding with the Serbian leadership and promoting the war in Croatia. In addition, Kadijevic had allegedly held secret meetings with Soviet Defense Minister General Yazov, before the failed August coup in Moscow, in order to arrange for the delivery of huge quantities of weapons to the YPA. The meetings were not sanctioned by the federal authorities.

In early October 1991, the pro-Serbian bloc in the federal presidency staged a takeover of government functions. This followed months of paralysis because of irresolvable differences between Serbian delegates and the Slovenian, Croatian, Bosnian, and Macedonian representatives. The objective was to exclude delegates from the rebel republics while providing a veneer of ongoing legitimacy to the federal authorities. President Stipe Mesic, a Croat, was barred from the proceedings; he asserted that the truncated Serbian-dominated leadership together with the army command was, in effect, staging a coup in collusion with the Milosevic regime. In November 1991, the Serbian authorities also made preparations to replace the federal government and to oust Prime Minister Markovic for his alleged Croatian sympathies. The resignation of Markovic in December 1991 ensured Serbian control over all remaining federal institutions.

In early 1992, a United Nations sponsored cease fire arrangement appeared to hold throughout Croatia. It was supported by the authorities in Zagreb and Belgrade and by commanders of the Yugoslav military. The only persistent opposition to the UN proposals came from Milan Babic, the Serbian President of the Krajina region. He feared that Serbian militia forces would be disbanded and the local population subjected to Croatian control once the UN troops were withdrawn. Babic was accused by some of his colleagues in the Serbian Democratic Party (SDP) of creating an autocratic system in Krajina and abusing the rights of the Serbian community.[12] In an internal power struggle, Babic was subsequently replaced as President of Krajina by Goran Hadzic, an avowed moderate who benefitted from the support of Belgrade. Although the Milosevic government, facing mounting opposition to the war in Serbia, appeared to back away from a "Greater Serbia" policy, suspicions persisted that this was a tactical play to subdue domestic criticism and elicit international support for the beleaguered regime.

Under the UN plan, about 14,000 troops were to be deployed to the combat zones, the Yugoslav army would be withdrawn from Croatia, and irregular Serbian and Croatian detachments were to be disarmed. Existing local authorities and police forces would function on an interim basis and under UN supervision, pending an overall political solution to the crisis. Croatian authorities also expressed some reservations about the UN mission, fearing that it could legitimize the separation of the Krajina region from Croatia and prevent them from retaking territory lost to the Serbian militia.

Slovenia

Slovenia was the most ethnically homogeneous republic in Yugoslavia and has not been embroiled in any significant territorial or minority conflicts with its Yugoslav neighbors. During the past two years, the republic has moved the furthest toward sovereignty and secession, or "disassociation," from Yugoslavia. The republican elections in April 1990, brought to power the pro-independence coalition DEMOS (Democratic Opposition of Slovenia), led by the Slovene Democratic Alliance (SDA). In July 1990, the Slovenian National Assembly adopted a proclamation on the republic's sovereignty and began to prepare a new independent constitution that would negate all Yugoslav federal laws in Slovenia.

In December 1990, a Slovenian plebiscite on independence was won overwhelmingly by pro-independence forces. The results further aggravated

Slovenia's dispute with the federal authorities. Ljubljana sought a much looser confederal arrangement with other republics; but in the event that an agreement on confederation could not be reached, Slovenia would move forward toward full independence. In February 1991, Ljubljana took a major step toward secession when the National Assembly annulled all federal laws and Slovenian obligations to Belgrade. The Slovenian government subsequently prepared for the republic's demilitarization and the removal of all Yugoslav troops from its soil. It also set June 1991 as the deadline for the formal declaration of independence if efforts to achieve a confederation of sovereign states finally collapsed.

The Slovenian authorities signalled that they would not be intimidated by the federal or Serbian governments. Before the declaration of disassociation from Yugoslavia, Defense Minister Ivan Jansa stated that Slovenia was prepared to defend itself against any attempted army crackdown. In fact, immediately after the Slovenian government's declaration of independence in late June 1991, the federal army mounted an armed intervention in the republic.[13] The YPA attempted to disarm Slovenia's territorial defense forces, to seize strategic military positions, and to regain control over the republic's frontiers with Italy, Austria, and Hungary. The army leadership calculated that Ljubljana could be cowered by a show of force to reverse its decision on independence without necessitating a full scale war with the republic's National Guard. It also wanted to demonstrate to the international community that Slovenia did not qualify as an independent state because the government did not control the republic's territory or its borders. But it quickly transpired that the YPA commanders seriously miscalculated the impact of their incursion. In fact, it served to stiffen Slovenian resistance and united virtually all the political groups behind the administration. Moreover, the YPA found itself operating in mountainous terrain unsuitable for conventional warfare, and the Slovenian forces effectively blocked the military intervention. Ljubljana's defense units proved to be sufficiently well armed, organized, and prepared to resist the assault, while the invasion force was too small, inflexible, and inexperienced. YPA formations were outmaneuvered by mobile and highly motivated Slovenian militiamen and proved unable to achieve their targets.

As the military situation on the ground deteriorated, YPA commanders realized that they would be unsuccessful without a substantial increase in troop numbers. Meanwhile, international condemnation mounted against the violent crackdown, and the military leadership together with the Serbian government calculated that the cost of escalation could be too high to bear. In response, they were willing to negotiate a ceasefire agreement sponsored by the EC countries and signed at Brioni on the Yugoslav Adriatic in early July 1991. In the Brioni agreement, both Slovenia and Croatia consented to suspend their declarations of independence for three months, pending a new series of inter-republican negotiations to restructure the federation. During the three month moratorium, federal military forces withdrew most of their contingents from Slovenia and relocated them in Croatia. The ceasefire in Slovenia allowed the EC to dispatch peace monitors to the republic.

Despite the termination of hostilities in Slovenia, leaders of the six republics and the country's collective presidency were unable to reach a workable compromise either on preserving the federation or forging a novel confederal arrangement. The moratorium on independence expired during the first week of October 1991 and the government in Ljubljana restarted its drive toward independence and separation from Yugoslavia. Despite the mounting conflict in Croatia and growing tensions elsewhere in the country, Ljubljana felt confident that the republic's determination, its record of resistance, and its territorial control would assure that Slovenia sooner or later gained international recognition.

The likelihood of any significant civil or ethnic conflicts in Slovenia has remained slight, particularly as the republic does not contain any sizable minorities that could become a source of rebellion against the incumbent government. The danger of another major military intervention against the republic has also receded significantly. Nonetheless, the possibility of a spill-over from the Croatian-Serbian conflict remained conceivable. This could take the form of a large scale refugee exodus, the use of Slovenian territory by various armed formations, and hot pursuit missions by the Croatian National Guard or the Yugoslav army. It could also not be discounted that the YPA would reorient its attention toward Slovenia, if and when the Croatian government was neutralized or disarmed. Hard-line Communist elements in the military leadership indicated that they may be unwilling to let Slovenia secede for strategic, economic, and ideological reasons, even if the Serbian regime were to accept a smaller federation.

One potential point of contention over Slovenian territory concerns the Istrian peninsula on the Adriatic coast, which the republic shares with Croatia. During 1990, the Italian Union for Istria and Rijeka (IUIR) and the Istrian Democratic Assembly (IDA) were formed to further the interests of the small Italian minority in the region that would seek to establish closer ties with Italy if Yugoslavia were to fissure.[14] Although the Italian population in Yugoslavia stands at only 15,000, the IDA has demanded either the autonomy of Slovenian and Croatian Istria, or the status of an "inter-republican" or "inter-governmental" region, with some assurances of outside protection in case of conflict or repression. Italian minority demands for sovereignty could become more strident following the secession of Slovenia and Croatia, particularly if economic conditions were to degenerate and minority aspirations were not satisfied by the new governments. However, some progress was evident in the early part of 1992 regarding the assurance of collective rights for ethnic minorities in both Slovenia and Italy.[15]

Belgrade has also become involved in the Italian issue in order to place additional pressure on the renegade republics. In early August 1991, leaders of the small neofascist Italian Social Movement (ISM) in Italy called for a revision of the Yugoslav-Italian border after a two day meeting with the Serbian government, legislature, and various opposition leaders. In particular, the ISM demanded the return of Istria and large parts of the Dalmatian coast if Yugoslavia disintegrated. Their calls were overtly supported by some Serbian leaders, including the self-proclaimed chief of the *Cetnik* party, Vojislav Seselj.[16]

Although Slovenia and Croatia have pushed for their independence in tandem, relations between the two republics have not developed completely smoothly. There has been a lack of full agreement on the content of their bilateral political and economic ties which delayed the signing of an agreement on full diplomatic relations. In addition, Zagreb has occasionally harbored suspicions over Slovenian-Serbian relations and Belgrade's willingness to only allow Slovenia to secede from Yugoslavia. Some marginal ultra-radical Slovenian groups have also expressed claims to Croatian lands in Istria by seeking autonomy for the peninsula, and to the Medjimura area next to the Hungarian border which contains a significant Slovenian minority. However, extremist claims by either side are unlikely to seriously effect relations between the two governments, especially as they both have more pressing concerns about their continuing survival.

Bosnia-Hercegovina

The republic of Bosnia-Hercegovina presents an even more intricate, divisive, and explosive problem for Yugoslavia than either Slovenia or Croatia. Any further aggravation of the Serb-Croat conflict will directly effect Bosnia, which has attempted to preserve a political balance between the three major nationalities—Muslims, Serbs, and Croats. Of the approximately 4.2 million Bosnian residents, Muslims form about 44%, Serbs 32%, and Croats 18%; the remainder belong to small nationalities or declared themselves as "Yugoslavs" in the census.

As Slovenia and Croatia pushed toward secession, Bosnia-Hercegovina found itself caught in the middle and leaders of the republic's chief ethnic groups have been increasingly pressurized to side with either Serbia or Croatia. Serbian republican authorities and Bosnian Serb leaders voiced fears over an emerging Muslim-Croat alliance. Such a coalition would form a clear majority in the republic and could even proceed to exclude Serbs from key posts in the administration. Serb activists also calculated that Muslims and Croats may seek some special links with Croatia if Slovenia and Croatia were to separate from Yugoslavia. Meanwhile, Bosnian Muslims and Croats grew concerned during the course of 1991 that Serbian minority leaders in league with the Milosevic regime in Serbia were planning a crisis in the republic similar to the one in Croatia.

In April 1991, a Community of Municipalities of Bosanska Krajina was carved out from 14 municipalities in western Bosnia, with its capital in Banja Luka, an area inhabited predominantly by Serbs and bordering the Serbian Autonomous Region of Krajina in Croatia.[17] At the same time, municipalities in the heavily Serb areas of south eastern Bosnia, near the Serbian and Montenegrin borders, also announced that they would form an autonomous "Community" to protect their interests. These moves were vehemently condemned by the government in Sarajevo, especially because the self-proclaimed authorities allegedly negated the rights of other minorities resident in Serbian community areas. They were viewed as the first steps toward the creation of a Serbian autonomous region that could presage the fracturing of the republic into contested ethnic zones. In such a scenario, the Croatians and Muslims would themselves seek to establish similar territorial units. Officials in Zagreb predicted that Belgrade would attempt to link up parts of Bosnia and Croatia, as a prelude to forming a new western Serbian state that would eventually gain formal attachment to Yugoslavia.

As the Serb-Croat conflict intensified at the federal level, and the war in Croatia escalated during the summer of 1991, rumors abounded about various conspiracies to divide up Bosnia-Hercegovina. They were fueled by several high level statements and allegations of secret meetings between Croatian and Serbian leaders, and they served to heighten the anxieties among Bosnia's Muslim officials. In July 1991, reports confirmed that Tudjman and Milosevic had held two clandestine meetings to discuss partitioning Bosnia between Serbia and Croatia, even though no agreement was reached. The Croatian Prime Minister Josip Manolic stated in June 1991 that a division of Bosnia-Hercegovina was "possible in principle," whereby municipalities inhabited predominantly by Serbs could join Serbia, primarily Croat areas would revert to Croatia, while the central Muslim area could form a separate republic.[18] In fact, various proposals have been issued during the past two years for the cantonization of the republic: for example, through a division into six mini-states (two Muslim, two Serb, and two Croat) whose administrations would decide on internal questions, such as the official language, education, culture, and state emblems.[19] But even in such a delineation, no ethnic group would account for more than 70% of the population in each canton. Widescale and costly resettlements would need to be conducted to sufficiently homogenize each area.

While Sarajevo grew concerned over political conspiracies to split the republic, the Serbian leadership in various parts of Bosnia proceeded to carve away more territory, placing it under the control of locally elected governments. At a joint session in June 1991, deputies of the assemblies of the Bosanska Krajina Municipalities and the Serbian Autonomous Region of

Krajina (in Croatia) adopted a "treaty on cooperation" and promulgated a "declaration of unification" of the two regions.[20] The local Serbian militia established armed "volunteer units" to control the territory and effectively eliminated Sarajevo's jurisdiction over the area. All these measures were supported by the Serbian Democratic Party (SDP), the strongest Serbian party in Bosnia-Hercegovina which had formed a coalition government with Muslim and Croat parties after the republican elections of November 1990. The Bosnian presidency, legislature, and all Muslim and Croatian organizations condemned the Serbian initiatives as illegal and provocative. But the Serbian leadership did not back down, and the Bosanska Krajina area was declared as the Serbian Autonomous Region of Krajina.

In mid-September 1991, Serbian activists announced the creation of a Serbian Autonomous Region of Eastern and Old Hercegovina; it covered eight municipalities inhabited mostly by Serbs in eastern Hercegovina, next to the Montenegrin and Croatian Dalmatian borders. In response, the largest Muslim party, the Party for Democratic Action (PDA), warned that it would form an autonomous Muslim region in the Mostar area of Hercegovina. According to the Bosnian press, Serb leaders were planning to link up the autonomous regions between Serbia and the Adriatic and to neutralize the Croatian and Muslim populations.[21] As evident proof of long-term Serbian designs, a Serbian Autonomous Region of Mount Romanija was established in an area between Sarajevo and the Serbian border. Two further Serbian autonomous regions were proclaimed in Northeastern Bosnia and in Northern Bosnia.

All these new territorial units threatened to secede from Bosnia, establish a unified Serbian Republic of Bosnia-Hercegovina, and remain in a federal Yugoslavia if the republic's national assembly failed to recognize their autonomy or if Muslims and Croats were to declare Bosnia-Hercegovina as an independent state. Sarajevo declared that no autonomous regions could be formed anywhere on the republic's territory and dismissed as null and void any planned referendums on autonomy. The Serbian leadership responded that Bosnia-Hercegovina would need to be divided into ethnic territories if civil war was to be avoided.[22] They proceeded to solidify the powers and jurisdiction of the new Serbian state, and in February 1992 adopted a "Constitution of the Serbian Republic of Bosnia-Hercegovina."

The creation of autonomous Serbian regions also served to energize the nearly 200,000 strong Croatian population in Hercegovina. Croatian political leaders claimed that they did not want to live outside of Croatia if a large wedge of Serbian controlled territory separated them from other republics. Some observers predicted that the Hercegovina Croats would also seek autonomous status and even unification with Croatia; this in turn would stimulate the nearly 600,000 Croats elsewhere in Bosnia to demand territorial self-determination and even unification with Croatia.[23] In November 1991, the largest Croatian political party in Bosnia, the Croatian Democratic Union (CDU), set up the "Croatian Community of Hercegovina-Bosnia" to include thirty municipalities with a large Croatian population. The "Community" was declared a political, economic, and cultural entity that would recognize the government in Sarajevo only as long as the republic upheld its sovereignty vis-à-vis Yugoslavia.[24] In the same month a "Croatian Community of the Bosnian Sava Valley" was also established and incorporated eight municipalities in northern Bosnia. During January 1992 a third "Croatian Community of Central Bosnia" was formed, comprised of four municipalities. Some leaders in these communities declared themselves in favor of union with Croatia, especially if Bosnia were to remain in Yugoslavia.

With armed conflicts intensifying in Croatia, the Yugoslav army increasingly used Bosnian territory to stage attacks on Croatian militia positions. The YPA also reportedly supplied arms to Serb irregulars in Bosnian Krajina, from where guerrillas also provided assistance to Serb units in Croatian Krajina and Slavonia. In September 1991, the Assembly of Bosnian Krajina adopted a decision for the general mobilization of the Serbian population under its control. Bosnia's Muslim leaders and government officials declared that the republic was incapable of defending itself against armed incursions or preventing the loss of territory to Serbian radicals. Underscoring the gravity of the situation, with a potential spillover from the war in Croatia, the authorities in Sarajevo announced the mobilization of the territorial reserve militia in regions most threatened by the actions of Serbian guerrillas.

The Serb-Croat conflict has also served to radicalize the Muslim population in Bosnia-Hercegovina, in a republic where every other adult male was believed to possess some kind of weapon; this in turn raised the likelihood of inter-communal clashes. The approximately two million strong Muslim majority in Bosnia has been revitalized during the past three years, both in the political and religious realms. The Muslim PDA leader Alija Izetbegovic was elected President in the republican elections of December 1990, while the new head of the Islamic Religious Community (IRC), Hadji Jakub Effendi Selimoski, proved to be a determined campaigner for Muslim rights throughout Yugoslavia.[25] Selimoski claimed that the Muslims were undergoing a religious revival in Bosnia by observing fasts, learning about their faith, and participating in Islamic rituals, thus necessitating the training of more *imams* (prayer leaders) and the building of new mosques. But Muslim leaders maintained that they were not fundamentalists and were not planning to create a theocratic state in Bosnia-Hercegovina.

During the spring and summer of 1991, Belgrade claimed that Muslim extremists were calling for the transformation of Bosnia-Hercegovina into a separate Islamic state. The new state was to exclude the predominantly Serbian and Croatian regions of Bosnia, but would purportedly incorporate other areas of Yugoslavia with a large Muslim population. In response, PDA leaders strenuously denied that they were planning to establish either an Islamic republic or a pan-Muslim state in the Balkans.[26] Despite these disavowals, the Serbian media vilified Bosnian President Alija Izetbegovic for his alleged pan-Islamic and pan-Turkic sympathies. He came under severe criticism for visiting Turkey, Iran, and Libya, and for requesting Bosnia-Hercegovina's membership in the Organization of the Islamic Conference. Ankara was also asked by Izetbegovic to supply direct financial aid to Sarajevo and to open up a consulate in the republic.[27] In the light of these developments, even the Croatian authorities warned the Muslim leadership against any attempt to turn Bosnia-Hercegovina into an Islamic republic.

Some divisions have also developed among Bosnia's Muslim leadership regarding their ethnic and political alliances. In July 1991, the Muslim Bosnian Organization (MBO), the second largest Muslim party led by Adil Zulfikarpasic, announced the conclusion of an "historic agreement" with Serbian political leaders. The move was vehemently attacked by President Izetbegovic, who opposed any kind of accord between any two ethnic groups in the republic that would exclude a third party. He reaffirmed that the PDA would not take sides in the Serb-Croat dispute, as this would endanger Bosnia's political integrity and provoke an all-out civil war.[28] While the MBO has supported preserving an indivisible Bosnia-Hercegovina within the Yugoslav federation, regardless of whether Slovenia and Croatia secede, the PDA favored a confederal Yugoslav arrangement without any loss of Bosnian territory. Meanwhile, Bosnia's Serbian leaders reiterated that they would not agree to live in an independent Bosnian state. Croat leaders were unwilling to remain in Bosnia if a smaller federation were allowed to survive after Croatia's secession, as this would avowedly place Serbia in a dominant position.

As tensions mounted within Bosnia, in October 1991 Muslim and Croat deputies in the republic's National Assembly voted to declare Bosnia's sovereignty and neutrality.[29] Serbian leaders boycotted the session and declared the vote illegal and announced that they would only recognize federal laws. The Muslim-Croat initiative allegedly broke a post-election agreement stating that all draft legislation required the consensus of all three ruling parties, including the Serbian Democratic Party. Meanwhile, Muslim and Croatian leaders prepared to hold a republic-wide referendum on Bosnian sovereignty and independence in February 1992. Although Serbs boycotted the ballot, over 64% of the electorate turned out and voted overwhelmingly for Bosnian sovereignty. The plebiscite was intended to legitimize the government's appeal for international recognition as an independent state.

Because Bosnia-Hercegovina is a complex mosaic of ethnic zones, any territorial divisions delineating exclusively Serbian, Croatian, or Muslim areas would prove extremely difficult to maintain without widespread population resettlements. Such efforts could meet with stiff local resistance and may provoke violent clashes between rival militia forces. Moreover, if Croatia and Serbia were to directly enter the ring to protect their co-ethnics or to claim Bosnian-Hercegovinian territory, the conflict could swiftly escalate. The republic could disintegrate or descend into prolonged inter-communal clashes involving armed irregular detachments, local militias, as well as the Yugoslav military. Despite, and some would argue because of, these destructive prospects, Serbian, Croatian, and Muslim leaders may ultimately be willing to reach compromises through administrative decentralization and territorial self-determination for national units without breaking up the republic.

Montenegro and Serbia

Montenegro (Crna Gora) faces fewer internal and external conflicts than the other Yugoslav republics. Since the "anti-bureaucratic revolution" engineered by Belgrade in early 1989, the government in Titograd (Podgorica) has largely supported Serbia's Milosevic regime. As in Serbia, Montenegro's first multi-party elections in December 1990 were comfortably won by reform Communists who changed their name to the Democratic Party of Socialists (DPS) in June 1991. The majority of the population has reportedly favored preserving the federation or, in the event of a Yugoslav rupture, retaining a close relationship with Serbia.

Montenegro's only sizable minorities are Albanians and Muslims; they are likely to be affected by developments among co-nationals in Kosovo, Bosnia-Hercegovina, Macedonia, and Albania itself. If the federation were to split and Montenegro moved closer to Serbia, fears among the approximately 41,000 Albanian and 90,000 Muslim residents can be expected to grow over possible onerous political restrictions and human rights violations, similar to those experienced in Kosovo. In the 1990 republican elections, Albanian and Muslim parties won 13 of the 125 seats in Montenegro's National Assembly, and inter-ethnic relations appeared to improve. But the specter of Albanian unrest and projected claims to Montenegrin territory was increasingly raised by pro-Serbian political leaders in Titograd. In fact, the largest Albanian party, the Albanian Democratic Alliance (ADA), simply asserted that it wanted a voice in determining the republic's future status in a Yugoslav federation. In response, leaders of the Montenegrin People's Party (MPP), which claimed to represent Montenegro's 57,000 Serbs, asserted that if Yugoslavia became a confederation then the republic's borders would need to be redrawn to advance Montenegro's unification with Serbia.

As Yugoslav instability intensified during 1991, leaders of various Montenegrin parties issued appeals to the republican government to prepare citizens for a potential civil war by creating self-defense detachments. In April 1991, the MPP issued warnings that Croats, Muslims, and Albanians were arming themselves throughout the country, with the latter avowedly demanding autonomy in parts of Montenegro.[30] In the meantime, Montenegro became more directly drawn into the war between Croatia and the Yugoslav-Serb armed forces. Thousands of Montenegrin recruits were called up into the YPA at the end of September, and armed clashes were reported between Montenegrin units and Croatian national guardsmen on Montenegro's borders with Croatia and Bosnia. The pro-Serb Montenegrin government simultaneously accused Zagreb of trying to extend Croatian borders along the Adriatic coast at Montenegrin expense. The key point of dispute has focused on the Prevlaka peninsula in the Bay of Kotor which Zagreb claims as Croatian territory.

Although Titograd has clearly sided with the Serbian authorities in the conflict with Croatia, signs of political disquiet have also become visible in the republic. In late September 1991, Prime Minister Milo Djukanovic affirmed that Montenegro was considering declaring its own sovereignty, even while it supported the retention of some federal structures and maintaining tight links with Serbia.[31] In mid-October 1991, the Montenegrin National Assembly began work on declaring the republic's sovereignty. The move seemed to surprise Belgrade as the Montenegrins were considered Serbia's most loyal allies.[32] However, Montenegrin President Momir Bulatovic explained that the affirmation of sovereignty did not equal a declaration of independence but simply a confirmation of Montenegro's internationally recognized position within the Yugoslav state.

An additional controversy between Titograd and Belgrade was stirred when Bulatovic called for the withdrawal of Montenegrin recruits from Croatian battle fronts. The move was sharply attacked by the strongly pro-Belgrade parties in the republic who felt that it was Titograd's duty to assist Serbia. It also served to revive traditional political rifts between the strongly pro-Serbian "Whites" and the more independence-minded Montenegrin "Green" forces. There are some indications that a rebirth of "Montenegrinism" is taking place in the republic. This has been visible in calls for the restoration of the Independent Montenegrin Orthodox Church, which was granted autocephalus status from the Serbian Orthodox Church in the 1850s but lost its position in 1920 after Montenegro was incorporated into Yugoslavia.[33] As dissatisfaction grew in the republic, in February 1992 about 10,000 people demonstrated in Titograd in favor of Montenegrin independence and against subservience to Serbia. A referendum on the republic's status was held in March 1992, but Albanian and Muslim leaders feared that the plebiscite would simply reaffirm Montenegro's continuing federation in a rump Yugoslavia. While Albanians and Muslims boycotted the referendum, a majority of the electorate approved the republic's continued membership in a federal Yugoslavia.

According to the 1991 census, out of Serbia's 9.7 million inhabitants, over 3.3 million belong to various minority nationalities.[34] Serbia thereby faces its own internal ruptures, especially in the predominantly Albanian region of Kosovo, the mixed-ethnic region of Vojvodina, and the Muslim-inhabited Sandzak area bordering on Montenegro and Kosovo. The first two issues are closely intertwined with Yugoslavia's foreign relations (see Chapter 5), whereas the Sandzak question is a predominantly internal one. The Sandzak region is actually divided between Serbia and Montenegro and contains about 260,000 Muslim inhabitants. The Serbian section includes approximately 170,000 Muslims, forming 90% of all Muslims in the Serbian republic. They inhabit a clearly defined territory, with its center in Novi Pazar, where they constitute over 50% of the population. But they do not enjoy any meaningful cultural or political autonomy and have grown alarmed at mounting Serbian government restrictions.

The victory of Milosevic in the Serbian elections in December 1990, heightened prospects for Serbian expansionism in a collapsing Yugoslavia. In response, Muslim organizations in the Sandzak became more active and anxious to protect their human and collective rights. Some of their leaders also became more outspoken on the question of political self-determination. The Party of Democratic Action (PDA), the largest Muslim-based organization in the Sandzak area, won all the electoral units in the region during the December 1990 Serbian elections. Its leaders became perturbed that Croatian and Slovenian secession could lead to more heavy-handed Serbian domination. As a result, they proposed Muslim autonomy in the Sandzak in case the federation were retailored. The PDA formed a Muslim National Council of the Sandzak (MNCS) in May 1991, for purposes of self-defense in case a state of emergency was declared in Yugoslavia. PDA leaders announced that they would declare autonomy for the Sandzak area if any republic were to secede from the federation.

According to MNCS chairman Sulejman Ugljanin, if there was a direct threat to the Muslim nation, the National Council would form a defense staff to take preventive actions. It would help defend Muslims from armed attacks in the event of civil warfare. Council leaders underscored that they saw no real future for Muslims in a Greater Serbia.[35] SDA leaders in Novi Pazar proceeded to call for a referendum on the status of the Sandzak, and specifically on whether the area should gain autonomous status if Yugoslavia was preserved or merge with Bosnia-Hercegovina if Yugoslavia fractured. If Belgrade refused to sanction such a plebiscite, then the PDA threatened to organize its own referendum asking residents whether they wanted to create a new republic within the Yugoslav federation or a larger state to encompass Bosnia and Kosovo.[36] Despite Serbian government warnings, a referendum was held in the region at the end of October 1991. Muslims in ten Sandzak municipalities balloted overwhelmingly in favor of political and cultural autonomy; out of 70.19% who participated, 98.92% voted in favor of Sandzak autonomy.[37] PDA leaders subsequently prepared to form a separate Muslim government in the region.

Serbian officials charged that the PDA was planning to form paramilitary units and to fracture Serbian territory, in collusion with Kosovo Albanians and other rebellious minorities. The depiction of such scenarios was intended to rally popular support behind the Milosevic regime. There were some indications that the PDA could form a coordinated front with Muslim organizations in Bosnia-Hercegovina and other republics. Nevertheless, the Slav Muslim question in Serbia may not be as potentially explosive as the Kosovo Albanian problem. Kosovan demands for self-determination remain diametrically opposed to the stance of all major Serbian political parties who contend that Kosovo must remain an integral part of Serbia whatever the future of Yugoslavia (see Chapter 5).

Serbia contains other restive minorities that remain fearful of Belgrade's policies and could seek to form united defensive fronts. About 180,000 Croats reside in the province of Vojvodina, forming approximately 6% of the population. Their leaders established the Democratic Alliance of Croats in Vojvodina (DACV), and in June 1991 proposed passing a law to enhance their cultural autonomy to terminate alleged Serbian discrimination and forcible assimilation. Some Croatian spokesmen also asserted that if the Krajina Serbs established formal links with the Serbian republic or achieved recognition as an independent region, then the DACV would seek political autonomy in Vojvodina. If the Serb-Croat conflict continues, border delineations will also come under increasing dispute both on the Slavonian and Vojvodinian sides of the frontier.

In their campaigns for self-determination, the DACV has established cooperative contacts with the large Hungarian minority in Vojvodina. Over 63,000 Slovaks also live in Vojvodina, and in 1991 they established a Slovak National Heritage Foundation (SNHF), with a membership of some 7,500 people. They have lodged complaints about restrictions on Slovak education, because the new Serbian education law did not guarantee separate schools or classes for ethnic minorities. SNHF leaders also pointed out that Serbia possessed a ministry that looked after the interests of Serbs outside the republic, but did not have a ministry for minority residents within Serbia.[38]

Post-Yugoslavia

The political and ethnic crisis in Yugoslavia also has profound economic, military, and security dimensions. Economic conditions have rapidly deteriorated in the country as armed hostilities escalated in Croatia. During 1991, the gross national product was projected to fall by some 20% and industrial production by nearly 30%. Hard currency reserves have evaporated, and according to some unofficial estimates the war in Croatia has cost Yugoslavia around $20 billion in lost earnings. Approximately $4 billion was lost in the tourist industry alone, while servicing the national debt will become increasingly difficult for Belgrade.[39] Meanwhile, unemployment is rapidly growing. It stood at over two million by the close of 1991, while a quarter of the Yugoslav population was officially registered below the poverty line as a result of economic decline. The secession of Slovenia and Croatia, the two richest republics, will further undermine the national budget and severely effect conditions in the poorer southern republics.

Deteriorating material conditions will also have profound political implications. Indeed, economic pressures within Serbia and other republics could spark industrial protests and social unrest and may further fuel ethnic tensions. Rather than promoting the democratization process, as witnessed in various parts of eastern Europe during the fall of 1989, economic grievances may radicalize a growing lumpenproletariat and provide opportunities for authoritarian nationalist forces to gain greater influence. Within Serbia itself, another point of conflict could emerge with regard to the role of the exiled King Alexander. Pressures to re-establish a constitutional monarchy in Yugoslavia could pit Socialists against Monarchists and lead to new splits with regard to the future shape of the federation and the status of Serbia and Montenegro.

In the military arena, both the Slovenian and Croatian governments, even before their declarations of independence, demanded an end to federal control over the armed forces. They wanted all YPA units subordinated to the republican authorities, but after the crackdown in both republics they increasingly favored a complete disbanding of the federal military structure. Some Serbian nationalist groups have also pressed for full Serbian control over the military; indeed, such a trend became visible during the summer of 1991 as the conflict spread in Croatia. These moves clearly ran counter to Yugoslav constitutional stipulations on security questions. All the republican authorities, outside of Serbia and Montenegro, have also objected to the military draft. Some have suggested alternatives to military service and proposed that troops only be stationed in their home republics.

The role of the Yugoslav military has proved critical in the country's development. While most of the federal institutions unravelled, YPA commanders increasingly viewed the military structure as the only remaining body capable of preserving the integrity of the country. In emphasizing the cohesiveness of the state, they evidently hitched their support behind Milosevic, because Serbia took the most forceful steps to maintain the federation. The army leadership, which was predominantly Serbian even before the outbreak of violence in Slovenia and Croatia, has opposed all separatist tendencies and the breakdown of central authority. Some elements of the officer core have simultaneously reasserted their commitment to Socialism and even established a revamped Communist Party within the armed forces, the Communist League–Movement for Yugoslavia (CL-MY). YPA commanders were also determined to preserve their privileges; the exalted position they have held in Yugoslav society would be seriously undercut if the federation were to crumble and the military were to shrink accordingly.

The danger persisted that inter-republican animosities would provoke an even more forceful military intervention to disarm the national militias operating in various republics. Such a scenario would not only intensify conflicts between republican and federal units, but could even presage armed clashes within the YPA itself. Any attempt to replace or overthrow the democratically elected republican governments would also trigger widescale violence, and could set in motion a chain reaction of ethnic and republican conflicts. Indeed, even if the democratically elected governments in Slovenia and Croatia were overthrown, activists in both republics would undoubtedly revert to a prolonged guerrilla struggle against the YPA. Such developments could also draw in outside powers either to protect co-nationals resident in Yugoslavia, to prevent a spill-over from the conflict, such as a major refugee exodus or provocative military incursions, and even to claim certain disputed territories.

A less violent resolution to the Yugoslav crisis could not be completely discounted. It depended primarily on whether some new association were devised between Serbia, Croatia, and Slovenia that would be acceptable to the other republics and nationalities. This could consist of a confederation of sovereign states that maintain some joint decision-making over key economic and security mechanisms. Post-Yugoslavia could also develop into a multi-tier structure, containing an inner union between Serbia and Montenegro, a looser federation embracing Macedonia and Bosnia-Hercegovina, and a more flexible confederal arrangement with Slovenia and Croatia. Alternatively, the next few years may witness the emergence of several new independent states with their own foreign policies and security structures, although maintaining some common economic links. However, following the violent conflict in Croatia, chances for a peaceful restructuring of the country dramatically receded. Both Slovenia and Croatia pushed ahead toward complete political sovereignty. Bosnia-Hercegovina began to fracture into pro-federal Serbian territories and Croat and Muslim areas whose governments proceeded to weigh the option of independence. Meanwhile, Serbia itself was increasingly racked by demands for Kosovan, Muslim, and Vojvodinian autonomy. In such volatile conditions, the federation was well on the road to disintegration, while the contours of what remained of Yugoslavia were still to be determined.

Notes

1. Background histories of Yugoslavia can be found in Fred Singleton, *A Short History of the Yugoslav Peoples* (Cambridge: Cambridge University Press, 1985); Ivo Banac, *The National Question in Yugoslavia: Origins, History, Politics* (Ithaca: Cornell

University Press, 1988); and Stevan K. Pavlowitch, *The Improbable Survivor: Yugoslavia and its Problems, 1918-1988* (Columbus: Ohio State University Press, 1988).

2. For a valuable recent article on Yugoslavia's ethnic intricacies see Patrick Moore, "The 'Question of All Questions': Internal Borders," Radio Free Europe, *Report on Eastern Europe,* Vol. 2, No. 38, 20 September 1991.

3. Croatian census figures for 1991 were issued by the Ministry of Information in Zagreb.

4. For the Charter of the Serbian Autonomous Region of Krajina see *Borba,* Belgrade, 4 January 1991.

5. *Tanjug,* Belgrade, 1 April 1991.

6. *Tanjug,* Belgrade, 4 April 1991.

7. See Blaine Harden, "Croats Field Militant Militia," *The Washington Post,* 10 October 1991.

8. *Tanjug,* Belgrade, 31 July and 8 September 1991.

9. For an analysis of the Serbian enclaves in Croatia see Paul Shoup, "The Future of Croatia's Border Regions," Radio Free Europe, *Report on Eastern Europe,* Vol. 2, No. 48, 29 November 1991.

10. *Tanjug,* Belgrade, 23 December 1991, *FBIS-EEU*-91-247, 24 December 1991.

11. D. Vucinic, "Ante Markovic Demands Resignation of Kadijevic and Brovet," *Borba,* Belgrade, 20 September 1991.

12. Radio Free Europe/ Radio Liberty, *Daily Report,* No. 24, 5 February 1992.

13. For useful media accounts of the armed confrontation in Slovenia check *The New York Times and The Washington Post* during July 1991.

14. For details see the interview with IDA president Ivan Parleto, "Istria: Why We are Demanding Autonomy," *Nin,* Belgrade, 11 January 1991.

15. See Boris Suligoj, "Minority Offers Agreement," *Delo,* Ljubljana, 7 January 1992, and Lojze Kante, "Slovenes Want Equal Rights for Everyone," *Delo,* Ljubljana, 9 January 1992.

16. See Radio Free Europe/ Radio Liberty, *Daily Report,* No, 147, 5 August 1991.

17. *Tanjug,* Belgrade, 29 April 1991, in *FBIS-EEU*-91-084, 1 May 1991.

18. *Tanjug,* Belgrade, 17 June 1991, in *FBIS-EEU*-91-117, 18 June 1991.

19. See Milan Andrejevich, "The Future of Bosnia and Hercegovina: A Sovereign Republic or Cantonization?" Radio Free Europe, *Report on Eastern Europe,* Vol. 2, No. 27, 5 July 1991.

20. *Tanjug,* Belgrade, 27 June 1991.

21. See Zoran Odic, "Constitutional Occupation of Bosnia-Hercegovina," *Oslobodjenje,* Sarajevo, 2 October 1991.

22. *Tanjug,* Belgrade, 13 September 1991.

23. Goran Moravcek, "The Opening of the Croatian Question," *Delo,* Ljubljana, 9 March 1991.

24. *Radio Croatia Network,* Zagreb, 18 November 1991, in *FBIS-EEU*-91-223, 19 November 1991. For details on the Croatian Communities see K. Kozar, "Self-Organization of the Sava Valley and Herceg-Bosnia," *Oslobodjenje,* Sarajevo, 20 November 1991.

25. For valuable background on the Muslim renaissance see Patrick Moore, "The Islamic Community's New Sense of Identity," Radio Free Europe, *Report on Eastern Europe,* Vol. 2, No. 44, 1 November 1991.

26. *Borba,* Belgrade, 27 May 1991.

27. *Tanjug,* Belgrade, 17 July 1991.

28. *Tanjug,* Belgrade, 31 July 1991.

29. See Milan Andrejevich, "Bosnia and Hercegovina Move Toward Independence," Radio Free Europe, *Report on Eastern Europe,* Vol. 2, No. 43, 25 October 1991.

30. *Tanjug,* 8 April 1991, Belgrade, in *FBIS-EEU*-91-068, 9 April 1991.

31. Reported in *Pobjeda,* Titograd, 24 September 1991, and *Tanjug,* Belgrade, 24 September 1991. For more details and analysis see Milan Andrejevich, "Montenegro Follows Its Own Course," Radio Free Europe, *Report on Eastern Europe,* Vol. 2, No. 47, 22 November 1991.

32. Radio Free Europe/ Radio Liberty, *Daily Report,* No. 200, 21 October 1991.

33. Hugh Poulton, *The Balkans: Minorities and States in Conflict* (London: Minority Rights Publications, 1991), p. 46.

34. *Tanjug,* Belgrade, 20 December 1991, in *FBIS-EEU*-91-245, 20 December 1991.

35. *Borba,* Belgrade, 24 May 1991.

36. S. Bakracevic, "Party of Democratic Action in Novi Pazar Calls for Referendum on Future of Sandzak: Either Autonomy or Accession to Bosnia," *Politika,* Belgrade, 10 July 1991.

37. *Radio Belgrade,* Belgrade, 30 October 1991, in *FBIS-EEU*-91-211, 31 October 1991.

38. Interview with Michal Sperak, chairman of the Slovak National Heritage Foundation in Yugoslavia, in *Pravda,* Bratislava, 26 July 1991.

39. See Milan Andrejevich, "The Economy on the Verge of Collapse," Radio Free Europe, *Report on Eastern Europe,* Vol. 2, No. 34, 23 August 1991.

5

The Yugoslav Crisis: External

The disruption and disintegration of the Yugoslav federation has contributed to heightening regional tensions throughout the Balkans, particularly with some of the neighboring countries. Fears of a major spill-over of the conflict have been fueled by the prospect that intra-republican and inter-republican hostilities in Yugoslavia will severely exacerbate economic decline, aggravate social turmoil, and degenerate into even more menacing armed clashes. The spill-over could take the form of cross-border incursions by military formations and the outflow of large numbers of distressed and displaced refugees. The escalating conflict has also increased anxieties among bordering states over the fate of co-ethnics residing in Yugoslavia or left within the new countries that emerge from the crumbling federation. In several instances, the Yugoslav crisis has raised aspirations for territorial adjustments, revived some irredentist ambitions among radical nationalists, and accelerated the search for novel political and security arrangements in the region. The Yugoslav divorce has also presented other European states and various multilateral institutions with the vexing problem of recognizing and absorbing several aspiring nation-states. In examining the strained relations between Yugoslavia and its neighbors, it is valuable to begin with some historical background to the most serious current conflicts.

Yugoslavia, Albania, and Kosovo

Animosities between Serbs and Albanians are underpinned by pronounced cultural, linguistic, and religious differences between the two ethnic groups, as well as by fervent mutual claims to the Kosovo region which currently belongs to Serbia. Kosovo-Metohija was a major cultural and religious center of medieval Serbdom and an important intellectual and political wellspring of Albanian nationalism.[1] Throughout the Ottoman Turkish occupation, the Serbs maintained a strong attachment to the territory, even while it gradually acquired an Albanian majority during the 19th century. Albania's decision in 1912 to press for full independence from the Turks was partly provoked by the fear that with the Ottoman empire shrinking, all of the Albanian-inhabited areas would be partitioned between Serbia, Greece, and Montenegro.[2] Albania's position was supported by Austria and Italy, who feared a strong south Slav state located astride the Adriatic coast. Although Serbian plans to gain an outlet to the Adriatic were thwarted and border disputes were settled by the mid-1920s, Belgrade successfully acquired the Kosovo area. Kosovo was administered as a virtual colony by Yugoslavia during the inter-war period in which the growing Albanian population was denied full political rights. Following the German conquest of Yugoslavia in 1941, Albania was given control over Kosovo under overall Italian supervision.

During World War Two, the Yugoslav Communists helped to sponsor an Albanian Communist resistance movement against German-Italian occupation; the movement gained power in Tirana at the end of the hostilities. The post-war Tito regime in Yugoslavia restored the previous borders with Albania and thereby regained the Kosovo region. Albania itself also became a virtual client-state of Yugoslavia until the Tirana regime formally broke with Belgrade in 1948. After Tito's expulsion from the Moscow-controlled Cominform, Tirana remained loyal to Stalin and used Moscow as a lever against Yugoslavian pressure. Although the 1954 Yugoslav constitution provided for substantial minority participation in the republican governments, Kosovo only achieved the status of an "autonomous province" within Serbia. The large Albanian population, forming about 80% of Kosovo's inhabitants at the time, became a source of simmering inter-state dispute between Belgrade and Tirana. The Albanian birth rate in Kosovo remained high, and local leaders demanded a share of power commensurate with their numbers, up to and including full republican status. By the late 1980s, Albanians constituted approximately 90% of the Kosovo population, while the Serb birth rate remained comparatively low. In addition, many Slavs left the area claiming discrimination and racial conflict and in search of better economic conditions in inner Serbia.

During the post-1966 liberalization, Albanian rights in Kosovo began to receive greater recognition by Belgrade, but this in turn spurred further nationalist demands. Tito's policy in the 1970s was one of measured appeasement, designed to give the Albanians some stake in the Yugoslav federation without provoking a Serbian backlash over concessions to the Kosovars. But Belgrade's policy failed and resentments grew on both sides: among Serbs over Albanian cultural and educational demands and the large sums invested in Kosovo, and among the Albanian intelligentsia over the lack of genuine self-government. Serbian leaders claimed that the 1974 Yugoslav constitution worked against Serbia's interests by allowing for the existence of *de facto* republics (Kosovo and Vojvodina) within Serbia, and favoring the non-Slav nationalities. Throughout the 1980s, Kosovo was convulsed by Albanian protest actions, inter-communal violence, and police crackdowns. Martial law was imposed at various junctures and the province assumed the appearance of a police state. Some Albanian leaders began to call for a Kosovo republic with the same status as Serbia in the Yugoslav federation, while a more radical minority proposed outright independence and unification with Albania.

Relations between Belgrade and Tirana stayed cool after the death of Marshall Jozef Broz Tito in 1980. Albania maintained its isolation from the outside world and the hard-line Marxist-Leninist government condemned Yugoslavia as a "revisionist" state that had veered away from the principles of Communism. Even after the death in 1985 of Enver Hoxha, Albania's Communist Party leader, and his replacement by the reformist Ramiz Alia, Tirana remained hesitant in establishing cordial relations with its neighbors. Contacts between the two states have been further undermined in recent years by the uncompromising position of the Serbian regime vis-à-vis its autonomous provinces and the mounting repression against the large Albanian population in Kosovo. Serbia's Socialist Party leader Slobodan Milosevic has successfully tapped Serbian nationalist sentiments, and much of this has been directed against the alleged Albanian threat to Yugoslavia's territorial integrity. Belgrade has pointed to the growing Albanian population in Kosovo as a direct challenge to the Serbian community, and as part of a pre-planned long-term program to detach the province from Serbia. Most of the major Serbian parties have supported Belgrade's hard-line stance toward Kosovo, while the presidential election victory of Milosevic in December 1990 contributed toward further ethnic polarization in the province.

Albanian political movements in Kosovo claimed that they were merely pursuing republican status for the region within a restructured Yugoslav confederation. Their goals have been supported by Slovenia and Croatia as a useful lever against both Serbian expansionism and Yugoslav centralism. Although Belgrade asserted that Kosovo Albanians received direct assistance from the government in Tirana in order to break up Serbia, there has been little evidence to confirm such charges. However, developments in Albania will undoubtedly have an impact on Kosovo, particularly as the country continues to open up to the outside world and the democratization process intensifies in Tirana.

If Yugoslavia continues to fracture, both the new administration in Tirana and the recently formed democratic parties may be tempted to provide direct support to the Kosovo Albanians, and even to press for closer links with the province in order to garner greater domestic popularity. This in turn could lead to a serious confrontation with the Serbian authorities, who remain fearful of Albanian irredentism and the creation of a "Greater Albania" at Serbian expense. If Albania were to evolve into a stable democracy following the political upheavals during the past two years, it could become a powerful magnet for Kosovo Albanians as a counterweight to Serbian domination in a shrunken Yugoslavia. This could also energize the sizable Albanian minority in western Macedonia to seek autonomy and some special relationship with both Kosovo and Albania.

The conflict between Yugoslavia and Albania focuses on the "autonomous province" of Kosovo in the republic of Serbia. According to the 1981 Yugoslav census, 1.7 million Albanians lived in Yugoslavia, of which over 1.2 million resided in Kosovo, making up about 90% of the region's population. The remainder of Kosovo's inhabitants consisted mostly of Serbs and Montenegrins. In the most recent unofficial estimates, the Kosovo Albanian populace has exceeded 1.5 million, with the number of Slav inhabitants dipping under 180,000. Albanians also form a majority in three neighboring municipalities of inner Serbia next to Kosovo. Ethnic Albanians held a referendum in the territory in March 1992 in support of political autonomy and the right to unite with Kosovo.

Serbian spokesmen, including leaders of the Serbian Orthodox Church, allege that thousands of Serbs have been pressured to leave the Kosovo region during the past few decades by an expansionist and hostile Albanian community. In fact, many families left the province for primarily economic reasons in order to seek better opportunities elsewhere in Yugoslavia. In addition, the Albanian birth rate in the region is calculated to be one of the highest in Europe, with some projections showing that the population in Kosovo will double within the next 20 to 30 years. During the 1980s, Albanian aspirations for self-determination and home rule were stifled by Belgrade. Student demonstrations and other public protests led to the periodic imposition of emergency measures and the closure of various educational and cultural institutions promoting Albanian autonomy.[3] Police crackdowns were also accompanied by manifestations of inter-ethnic conflict. The hostilities have been aggravated by economic decline and accompanied by charges that federal and Serbian development funds for the region have been deliberately curtailed to punish the Albanian inhabitants.

Since 1987, the Serbian regime has strengthened its direct controls over Kosovo. According to Belgrade, the over-assertive regional government was dominated by Albanians who excluded Serbs and Montenegrins from all important positions of authority. Moreover, Albanian separatists had allegedly endeavored to thoroughly albanianize the province.[4] Serbian leaders uphold the position that they will not allow the detachment of any part of Serbian territory and have threatened civil warfare and a violent crackdown if unrest persists. According to official Serbian propaganda, the anti-Yugoslav Albanians have been divided in two broad factions: a "right wing" pro-monarchist group and a "left wing" pro-Tirana contingent. Both allegedly supported the secession of Kosovo and its reunification with Albania; they have purportedly combined their forces in recent years as the crisis in Kosovo has deepened.

Serbian government spokesmen have outlined the ostensible Albanian strategy for separating Kosovo from Serbia. It includes "peaceful struggles" such as escalating political demands, the takeover of local institutions, and a propaganda barrage designed to conceal secessionist aims. It also allegedly involves "armed struggle" by way of demonstrations, riots, assassinations, sabotage, and terrorism against Serbian community leaders. The avowed creation of illegal armed units has been assisted by Tirana's security forces and Albanian émigré organizations. According to the Serbian media, weapons have also been stolen by Albanian activists from police and army depots or smuggled in from abroad.[5] As a result of these supposedly deadly threats, Belgrade has imposed states of emergency in the region and taken preventative actions in order to forestall civil war.

For several years, periodic demonstrations and clashes occurred between Albanian protesters and the Serbian police, and in some cases, as in February 1990, a number of deaths were reported. Since then Belgrade has taken numerous steps to restrict or control all aspects of Albanian political and social life. In March 1990, Serbia took over all public security organs in Kosovo and claimed the right to appoint and dismiss all judicial and legislative bodies. In July 1990, Belgrade suspended the Kosovo Provincial Assembly days after the legislature had declared the region's independence from Serbia as a sovereign Yugoslav republic.[6] Albanian legislators from the dissolved parliament met secretly in September 1990 to pass a basic law on Kosovo's republican status, known as the "Kacanicka constitution." Some Albanian deputies were imprisoned or exiled while Serbian authorities also suspended the operations of much of the Albanian-language media. Under the new Serbian constitution, Kosovo's autonomous statehood was eliminated. In March 1991, Kosovo's provincial presidency was abolished, thus sealing the province's full political integration into Serbia. At the start of the new school year in September 1991, several thousand Albanian teachers were barred from teaching in secondary schools and other pressures were applied to further restrict Albanian formal education. This provoked demonstrations by thousands of students demanding the reinstatement of the Albanian language in schools and colleges.

During the past three years, there has been a significant growth in Albanian political activism in the province. The largest political force, the Democratic Alliance of Kosovo (DAK), claimed over 100,000 members by mid-1990. DAK leaders denied that they were separatists, and their chief programmatic planks have included an end to repression in the region, the withdrawal of Serbian security forces and army units, and free elections in Kosovo. Alliance president Ibrahim Rugova denied that the DAK sought Kosovo's unification with Albania, but simply the establishment of good relations between a Yugoslav Kosovo republic and a democratic Albania.

Before its dissolution, the Kosovo Provincial Assembly had pressed for Kosovan sovereignty and a new constitution giving the region equal status with the other Yugoslav republics. Albanians were to be declared a nation and not merely a "national minority," in recognition of the fact that they constituted the third largest ethnic group in Yugoslavia and were thereby entitled to their own republic. Belgrade envisaged such moves as unconstitutional and as a direct assault on Serbian and Yugoslav territorial integrity. The subsequent crackdown alienated all Albanian parties from the political process and resulted in a comprehensive boycott of Serbia's republican elections in Kosovo in December 1990. The DAK and other Albanian parties continued to press for Kosovan sovereignty and republican status, although explicitly opposing the use of violence despite the ongoing Serbian clampdown.

Following the declaration of independence by Slovenia and Croatia in June 1991, DAK leader Rugova declared that Albanians would not remain in a truncated Yugoslavia. But he also insisted that only political means would be used to promote Kosovar interests. During the summer of 1991, a Coordinating Council of Albanian Political Parties in Yugoslavia (CCAPPY) was formed in the Kosovo capital of Pristina to help coordinate self-defense and prepare contingencies for creating a provisional "government of national salvation."[7] Its leaders demanded the withdrawal of Yugoslav army units from Kosovo, the abandonment of the military by Albanian conscripts, and the creation of a Kosovo defense system as a precaution against a major crackdown.[8] Some more radical groups were also formed in Kosovo. For example, in May 1991 an Albanian Christian Democratic Party (ACDP) openly advocated the union of Kosovo with Albania if Yugoslavia continued to disintegrate: it claimed a membership of some 130,000, including both Christians and Muslims.[9]

As the armed conflict intensified in Croatia and threatened to spill over into other republics, the Assembly of the Republic of Kosovo in exile (some of whose members were reportedly residing in Croatia) endorsed a resolution confirming that Kosovo would become a sovereign republic with the right to participate in forming alliances with other Yugoslav republics. It also announced the holding of a referendum on Kosovo's sovereignty in late September 1991, as well as plans to form a new government in the province.[10] Despite police intimidation, about 87% of the Albanian population voted in the referendum, of which over 95% reportedly came out in favor of sovereignty and independence. A few weeks later the Kosovo Republican Assembly elected a new provisional coalition government, headed by Bujar Bukashi; the single-party Executive Council was replaced by a multi-party governing body.[11] Multi-party elections were scheduled for the Kosovo Assembly regardless of the Serbian response. Kosovo's Albanian leaders also demanded a new agreement between the Yugoslav republics that would provide Kosovo with equal status in a confederal arrangement.

The Kosovo crisis could become increasingly linked with Muslim disquiet in Bosnia-Hercegovina and in the Sandzak region of Serbia. In August 1991, the Kosovo branch of the Bosnian Party of Democratic Action (PDA) announced that it had set up a Muslim Defense Council in the city of Pec in Kosovo to counter the danger of "physical extermination" of Muslims by the Serbian regime and the Yugoslav army. It would operate within the framework of the Council for the National Defense of Muslims established in the Bosnian capital of Sarajevo during that summer.[12] The Serbian authorities responded by asserting that the PDA was colluding with Kosovo Albanians in order to carve out a large Islamic state from parts of Yugoslavia, consisting of Bosnia-Hercegovina, Sandzak, parts of Montenegro, and sections of Macedonia. According to the Belgrade media, weapons stocks were being amassed in Kosovo and some Albanians were organizing paramilitary units in preparation for an insurrection.[13] In addition, Albanians from Kosovo were allegedly being recruited by the Croatian National Guard in a broader conspiracy against the Yugoslav federation.

In order to try and alter the demographic balance in its favor, Belgrade has sponsored the resettlement of Serbs and Montenegrins in Kosovo and has reportedly begun to distribute land to willing settlers from inner Serbia. Although some proposals have been floated to move over 200,000 Serbs and Montenegrins into the region, the idea may not be practical or attractive to most Serbian families. Aside from the Socialist Party, several other Serbian political organizations have spoken out over the Kosovo issue. The ultra-nationalist Serbian Radical Party (SRP), the strongest non-Socialist party in the republic, has called for the expulsion of those Kosovo Albanians who do not recognize the Serbian legislature and who continue to agitate for an Albanian republic. If the SRP's popularity continues to grow, its militant anti-Albanian stance could also heighten tensions in the region and further polarize inter-ethnic relations.

With the Serb-Croat rift widening during the past two years, Belgrade has capitalized on the turmoil in Croatia to beef up its security presence in Kosovo. Reports also surfaced in May 1991 that army and police units had begun to distribute weapons to Serb volunteers in the province.[14] A Kosovo-based Serbian Peony Association (SPA) was formed at about this time and called for the creation of paramilitary groups to protect the local Slav population. Several Serb parties reportedly also established armed formations in the province as tensions heightened. Kosovo's Albanian leaders alleged that Serbia was moving thousands of its militia and army reservists into the province to intimidate the population and prepare for a military crackdown. Increased repression in the region, especially if coupled with the growth of irregular Serbian units, could provoke a more violent Albanian response. In such a scenario, the DAK and other moderate Albanian parties could be left on the sidelines while more radical Kosovar groups gained prominence to actively resist Serbian repression. The Belgrade authorities could also try to deliberately manufacture and provoke clashes in the region, in order to justify a more comprehensive clampdown against Albanian activism. In the summer of 1991, reports also surfaced of a Serbian plan to divide the region into two, by pushing out a large proportion of Albanians into the poorer Metohija area in western Kosovo while repopulating the rest of the territory with a Serb and Montenegrin majority.

The Kosovo crisis has seriously aggravated relations between Yugoslavia and Albania, particularly between the Serbian regime and the new government in Tirana. Officials in Belgrade have continued to accuse Albania of expansionist pretensions and of seeking to dismember Yugoslavia. Previously, they had claimed that the Communist regime had direct links with all Albanian separatist groupings in Kosovo, supplying them with funds, equipment, propaganda material, and weapons. As the pace of political change quickened in Albania during 1991, the Serbian authorities grew concerned that internal turmoil would push both the Labor (subsequently Socialist) Party government and the newly formed opposition parties to focus on external issues as a rallying point to harvest popular support.

Kosovo's Albanian organizations have welcomed the changes in Tirana. DAK leaders confirmed that developments in the country provided encouragement for the struggle of Albanians throughout Yugoslavia. Belgrade itself lodged protests over Tirana's tolerance of pro-Kosovo demonstrations, interpreted as unwarranted interference in Yugoslavia's internal affairs. Serbian spokesmen accused Albanian organizations of planning to form a single parliament in Tirana, in which delegates from Kosovo and western Macedonia would also be represented. Rugova's visit to Tirana in February 1990 and subsequent visits by Albanian leaders from Kosovo and other Yugoslav republics were depicted as steps in this direction and intended to coordinate anti-Serbian policies culminating in the creation of a "Greater Albania."

In the midst of the democratic upheavals in Albania throughout early 1991, both the ruling Socialist Party and the recently established opposition parties began to speak publicly about the Kosovo question. Leaders of the Albanian Democratic Party (ADP), the strongest non-Communist organization, announced that they would work for a gradual and peaceful "democratic union" between Albania and Kosovo. After the first free elections in March 1991, the Democrats became more outspoken over Kosovo than the ruling Socialists. This in turn encouraged the latter to take aboard the Kosovo issue, whereas prior to the democratic changes Tirana avoided direct confrontations with Belgrade to forestall any spill-over of the conflict. Socialist leaders began to express support for the "legitimate rights" of Kosovo Albanians. Despite this verbal backing, the Democratic Party condemned the Socialists for failing to formally recognize the proclamation of the republic of Kosovo by the exiled Kosovo Assembly. Paradoxically, in August 1991 ADP chairman Sali Berisha also accused the Socialist "crypto-Communist" leadership of seeking to provoke a war with Serbia because they were afraid of losing power and hoped to rally the nation on a foreign policy issue.[15] After the Democrats' election victory in March 1992, Berisha declared that the government would be more assertive in defending the rights of Albanians abroad.

Several militant pro-Kosovar groups have also formed in Albania. In June 1991, the Kosovo Patriotic and Political Association (KPPA) held its founding congress in Tirana and claimed a membership of 12,700 people. Delegates spoke out for the "national unification" of all Albanians and the peaceful creation of a single Albanian state.[16] Other pan-Albanian organizations were established during 1991; they included the National Unity Party (NUP) and the Motherland Political Association (MPA).[17] Their programs included calls for the creation of a pan-Albanian confederation encompassing all the territories inhabited by Albanian majorities. The KPPA, NUP, and the MPA wanted Tirana to take a more active role in support of Albanian rights in Kosovo and unreservedly recognize the independent Kosovo constitution passed in September 1990 by the Kosovo Assembly. Albania's multi-party National Assembly condemned Serbia's suppression of Kosovo Albanians as the Yugoslav crisis escalated. In September 1991, Tirana's coalition government formally endorsed the resolution of the exiled Kosovo Assembly that defined Kosovo as a sovereign republic within Yugoslavia.[18] Moreover, in October 1991 the Albanian National Assembly voted to recognize Kosovo as an independent republic, once the final results of the republican referendum were made public.

The authorities in Tirana expressed concern that Belgrade aimed to turn a truncated Yugoslavia into a large Serbian state while ignoring Albanian demands for equal national status and Kosovan sovereignty.[19] Since early 1991, an increasing number of official Albanian commentaries have appeared on the Kosovo issue. Public opinion surveys indicated that most Albanian citizens considered a merger with Albania to be the optimal solution to Kosovo's problems. This position was underscored by the Serbian media, which openly charged that a growing number of Albanians supported a forceful intervention in Yugoslavia while Tirana was demanding that Albanians in Yugoslavia establish their own republic. Such accusations were intended to rally the Serbian population behind the Belgrade authorities. According to some political sources in Belgrade, Albania was waiting for the opportune moment when Yugoslav forces were embroiled in another trouble spot in order to organize an armed uprising in Kosovo to be followed by Albanian intervention.[20] Albanian observers pointed out during the summer of 1991 that Yugoslav army units were concentrating on the Albanian border and provoking violent incidents in order to accuse Tirana of military aggression.

In the battle of words against Tirana, Serbian leaders also raised the issue of Slav minorities in Albania, which included about 50,000 Serbs, Montenegrins, and Macedonians. Belgrade asserted that these minorities had been denied nationality status and continued to suffer from severe government repression. During the refugee exodus in late 1990 and early 1991, thousands of Slavs from Albania reportedly crossed the border into Yugoslavia in order to escape from poverty and political oppression.

The development of Serb-Albanian relations will also have a Macedonian dimension. Approximately 20% of the population of former Yugoslav (or Vardar) Macedonia, numbering over 400,000 people, are ethnically Albanian. Some Albanian spokesmen claim the true figure may be closer to 40%, and local Albanian leaders calculate that the actual population may be nearer to 800,000. They reside primarily in the western part of the republic, known as the Dzamija area in Albanian, next to the Albanian border. The Albanian demographic growth has far exceeded that of the Macedonian Slavs, and in recent years increasing numbers of Albanians have been settling in other parts of the republic. Albanian leaders claim that they have been denied the most fundamental civil, cultural, educational, and political rights in Macedonia, and have been subjected to incessant assimilationist pressures particularly since the purge of Albanian officials in 1987. Macedonian nationalists in turn charge that the Albanians are planning to numerically overrun the republic and declare the Dzamija area an autonomous region prior to annexation by an expansionist Albania. Demands for Albanian minority rights have therefore been interpreted in Skopje as the first steps toward secession. The Party for Democratic Prosperity (PDP), which captured most of the Albanian vote in the republican elections in November 1990, has been accused by Macedonian nationalists of deliberately fanning ethnic conflicts, displaying separatist tendencies, and of being an appendage of the Kosovo-based DAK.[21]

PDP leaders complained that the Albanians did not enjoy equal rights with the Slav Macedonians. They claimed that Albanians should not figure in the constitution as a "national minority" but as a distinct "nation" with equal rights vis-à-vis other nations. PDP chairman Nevzat Haljilji asserted that he would wait until after the new Macedonian constitution was adopted to introduce changes in the definition and rights of the Albanians. He warned that if constitutional stipulations proved unsatisfactory then the Albanians would organize a separate referendum, declare the Macedonian constitution non-binding, and take steps toward "cultural and territorial independence."[22] This could culminate in the proclamation of an Autonomous Region of Western Macedonia, with the right to enter into alliances with other states. Indeed, in early January 1992 a referendum was held among the Albanian minority despite strong government opposition. Although the turnout was reportedly below expectations, over 90% of the ballots cast favored political and cultural autonomy for Albanian areas in Macedonia and their eventual unification with Kosovo. After the voting, several predominantly Albanian municipalities in western Macedonia declared the region as the "Republic of

Illirida," but this initiative was condemned by the PDP leadership. At its first congress in February 1992, the PDP passed a resolution asking the Macedonian authorities to recognize the independence of Kosovo and the autonomy of Albanian western Macedonia, which would eventually unite with Kosovo.[23]

The leading Macedonian nationalist party—the Internal Macedonian Revolutionary Organization–Democratic Party for Macedonian National Unity (IMRO-DPMNU)—entered the coalition government in December 1990. It gained broad public support even in the western regions of the republic, partly because it adopted a militant stance toward the Albanian minority and criticized Skopje's previous "indulgent policy" toward the Albanians. It opposed any extension of educational rights for Albanians, demanded new republican elections, and proposed resolute moves against alleged "Albanian pressures" in western Macedonia.[24] Albanian leaders in Macedonia have been hesitant in supporting the republic's independence, fearing that a sovereign Macedonia will further erode minority rights in the drive for a "uni-national" state. The PDP successfully called for an Albanian boycott of the Macedonian referendum on independence in early September 1991. But it did not discount the possibility of eventually supporting Skopje's sovereignty if the republic was to guarantee Albanian "collective rights" in legislation, education, culture, and language use. PDP leaders also realized that Serbian nationalists and Yugoslav federalists were purposively stirring Macedonian-Albanian conflicts to preserve Belgrade's control over the region.

There are strong suspicions that Serbian leaders have deliberately exacerbated Macedonian-Albanian tensions in order to pose as defenders of Macedonian sovereignty and integrity against alleged Albanian irredentists. Any form of autonomy in Kosovo could act as a magnet for Macedonian Albanians, especially if the Kosovo republic were to canvas for closer links with Albania and press for the unification of all lands containing substantial Albanian populations. Such pretensions could even bring Belgrade and Skopje closer together against the perceived Albanian threat, with the possibility of some new Serbian-Macedonian political arrangement even if Yugoslavia were to continue disintegrating.

The Serb-Albanian conflict has also entangled other Yugoslav republics. According to the 1981 census, approximately 40,000 Albanians live in Montenegro, particularly in areas close to the northern Albanian border. The threat of Albanian demands for self-determination, political autonomy, and even territorial revisions has contributed to reinforcing Montenegro's solidarity with Belgrade. The federal and Serbian authorities have linked the Albanian drive for Kosovan self-determination with the Croatian and Slovenian push for independence. According to Belgrade, both Zagreb and Ljubljana have provided direct support and material assistance to Albanian separatists to buttress their plans for secession in the event of escalating Croatian-Serbian hostilities. Although allegations concerning preparations for armed confrontation within Kosovo are clearly exaggerated, the Kosovo card has undoubtedly been played by Croatia and Slovenia against both Serbia and the federal government. The authorities in Zagreb recognize Kosovo as a separate republic, maintain close contacts with Albanian activists in Kosovo, and have established high-level ties with Tirana. Albania itself could become a valuable future ally for both Croatia and Slovenia, especially as a useful counterpoint to Serbian influence in the region.

The collapse of the Yugoslav federation and the secession of any republic will directly involve Albania. Serbian claims on the remaining republics have visibly increased since the summer of 1991, provoking fears of intensified repression in Kosovo and western Macedonia, and stiffening demands for Albanian secession. Albania could sooner or later be faced with a large outflow of refugees, major civil unrest, and escalating violence on its borders. It may even become embroiled in providing direct aid to co-ethnics in Kosovo or even in sheltering armed detachments in conflict with the Serbian militia and the Yugoslav army. A scenario of escalation could involve clashes between Yugoslav and Albanian military units along the frontier areas.

Serbian nationalists have also predicted the emergence of regional religious alliances in which the Serbian-Orthodox and Albanian-Islamic rift occupies a central role. The Milosevic regime has warned about the avowed threat of Islamicization in the Balkans, which is currently masking behind demands for human rights and Albanian and Turkish autonomy. Such a program is reportedly financed from abroad by Islamic states and apparently takes the form of a covert *jihad* in Kosovo and other Albanian-populated regions. In order to counter the alleged Islamic threat in Yugoslavia and in neighboring states, some Serb ultra-nationalists have put forward proposals for a grand alliance of Orthodox Christian countries. For instance, the Serbian Renewal Movement (SRM) has proposed an association between Serbia, Bulgaria, and Greece to resist the "Islamic advance" from Turkey, Albania, and the Muslim minorities in Yugoslavia and Bulgaria.[25] There is little hard evidence of any fundamentalist religious revival among Islamic populations in the region, let alone of an international pan-Islamic or pan-Turkic conspiracy. Nonetheless, such allegations could elicit some popular resonance in countries and republics experiencing severe political, economic, and ethnic strains. They could be increasingly employed by governments in search of convenient scapegoats for their internal and external problems.

Yugoslavia, Hungary, and Vojvodina

Animosities between Hungarians and the south Slavs can be traced back to the early years of Magyar penetration into Central Europe. The most substantial Hungarian contacts were with the Croatians, who had an independent state in the 10th and 11th centuries before their absorption into the Hungarian kingdom, and subsequently into the Habsburg empire. During the 19th century, the Croats struggled for recognition of their federal status within Austro-Hungary. Budapest eventually granted Zagreb limited autonomy, recognized the Croatians as a distinct people, and gave them some control over the Slavonian region along the Hungarian border. From the middle of the 19th century, Croatia amplified its calls for independence and sought to consolidate south Slav unity by bringing together non-Catholic Serbian and Bosnian populations. Such pressures aggravated Hungarian-Croatian antagonisms while laying the basis for the future Yugoslav state.

With the collapse of the Austro-Hungarian empire in 1918, Budapest relinquished its hold over Croatia-Slavonia and the Vojvodina area in southern Hungary which were incorporated in the newly established Yugoslav state. Some tensions appeared between the two states, particularly over Vojvodina where a large Magyar minority was left at the close of World War One. Budapest seized Vojvodina during World War Two during its war-time alliance with Hitler, who carved up Yugoslavia after the 1941 German conquest. But the territory was ceded back to Belgrade at the close of the war. Hungarian minority rights were recognized in the 1950s, when Vojvodina was awarded the status of an "autonomous province" within the Yugoslav federation. The area experienced a significant shift in ethnic composition after the expulsion of Germans and the settlement of Serbs and other Slavs. Magyar numbers fell to about 20% of the population, but the community benefited from a good measure of administrative and economic decentralization with extensive linguistic and educational rights.

During the Communist period, the Vojvodina question did not become a major source of conflict between Hungary and Yugoslavia, and the minority issue played a secondary role. This was assured by the relative economic prosperity of the region, Magyar loyalty to the Yugoslav state, and the absence of any overt Hungarian territorial ambitions. The only visible problems emerged after Tito's expulsion from the Cominform in 1948, when the Soviet bloc states under Moscow's direction imposed an economic blockade on Yugoslavia. The blockade was formally lifted after Stalin's death in 1953, but differences of opinion persisted about the amount of compensation that should accrue to Belgrade for the costly sanctions. Since the accession of Slobodan Milosevic to the Serbian leadership in the late 1980s, the Vojvodina question has resurfaced as an important bone of contention between Hungary and Yugoslavia.

Relations between the two states have been aggravated as the fractures in the Yugoslav federation deepened. Even starker disputes are likely as Budapest readjusts and improves its relations with the increasingly independent south Slav republics. Two sets of problems have preoccupied inter-state contacts: the treatment of the Hungarian minority in Serbia's autonomous province of Vojvodina, and Budapest's new relationships with two post-Yugoslav republics bordering on Hungary—Slovenia and Croatia. Hungarian activists have grown concerned that as Serbia strengthens control over its autonomous provinces and attempts to assert Serbian dominance in the remainder of the federation, the rights of the Magyar minority will be seriously undermined. In such an eventuality, more forthright defense of the Vojvodina Hungarians by Budapest cannot be discounted. Furthermore, as Hungary seeks to improve its relations with the neighboring Slovenian and Croatian republics, historical animosities between Budapest and Belgrade could be revived.

In the last few years, the Serbian regime has buttressed its powers in the autonomous region of Vojvodina. In the summer of 1988, the Vojvodina authorities were replaced in a purge orchestrated by the Milosevic leadership against "pro-autonomist" forces who were allegedly conspiring against Belgrade. These moves intensified tensions in the region where approximately 341,000 Magyars resided (according to the 1991 census), making up about 16% of the population. The figure constituted a reduction of some 11.5% since the 1981 census, although Hungarian sources estimated the total at about 500,000 with clear Magyar majorities in some municipalities. Other minorities have also decreased in size in Vojvodina during the past decade, as a result of assimilation, declining birth rates, emigration, and the non-disclosure of ethnic identity because of fears of government reprisals.

Since 1989, the Hungarian minority has stepped up its organizational efforts in order to protect its interests. In March 1990, the Democratic Community of Hungarians in Vojvodina (DCHV) was founded and its leaders strongly criticized Serbian policy in the province. The DCHV claimed a membership of some 25,000 and decided to push for the development of a civic society and for cultural autonomy in Vojvodina. This was to include the equal use of the Hungarian language and the expansion of a free Magyar press. DCHV leaders also began to discuss the possibility of minority self-rule, thereby directly opposing Serbia's new constitutional provisions that further weakened provincial self-government.[26]

Magyar minority leaders in Vojvodina as well as government officials in Budapest have complained about Belgrade's discriminatory policies, assimilationist pressures, and its deliberate erosion of minority rights. There were also problems with the new Serbian educational laws, which since early 1990 have imposed a uniform schooling system throughout Serbia.[27] The new legislation rescinded existing minority educational rights and reinforced Belgrade's integrative policies. The number of Hungarian schools dropped from 197 in 1966 to 127 by 1987, and many Magyar language classes were discontinued under the pretext of school reorganization. The Serbian government also began to exercise direct supervision over the Hungarian media by approving the directors of the local press, radio, and television. In July 1991, a new law was passed making Serbian the sole official language in the republic, thus ruling out the use of Hungarian in public life.[28] Reacting to these measures, the DCHV presidium condemned the growing political pressures on the Magyar population and demanded the restoration of Vojvodinian autonomy.

Criticisms were also lodged by Hungarian leaders in late 1990 over the Serbian election laws, in which the formation of electoral districts worked to the disadvantage of minorities. In the December 1990 republican elections, the DCHV only won 8 out of 250 seats to the Serbian National Assembly, even though it obtained over 80% of the Hungarian vote. DCHV leaders remained anxious that the Serbian authorities would further gerrymander electoral districts in Vojvodina, in order to dilute the Hungarian vote and reduce Magyar representation in the republican parliament.

In September 1990, a group of opposition parties representing Hungarian, Slovak, Croatian, and Ruthenian minorities adopted a resolution condemning the new republican constitution for undermining the political autonomy of Vojvodina and intensifying Serbian centralism.[29] DCHV leaders favored a looser confederal arrangement in Yugoslavia, but were worried that as the federation collapsed Serbia would step up its repressive policies in the province. They contended that if Serbia democratizes, the DCHV will become actively involved in local government within the republic. On the other hand, if Belgrade's policies become more despotic they will form a front with other groups to ensure the "self-defense" of Vojvodina's minorities.

About 50,000 south Slavs reside in southern Hungary, comprised mostly of Croats, with a few thousand Serbs and Slovenes. The Slav minority has not been a source of dispute between Budapest and Belgrade. It has begun to organize more effectively in the past year in order to claim various educational and cultural benefits. In the wake of the democratic changes in Hungary, the Communist-sponsored Democratic Alliance of Southern Slavs (DASS) split into several national components, including the Croatian Democratic Alliance (CDA) and the Serbian Democratic Alliance (SDA). Both associations were allowed to operate without hindrance and were not perceived as a threat by the Hungarian administration. Approximately 26,000 Hungarians also live in Croatia and a further 10,000 in Slovenia. In both republics they benefit from government support, expanded language instruction, and an independent mass media and harbor no outstanding grievances against the Croatian and Slovenian governments.

Relations between Hungary and the Serbian regime have come under mounting strain recently partly over the situation in Vojvodina, over the escalating war in Croatia that has affected several Hungarian communities, and over Budapest's developing ties with Zagreb and Ljubljana. Contacts sharply deteriorated in January 1991 when Budapest was accused of secretly selling arms to the Croatian government to help build up the republic's national guard in its struggle with the Yugoslav army. The Hungarian authorities initially denied the allegations, which Serbia depicted as part of an international conspiracy to undermine and unseat the Yugoslav government.[30] As the controversy continued, Budapest admitted that a Hungarian foreign trade enterprise, with the involvement of some middle-level officials, had indeed sold quantities of automatic weapons to Zagreb. But it dismissed charges that the deal was either significant, illegal, or arranged between high-ranking Croatian and Hungarian officials to challenge the integrity of the Yugoslav state.

As the Croatian-Serbian crisis mounted, the Yugoslav army command and the Serbian regime accused Hungary of open interference for revanchist purposes and of being at the center of a NATO-directed conspiracy against the federation and the socialist system.[31] Budapest lodged a strong protest with Yugoslavia when Belgrade television aired a provocative documentary on alleged plans for Croatian militia attacks on the Yugoslav army, in which Hungary was heavily implicated. The Yugoslav authorities were in effect accusing Budapest of trying to capsize Yugoslavia while laying territorial claims to Vojvodina. This charge was reinforced in July 1991 when Hungarian Prime Minister Jozsef Antall came under severe criticism for stating that Vojvodina joined Yugoslavia and not Serbia earlier in the century. This statement appeared to imply that the province could become an independent republic if the federation disintegrated.[32] Antall himself was attacked by the political opposition in Budapest for allegedly creating false illusions for Magyars in Vojvodina about possible future links with Hungary and for contributing to spurring Serbian nationalism. Belgrade's charges against the Hungarian government were repeated throughout the summer and fall of 1991. Budapest stood accused of clandestinely transporting arms to Croatia and of training "saboteurs, terrorists, well-known *Ustasas* and extremists on its territory."[33]

The Croatian arms controversy placed the Magyar minority in Vojvodina in a difficult predicament. Some nationalist Serbian leaders depicted the Hungarians as potentially untrustworthy and supportive of Croatian separatism. Reports also emerged of growing anti-Hungarian sentiments in Serbia and in Vojvodina itself, with local press attacks questioning the loyalty of Magyar leaders.[34] In February 1991, the Serbian government demanded that the DCHV "take a stand in the arms sale episode" and condemn Budapest's involvement in internal Yugoslav affairs. Belgrade orchestrated a media campaign against the DCHV for its alleged involvement in the arms sales to Croatia, and even for storing weapons in Vojvodina. Ferenc Csubela, a Hungarian deputy from Vojvodina, publicly denied accusations that he had asserted that a part of Vojvodina should be incorporated in Hungary if Yugoslavia collapses.[35]

DCHV spokesmen claimed that the Magyar minority had found itself in a critical position due to the arms sale incident and because of Serbian contentions that the Hungarians sympathized with Zagreb. The minority has been depicted as a virtual fifth column seeking to profit from Yugoslav instability in the midst of re-emerging Hungarian territorial aspirations.[36] During the summer of 1991, the Serb authorities in Vojvodina established a front organization for Hungarians, the Association of Hungarians for the Homeland of Serbia and Yugoslavia (AHHSY). Its leaders declared that the DCHV did not represent the Magyar population and was conspiring to create rifts with the Serbs; it also attacked the Hungarian media for its purported anti-Serbian bias.[37] DCHV Secretary-General Andras Agaston revealed that Serbian leaders had a program to completely abolish Vojvodina's autonomy and to divide up the province into four districts governed by commissioners appointed in Belgrade. To defend itself from such centralizing pressures, the DCHV proposed the formation of a minority council among Vojvodina Magyars that would insure minority self-government with separate jurisdiction over culture, education, and the local media.[38]

While Hungarian contacts with Croatia and Slovenia developed smoothly, through the opening up of consulates, high level visits by government leaders, the pursuit of economic and cultural cooperation, and programs for the mutual protection of minorities, relations with Serbia continued to deteriorate. Closer Hungarian-Croatian ties sparked accusations by Belgrade that Budapest was actively supporting Croatian separatism, while negotiations over a bilateral military agreement between Yugoslavia and Hungary were frozen. As the war in Croatia escalated, the Hungarian government condemned Yugoslav army actions and air force incursions on to Hungarian territory that were said to endanger European stability. Budapest also grew alarmed as Magyar villages in Croatia became caught up in the conflict and several thousand refugees from Yugoslavia sought shelter in Hungary to escape the war.

Hungarian-Serbian relations could further deteriorate, especially if the armed conflict spreads to other republics, and if Yugoslavia breaks up into separate and mutually antagonistic states. In such a scenario, the Serbian regime could intensify its controls over Vojvodina and further endanger the dwindling "cultural autonomy" of the Hungarian minority. This could entangle Budapest in the conflict amidst mounting Hungarian condemnations of the Serbian authorities and increasing public pressures for the protection of vulnerable ethnic kinsmen in the remainder of Yugoslavia.

Yugoslavia, Bulgaria, and Macedonia

During several centuries of Turkish domination, the Serbs and Bulgarians maintained relatively peaceful relations while retaining their distinct national identities and separate Orthodox Churches. But in the latter part of the 19th century, the territory of Macedonia adjacent to the Serbian-Bulgarian border became a major source of antagonism between the newly recreated states. Bulgaria achieved independence from Ottoman rule in 1878, following a Russian intervention against Turkish forces.[39] The Treaty of San Stefano ceded the whole of Macedonia to Bulgaria, but this decision was annulled a few months later by the Congress of Berlin. The major European powers dictated the revision of borders throughout the Balkans because they feared Russian expansion toward the Mediterranean. Macedonia was again separated from Bulgaria and Serbia was allocated some of its districts, while other areas were placed under Ottoman protection. This set the stage for bitter conflicts between Serbia and Bulgaria over the Macedonian region.[40]

After the defeat of Turkey in the First Balkan War of 1912, the victors disagreed over the division of territorial spoils in Macedonia and Thrace. In 1913, Serbia and Greece signed a secret treaty to divide former Turkish lands among themselves because both states feared a strong and enlarged Bulgaria. Violence escalated as the Central Powers sought to undermine Slavic unity in the Balkans, which they perceived as a potential threat to their own imperial ambitions. During the Second Balkan War in 1913, Bulgaria attacked both Serbia and Greece, dragging Romania and Turkey into a struggle which the Bulgarians quickly lost. Sofia was forced to accept further territorial losses as Serbia and Greece divided most of Macedonia, while Bulgaria was only left with some small eastern portions. Sofia sided with the Central Powers during World War One in the hope of recovering Macedonia, but ended up relinquishing even more territory to Serbia in the Rhodope mountains. As a result of these war losses, Bulgaria's frustration and hostility toward its Balkan neighbors intensified.

During the inter-war years, Bulgarian and Macedonian irredentists applied pressure on the Sofia government not to neglect the Macedonian issue. Their paramilitary arm, the Internal Macedonian Revolutionary Organization (IMRO), engaged in numerous acts of terrorism and sabotage in Yugoslav and Greek Macedonia as well as in Bulgaria. Their goal was either to incorporate Macedonia into Bulgaria or to create an independent Macedonian state. IMRO was eventually combated by Sofia, which arranged a rapprochement with Belgrade in 1937. Bulgaria sided with the Germans in World War Two, and after the Nazi dismemberment of Yugoslavia in 1941, Sofia obtained a large share of Macedonia. It lost these territories once again at the end of the war when the Yugoslav state was restored.

During the early post-war period, the Soviets sought to prevent any resurgence of territorial conflict between Communist governments in the Balkans. As a result, Bulgaria engaged in a more conciliatory foreign policy toward Yugoslavia and played down the Macedonian question. Even though the Bulgarians considered Macedonians to be simply western Bulgarians, the

Communist regime in Sofia accepted the creation of a separate Macedonian republic in Yugoslavia and accorded its own Macedonians national minority status. As Moscow's relations with Belgrade deteriorated, Sofia stepped to the forefront of the anti-Yugoslav campaign and revived its claims to Macedonia while eliminating the separate status of its own Macedonians. This campaign was pursued at a time when Belgrade was strenuously promoting a distinct Macedonian identity within Yugoslavia. For example, during the 1960s an autocephalus Macedonian Orthodox Church was established in a government-engineered schism with the Serbian Orthodox Church. This was part of Tito's strategy to maintain an inter-ethnic balance in Yugoslavia and prevent the domination of any single republic.

The Macedonian issue was played down during the 1960s, while Moscow attempted to re-establish closer relations with Belgrade and held Sofia in check. It was revived again during the 1970s and 1980s, particularly as the Bulgarian Communist regime began to employ the nationalist card. Belgrade periodically charged Sofia with violating the U.N. Charter and the Helsinki agreements by refusing to recognize Macedonians as a distinct national minority and of undermining the integrity of Yugoslavia by denying legitimacy to one of its republics. Although Bulgaria's Communist leader Todor Zhivkov asserted that Sofia had no territorial claims on Yugoslavia, Belgrade refused any formal discussions on the issue until Bulgaria recognized the Macedonian minority in its own country. The dispute remained in a stalemate.

Bulgarian-Yugoslav relations have grown more strained over the past few years, particularly as Serbia asserted its authority in the Yugoslav federation and the Macedonian issue re-emerged on the international arena. Yugoslavia's prolonged political crisis fuelled inter-ethnic tensions and energized nationalist demands in all six constituent republics. The republican elections in Yugoslav Macedonia in November and December 1990 witnessed the unexpected success of a pro-sovereignty party that sought to protect itself from federal government domination and Serbian control. The danger existed that if the country were to fracture and Slovenia and Croatia were to successfully break away, the Serbian authorities could attempt to tighten their control over the southern republics, including Macedonia. Such developments could further ignite Macedonian demands for full independence, separation, and even for closer association with Bulgaria as a source of patronage and protection against Belgrade.

The authorities in Sofia have remained prudent by not pushing the Macedonian issue too forcefully, but a crackdown against the sovereign republic by Yugoslav-Serbian forces could increase the likelihood of Bulgarian involvement. Nationalist pro-Macedonian groups have also become more active inside Bulgaria since late 1990. Their programs for an economic association between the divided Macedonian territories could eventually escalate into demands for pan-Macedonian independence and even for re-annexation by Bulgaria.

About 30,000 Bulgarians reside in five municipalities in south eastern Serbia, in an area which belonged to Sofia before the Second Balkan War. They have not constituted a major focus of dispute in recent years, but their predicament in a fast changing Yugoslavia could also be a factor in heightened Serb-Bulgarian tensions. In October 1990 a Democratic Foundation of Bulgarians in Yugoslavia (DFBY) was founded in Nis in south eastern Serbia, but its leaders expressed general satisfaction with the situation of Bulgarians in the republic.[41] The future of Macedonia remains the outstanding area of conflict between Yugoslavia and Bulgaria. The federal Yugoslav Communist regime has cultivated Macedonian ethnic and republican identity since the 1940s, partly in order to counter Bulgarian claims to the region. According to the 1981 census, about 67% of the population, or nearly 1.3 million people in Macedonia were registered as ethnic Macedonians. Yugoslavia also claimed that over 350,000 Macedonians lived in the Pirin region of western Bulgaria, although Macedonian identity is no longer recognized by Sofia as it was in the 1950s, when over 150,000 Macedonians were recorded in the Bulgarian census. An undetermined number of ethnic Macedonians also resided in northern Greece.

As the fissures in Yugoslavia deepened, the Macedonian republican authorities and various new political organizations became more assertive of Macedonian statehood. During the summer of 1989, the National Assembly amended the 1974 constitution, changing the definition of the republic from "a state of the Macedonian people and the Albanian and Turkish minorities" to the "state of the Macedonian nation." Such internal Macedonian developments coupled with growing turmoil throughout Yugoslavia, the rise of Serbian nationalism, and the democratic changes in Bulgaria, have brought Macedonia to the forefront of relations between Belgrade and Sofia. Macedonian leaders have in the past generally supported the federal Yugoslav structure, as it recognized their ethnic distinctiveness, provided protection against outside claims to the region, and helped supply important economic aid. But with nationalism on the rise throughout Yugoslavia and with the breakdown of federal authority, Macedonians became more remonstrative although divided about the future status of the republic.

Several new nationalist groups were established during 1990 to press for Macedonia's sovereignty and security in the face of mounting Yugoslav turmoil. The Internal Macedonian Revolutionary Organization–Democratic Party for Macedonian National Unity (IMRO-DPMNU) held its founding congress in June 1990. Although renouncing the IMRO's pre-war terrorist heritage, it pledged to continue its political traditions and opposed any amendments to the republican constitution that would limit Macedonian sovereignty. IMRO leaders also called for the recognition of Macedonian minorities by neighboring states and appeared to depart from IMRO's traditional pro-Bulgarian orientation by calling for a sovereign Macedonia in a future Balkan confederation. Its leaders supported a looser political arrangement in Yugoslavia, but expressed apprehensions about Serbian domination in a smaller federation. Some IMRO factions also expressed more ambitious objectives by seeking the union of all former Macedonian territories in Yugoslavia, Bulgaria, and Greece.

The nationalist Movement for All-Macedonian Action (MAAK) was set up by Macedonian intellectuals in February 1990, and a few months later issued a manifesto calling for Macedonian sovereignty. It too supported a confederal Yugoslav state and voiced fears over a perceived Serbian threat to "recolonize" the republic. More radical groups have also been formed during the last few years, unequivocally calling for a "united Macedonia" to embrace the Aegean (Greek), Pirin (Bulgarian), and Vardar (Yugoslav) regions, together with some border adjustments with Serbia in favor of Macedonia.[42] They could have an increasing appeal in the republic, especially among young people experiencing economic deprivation in one of post-Yugoslavia's poorest regions. Both IMRO and MAAK took aboard the nationalist cause in the republican elections held in November and December 1990. IMRO performed remarkably well, gaining more seats than any other party although falling well short of a clear majority. A fragile coalition government was subsequently put together in the republic and its viability was put to the test as Yugoslavia's internal crisis deepened.

The IMRO organization in Skopje has remained divided on the Bulgarian issue with some factions appearing to be more pro-Bulgarian than others. Although it declared itself an "inter-state party," that would also operate on Bulgarian and Greek territories, each faction differed in its stance toward both Belgrade and Sofia.[43] After an IMRO group was established in Sofia in December 1990, some IMRO representatives in Skopje condemned it for seeking to seize Macedonia and accused it of "Bulgarian elitism." Meanwhile, IMRO (Sofia) claimed it supported the goals of IMRO (Skopje) for a sovereign Macedonia, but envisioned this as a stepping stone toward secession and eventual reunification with Bulgaria. IMRO (Skopje) denied that it maintained close links with Sofia. However, it did admit to seeking the eventual unification of all Macedonian lands, although not under Bulgarian patronage or supervision.

The post-Communist government in Sofia, and virtually all political parties in Bulgaria, have asserted that there is no separate Macedonian nation. Macedonian parties were prohibited from registering in the Bulgarian elections in June 1990 and October 1991, or from organizing any separate political or cultural movements. The Bulgarian Orthodox Church has refused to recognize either the distinctive ethnicity of Macedonians or the autocephaly of the Macedonian Orthodox Church. Indeed, Church leaders in Sofia upheld that Macedonia was the cradle of Bulgarian culture and religious tradition. The authorities in Sofia asserted that Belgrade was afraid of the revival of "Bulgarian identity" in Macedonia, and that Serbia engaged in anti-Bulgarian propaganda to deflect attention from its own internal problems.[44] Serbian leaders have been accused of trying to destabilize Bulgaria by aiding the marginal and illegal separatist organizations in the country with a view to annexing the Pirin region to Yugoslavia.

Sofia considers the Illinden group, or the United Macedonian Organization (UMO), as a virtual Serbian front and a manufactured provocation designed to dismember Bulgaria. UMO was established in November 1989, and its small membership has been particularly active in the Blagoevgrad and Sandanski areas of Pirin Macedonia in western Bulgaria. The group has been declared illegal by Sofia and condemned for violating the Bulgarian constitution and undermining the unity of the Bulgarian nation by aiming to establish an enlarged Macedonian republic.[45] UMO denies that it has any territorial pretensions, but is simply struggling for the recognition of Macedonian linguistic and cultural rights in Bulgaria and elsewhere. Illinden has been holding semi-clandestine meetings, disseminating leaflets, and gathering signatures for the recognition of a Macedonian minority in Bulgaria. In April 1991, UMO issued sixteen demands to the Bulgarian government, including the restoration of the Macedonian language and culture in all educational institutions in the Pirin region, full access to the mass media, and the placement of a Macedonian bishop in Pirin independent of the Bulgarian Orthodox Church but united with the Macedonian Autocephalic Church in Ohrid (in Vardar Macedonia). It also demanded the withdrawal of "Bulgarian occupation troops" and full cultural, economic, and political self-determination for the Pirin area.[46]

According to Bulgarian commentators, the UMO has benefitted from substantial material assistance from Belgrade and Skopje and capitalized on the weakened administrative structures in the Pirin region following the collapse of Communist rule.[47] Its leaders have held meetings with some like-minded Yugoslav Macedonian organizations denounced by Bulgaria as Serbian fronts. These have included MAAK, which the Bulgarian media alleges is channelling material aid to UMO. In addition, the smuggling of weapons into the Yugoslav republics from Hungary and elsewhere has been described in Sofia as a "major threat to Bulgarian security."[48]

Serbian nationalist groups have also revived the notion that Macedonians are in reality south Serbs, as they were often referred to in the inter-war Yugoslav kingdom. Such a position exacerbates animosities with both the Bulgarians and Macedonians. Serbian parties, including the Serbian Radical Party, contend that Macedonia was artificially separated from Serbia by Titoist Communists in league with the Moscow-directed Comintern, while thousands of Serbs were forcibly expelled from the region. Some Macedonian spokesmen have warned about a revival of Serbian expansionism with clear designs on Macedonian territory, even including the Pirin area of Bulgaria.[49] They feared that the current Serbian regime would act upon its claims to Macedonia if the Yugoslav federation were to split. The government in Belgrade could also engender problems with Macedonia's Serbian minority, estimated at well under 10% of the population and situated primarily in the northern border region. In February 1992, a referendum on Serbian autonomy was held in thirteen districts of northern Macedonia.

The Yugoslav and Serbian authorities assert that they hold no territorial pretensions to Bulgaria but remain anxious over potential Bulgarian claims to Yugoslav lands. Belgrade has alleged that Sofia stepped up its discrimination against ethnic Macedonians since the fall of Zhivkov, and that the resurgence of Bulgarian nationalism also threatens the Macedonian republic. The nationalist All-Bulgarian Association (ABA), based in Sofia, has been active since early 1990 in campaigning for Bulgarian "cultural integrity." It has pledged to lead a legal struggle against "pan-Serbian chauvinism and Macedonianism" and Yugoslav attempts to assimilate the "Bulgarians" in Vardar Macedonia. In December 1990, at its first national congress the Union of Macedonian Cultural and Educational Societies changed its name to IMRO-UMS (Union of Macedonian Societies) and adopted a more forthright anti-Yugoslav stance.

Both ABA and IMRO-UMS support the expansion of Bulgarian social, cultural, and economic links with a sovereign Macedonian republic. This will apparently bring the Vardar region closer to Bulgaria. In the event that Yugoslavia disintegrated, this would also lay the groundwork for political absorption or the creation of a new confederation. The ABA has also pledged to defend the interests of "Macedonian Bulgarians" in Thrace (Greece) and northern Dobrudja (Romania), and to support the independence drive of Slovenia, Croatia, and other non-Serb republics. For example, a Union of Thracian Cultural and Educational Associations (UTCEA) was formed in 1991 to campaign for the rights of "Bulgarian Macedonians" in the Thrace region of northern Greece. In Yugoslav Macedonia itself, a Society of Bulgarians (SOB) has been established to support the ABA and IMRO-UMS positions. It has remonstrated with the new administration in Sofia to intercede and protect the Macedonians' avowed Bulgarian heritage. It also issued an appeal to the Bulgarian people denying the entire concept of a Macedonian nation.

In early 1991, the coalition government in Sofia declared that it supported Macedonia's autonomy in Yugoslavia, even though it did not recognize a separate Macedonian nationality within Bulgaria. Bulgarian Foreign Minister Viktor Valkov affirmed in August 1991 that all Yugoslav republics that declared their independence, including Macedonia, should be recognized.[50] He underscored that Sofia would only recognize a Macedonian republic within its current borders, but not a Macedonian nation or a Macedonian minority in Bulgaria. Belgrade capitalized on this stance to accuse Sofia of interfering in its internal affairs and of seeking to create a second Bulgarian state in preparation for future annexation. In January 1991, the Yugoslav authorities also lodged protests against joint statements by the Bulgarian and Greek Prime Ministers which "negated the existence of Macedonian national minorities in their countries." Such statements apparently contradicted their declared intention to promote Balkan cooperation, and contravened the principles of the Helsinki accords which underscore respect for the rights of all national groupings.[51]

The dispute with Bulgaria has been compounded by reportedly high-level meetings between Croatian and Bulgarian officials. This presents Serbia with an alleged conspiracy on both its northern and southern flanks, designed to decouple Yugoslavia's restive republics. If such contacts develop, Serbian leaders may feel increasingly surrounded and embattled and could stage some major provocation in Macedonia to justify a military crackdown. They could also exploit the Albanian issue to their advantage by posing as the protectors of Macedonian sovereignty against alleged Albanian expansionism disguised as appeals for Albanian autonomy in western Macedonia.

In late January 1991, the Macedonian republican assembly adopted a declaration on sovereignty and self-determination, despite the concerns of Albanians and other minorities over growing ethnic discrimination. In September 1991, over 95% of the 71.85% of the population that participated in a republican referendum voted for Macedonian independence, while Prime Minister Nikola Kljusev declared that Skopje harbored no claims on Bulgarian, Greek, or Albanian territory. The Milosevic government in Serbia responded by declaring that Macedonia would not be permitted to leave Yugoslavia, while the Belgrade authorities were prepared to use force to prevent secession.[52] The Skopje government initially adopted a more cautious approach than Slovenia and Croatia toward independence, fearing a possible Yugoslav army assault. Moreover, IMRO has only maintained a slim majority in the republican parliament and could not unilaterally push for independence. Although Skopje did not immediately declare its secession from Yugoslavia, it clearly reserved that option if conditions in the crumbling federation warranted such a move.

Once the EC announced in December 1991 that it was willing to recognize the independence of any Yugoslav republic that fulfilled certain political and territorial criteria, the Macedonian authorities declared the republic's independence and requested international recognition. By February 1992 only Bulgaria and Turkey had recognized Macedonia's independence. Sofia underscored that it was only recognizing the existence of a Macedonian state and not a distinct Macedonian nation. The EC did not automatically recognize Macedonian independence largely because of Greek opposition. Although Skopje formally renounced any claims to neighboring territories in the republic's constitution, Athens demanded that Macedonia change its name and thereby eliminate all possible pretensions to Greek soil.

IMRO called for the Yugoslav army to withdraw from Macedonia and for the creation of a territorial defense force; but during the course of 1991, the legislature rejected both proposals. Nonetheless, in late 1991 Skopje prepared a new law on national defense providing for the formation of a Macedonian army general staff. According to Belgrade, IMRO was also allegedly illegally importing arms from Poland and other foreign sources.[53] In January 1992, after declaring Macedonia's independence, the government in Skopje adopted a draft law paving the way for the establishment of a national army to number between 25,000 and 30,000 troops.

Some radical Macedonian nationalists have also proposed "solving the Albanian problem" through deportations to Kosovo and by denying full citizenship rights to the Albanian minority. Such propositions have exasperated Albanian political leaders in the republic and could in turn be exploited by Belgrade. If ethnic relations deteriorate in Macedonia, Serbia may try to forge a common front with Macedonian nationalists by claiming Albanian internal subversion and foreign aggression against both republics. Bulgaria's reaction to such moves could prove critical, especially if it can offer a viable alternative to Serbian influence in Macedonia. Meanwhile, the Serbian government and Yugoslav leaders have voiced increasing concern over Sofia's support for the dismemberment of Yugoslavia and over growing Bulgarian influence in the Balkans.[54]

Yugoslavia and Romania

Relations between Romanians and neighboring Serbs remained reasonably amicable over the centuries. Both groups were preoccupied with more menacing rivals and harbored no territorial ambitions against each other. Contacts between Bucharest and the newly formed Yugoslav state were also cordial throughout the post-World War One period. The former Hungarian Banat region was equitably divided between the two states along national lines and the Romanian-Yugoslav frontier became one of the most stable borders in eastern Europe. Indeed, when Romania entered World War Two on the Axis side, it chose not to participate in the carve up of Yugoslavia by claiming more of the Banat region. The area was not in dispute and only contained a small Romanian population.

In the early Communist period, relations between the two states were soured by Tito's expulsion from the Moscow-directed Cominform. But as Romania asserted greater independence from the Soviet Union in the early 1960s, Bucharest's relations with Belgrade warmed up. Yugoslavia itself was seeking closer ties with its socialist neighbors to break out of its international isolation. After Ceausescu's accession to the Romanian leadership, regular high-level meetings were held with Belgrade and economic cooperation was enhanced. Good relations were also maintained after Tito's death and throughout the 1980s.

Even before the overthrow of Ceausescu, contacts between Romania and Yugoslavia were reasonably amicable. There was an absence of territorial claims and the only simmering dispute focused on the deteriorating treatment of Yugoslav minorities in the Banat region of western Romania. Belgrade complained about the discriminatory and assimilationist pressures applied by Bucharest against Serbian and Croatian populations, which resembled the policies pursued toward the Hungarians of Transylvania. Relations have improved since Ceausescu's ouster, as has the treatment of the Yugoslav minorities in Romania. But great uncertainty remained in Bucharest over the survivability of the Yugoslav federation. The country's future shape and internal structure will determine its relations with all neighboring states, including Romania. The policies of the Serbian government are considered to be crucial in this equation.

About 80,000 Yugoslavs live in the Banat border region of Romania; the majority are Serbs and Croats. During the last years of the Ceausescu regime, Belgrade accused Bucharest of attempting to assimilate its south Slav population. Conversely, the Romanian regime periodically accused the Yugoslavs of siding with the Hungarians over the Transylvanian question. Since the Romanian uprising of December 1989, Belgrade has become more active in aiding the Yugoslav minorities in the Banat area, particularly in the cultural and publishing fields. The Romanians have been reasonably tolerant of such endeavors, because the self-assertion of the small Slavic populations was not viewed as a threat to Romania's territorial or political integrity. During President Ion Iliescu's visit to Yugoslavia in September 1990, the Romanian leader agreed to improve the position of Slav minorities by developing language classes, establishing libraries, and aiding various cultural institutions. In addition, the Serbian authorities proposed a plan to resettle some of the 50,000 Serbs from the Banat area in Yugoslavia's Kosovo region; the idea has not been publicly opposed by Bucharest.

The few thousand Romanians in Serbia's Vojvodina province have also embarked on organizing their own associations. For instance, a Democratic Alliance of Vojvodina Romanians (DAVR) was formed in early 1990. Several thousand Vlachs, or ethnic Romanians, also live in the Homoljski region of eastern Serbia, although precise numbers cannot be confirmed as many Romanian-speakers in the republic have not declared themselves as non-Serbs in the Yugoslav census. Some Romanian minority leaders have expressed reservations about Serbian policy toward the minorities, especially if Yugoslavia dissolves into its component republics. However, the small size of the Romanian minority and the absence of autonomist or territorial claims indicates that the situation in Vojvodina and Homoljski is unlikely to grow into a major dispute between Belgrade and Bucharest. On the contrary, both

Serbia's and Romania's search for future Balkan allies, particularly vis-à-vis the perceived Croatian-Hungarian challenge, could actually bring the two Orthodox Christian semi-authoritarian states closer together.

Yugoslavia and Greece

Greek-Yugoslav animosities have focused on the Macedonian region and on the identity of the Macedonian population that Belgrade considered to be Slavic and Athens as ethnically Greek. To counter Greek claims to Yugoslav Macedonia, the Communist government in Belgrade occasionally pressed for ethnic recognition and full cultural rights for the Aegean Macedonians under Greek administration. Athens continued to discriminate against those who declared themselves Macedonians and pressed forward with its assimilation policies. It also continued to resettle Greeks in traditionally Slav areas to dilute the Macedonian population. After Tito's break with the Soviets in the late 1940s, contacts improved between Yugoslavia and its non-socialist southern neighbors. Friendship treaties were signed with Greece and Turkey in 1953. These were later transformed into security agreements even though Yugoslavia avoided entangling itself in any military commitments with NATO members.

Yugoslav-Greek relations have remained relatively cordial, but the interlinked Albanian and Macedonian issues could create some future problems. Democratization in Albania has encouraged Macedonia's Albanians to push for autonomy and even closer links with Tirana. This will increase pressures on the Macedonian republic, whose perceived vulnerability could accentuate calls for the unification of the three traditional areas of Macedonia: Vardar (in Yugoslavia), Pirin (in Bulgaria) and Aegean (in Greece). But any moves toward Macedonian unity will undoubtedly worsen Skopje's relations with Athens, as the Greek authorities refuse to recognize the existence of a Macedonian minority anywhere on their territories. Macedonian self-assertion would also complicate relations between the federal Yugoslav authorities, the Serbian government, and the Greek administration. All these factors will have a significant effect on emerging Balkan alliances. They could lead to new realignments with each state seeking to establish advantageous international relations.

The Yugoslav federal government has contended that about 150,000 Slav Macedonians still inhabit parts of northern Greece. Macedonian estimates range between 200,000 and 350,000. Belgrade has periodically called upon Athens to recognize their existence and grant them internationally sanctioned minority rights. By contrast, Athens claims that the Macedonian question is a non-issue. According to Greek officials, the Macedonians are actually "Slavophone" or bilingual Greeks who have undergone Slav cultural and linguistic pressures over the centuries but have since reverted back to their Greek heritage.[55] Yugoslavia has raised the Macedonian issue at the United Nations and other international forums, demanding that Greece recognize the existence of this distinct minority. Athens has persistently refused and counter-attacked by lodging various complaints against Belgrade with the European Commission and other international bodies.

During the past few years, Yugoslavia has complained about Greek travel restrictions between Macedonia and Aegean Greece. Athens has persistently hindered Yugoslav Macedonians from crossing the frontier to visit their families or obtain seasonal work. It has curtailed the issue of entry visas and increased entry charges. In retaliation, Belgrade limited the number of transit permits issued to Greek truck drivers, contending that Athens feared inter-Macedonian contacts would spur minority demands. In reply, Greek government spokesmen warned about unacceptable Yugoslav territorial demands and Belgrade's alleged incitement of inter-state tensions by resuscitating the Macedonian issue.[56]

Yugoslavia's increasingly assertive Macedonians have become more outspoken in recent years over the fate of co-nationals in Greece, regardless of how this affects relations between Belgrade and Athens.[57] IMRO-DPMNU and other Macedonian nationalist groups have assisted in organizing the Greek Macedonians. During 1990, an Assembly of Aegean Macedonians (AAM) established its headquarters in Skopje as did *Dostoinstvo* (Dignity), a human rights organization focusing on violations of Macedonian rights in northern Greece. In Greece itself, an organization styling itself as the Central Committee for Macedonian Human Rights (CCMHR) appeared in Thessalonika in 1989. The AAM has regularly issued protests against Greek policy and the non-recognition of minority rights. Although the AAM and IMRO have not called for the outright annexation of the Aegean region, they have supported forging closer cross-border ties and developing Macedonian "cultural self-determination." They have also proposed convening a world Macedonian congress in preparation for an international conference on the future of Macedonia.

Nationalist Macedonian groups have sponsored protest actions on the Greek-Yugoslav border in order to draw attention to Greece's disavowal of its Macedonian minority. For example, in May 1990, 50,000 Macedonians blocked several border crossings with the full support of the republican authorities. Crowds of Macedonians reportedly also gathered in some northern Greek towns. In June 1991, Macedonian President Kiro Gligorov asserted that the republic would continue to raise the question of Macedonian human rights in Greece.[58]

Macedonian nationalist leaders have also criticized Belgrade's cautious approach toward the minority issue. They have pressed the Yugoslav government to demand that Greece grant full ethnic and cultural liberties to the Aegean Macedonians. Athens in turn charged that Belgrade and the Serbian regime were behind the recent upsurge in Macedonian activism and anti-Greek invective. It speculated that the disruptive upheaval in Yugoslavia had led Belgrade to reach for sensitive foreign policy issues to rally support in the republics and thereby to deflect attention from its severe internal problems. Athens feared that Yugoslav conditions would further deteriorate and push the Macedonians and even the Serbs toward more provocative actions against Greece. Some Greek spokesmen also claimed that Skopje was supported by Ankara over the Macedonian question, and issued warnings about a prospective Macedonian-Turkish alliance against Greece.

Concerned about instability on its northern borders, in September 1991 the Greek authorities planned to hold a regional conference on Yugoslavia, with the participation of Bulgarian, Romanian, Greek, and Serbian leaders. The session was eventually cancelled following substantial international opposition to the selection of participants, particularly over the exclusion of Macedonian representatives. Some observers charged that the conference was a Greek plot to divide up Yugoslavia and quash Macedonian aspirations in the region. Athens also become increasingly worried about an overflow of refugees from Macedonia if Belgrade were to impose an economic blockade on Skopje or resort to force to keep the republic within Yugoslavia. Greek troop reinforcements were reportedly dispatched to the border areas in September 1991.[59]

According to some reports, as the Serb-Croat war intensified in the fall of 1991 and threatened to spill over into other Yugoslav republics, the Greek authorities began to reconsider their hard-line stance on the Macedonian question. While still supportive of preserving Yugoslav unity, Athens evidently did not want to be too far out of step with its EC partners and other Western allies. Speculation increased that the Greek government would be prepared to recognize the sovereignty of Macedonia, if it obtained firm guarantees that the existing borders were unchangeable, that Macedonia had no claims on Greece, and that Skopje would desist from campaigning on behalf of the Macedonian minority in the Aegean region.[60] But Skopje suffered a setback near the close of 1991, when Athens rejected a request from Macedonia's President Kiro Gligorov for the republic's recognition and effectively blocked EC recognition of Macedonia's independence. Athens demanded that the republic change its name and incorporate constitutional guarantees that it had no territorial pretensions toward Greece. Skopje refused to consider what it viewed as Greek interference in its internal affairs. The Greek position will continue to complicate Balkan relations. Any recognition of Macedonian independence could undermine Greek relations with Serbia, while continuing non-recognition could worsen relations with Bulgaria and heighten Macedonian suspicions of an aggressive "Belgrade-Athens axis."

Notes

1. For background on Kosovo see Alex W. Dragnich and Slavko Todorovich, *The Saga of Kosovo: Focus on Serbian-Albanian Relations* (Boulder: East European Monographs, 1984).

2. Accounts of Albanian history can be found in Anton Logoreci, *The Albanians: Europe's Forgotten Survivors* (Boulder: Westview, 1977); and Stavro Skendi, *The Albanian National Awakening, 1878-1912* (Princeton: Princeton University Press, 1967).

3. For background see Stefan K. Pavlovitch and Elez Biberaj, "The Albanian Problem in Yugoslavia: Two Views," *Conflict Studies*, London, No. 137/138, 1982.

4. The Serbian government position is outlined in *Kosovo and Albanian Separatism: The Defence of Kosovo,* published by the Secretariat for Information of the Socialist Republic of Serbia, Belgrade, 1990.

5. Check Milovan Milutinovic, "Secret Armed Units," *Narodna Armija,* Belgrade, 13 September 1990.

6. See Milan Andrejevich, "Serbia Cracks Down in Kosovo," Radio Free Europe, *Report on Eastern Europe,* Vol. 1, No. 30, 27 July 1990.

7. See *Bujku,* Pristina, in Albanian, 21 July 1991, in *FBIS-EEU*-91-151, 6 August 1991.

8. *ATA,* Tirana, 5 August 1991, in *FBIS-EEU*-91-151, 6 August 1991.

9. See the interview with Ramush Tahiri, Secretary of the Albanian Christian Democratic Party, in *Vjesnik,* Zagreb, 18 May 1991.

10. See *Radio Tirana Network,* Tirana, 13 September 1991, in *FBIS-EEU*-91-185, 24 September 1991.

11. Reported on *Radio Croatia,* Zagreb, in Albanian, 19 October 1991, in *FBIS-EEU*-91-203, 21 October 1991. See also Milan Andrejevich, "Kosovo: A Precarious Balance Between Stability and Civil War," Radio Free Europe, *Report on Eastern Europe,* Vol. 2, No. 42, 18 October 1991.

12. *Tanjug,* Belgrade, 14 August 1991.

13. Milovan Drecun, "Preparations of the Skipetars for an Armed Rebellion," *Politika,* Belgrade, 14 July 1991.

14. *Radio Croatia,* broadcast in Albanian, Zagreb, 20 May and 21 May 1991.

15. Boris Kalnoky, "Threat in Albania: You Will Fare As Badly as Gorbachev," *Die Welt,* Hamburg, 31 August 1991, *FBIS-EEU*-91-171, 4 September 1991.

16. See the "Program and Statute of the KPPA," issued in Tirana on 9 June 1991 in *Kosova,* 21 July 1991.

17. Check *Radio Tirana Network,* Tirana, on 24 September 1991 in *FBIS-EEU*-91-188, 27 September 1991.

18. *ATA,* Tirana, 29 September 1991, in *FBIS-EEU*-91-189, 30 September 1991.

19. See Kristaq Prifti, "The Truth About Kosovo and the Albanians in Yugoslavia," *Zeri i Popullit,* Tirana, 9 February 1991.

20. For example, see *Belgrade Domestic Service,* Belgrade, 10 February 1991, in *FBIS-EEU*-91-029, 12 February 1991.

21. *Tanjug,* Belgrade, 8 March 1991.

22. See the interview with Haljilji in *Kossuth Radio Network*, Budapest, in Hungarian, 9 September 1991, in *FBIS-EEU*-91-178, 13 September 1991.

23. Radio Free Europe/ Radio Liberty, *Daily Report*, No. 28, 11 February 1992.

24. See *Borba*, Belgrade, 31 May 1991.

25. Radio Free Europe/ Radio Liberty, *Daily Report*, No. 210, 5 November 1990.

26. See Tibor Bogdan, Vince Toth, and Evelyn Forro, "The Pathogens: Anti-Hungarianism and Nationalism," *Magyar Hirlap*, Budapest, 1 March 1991.

27. For details on recent developments see Edith Oltay, "Hungarians in Yugoslavia Seek Guarantee for Minority Rights." Radio Free Europe, *Report on Eastern Europe*, Vol. 2, No. 38, 20 September 1991.

28. Milan Andrejevich, "Vojvodina Hungarian Group to Seek Cultural Autonomy," Radio Free Europe, *Report on Eastern Europe*, Vol. 1, No. 41, 12 October 1990.

29. "Constitution That Ignores the Truth," *Borba*, Belgrade, 26 September 1990.

30. For an overview of the episode see Judith Pataki, "Relations with Yugoslavia Troubled by Weapons Sale," Radio Free Europe, *Report on Eastern Europe*, Vol. 2, No. 8, 22 January 1991.

31. See the report on the document issued by the Political Department of the Federal Secretariat for National Defense on the tasks of the People's Army, entitled "Only a Federal Yugoslavia," in *Borba*, Belgrade, 1 February 1991.

32. *Tanjug*, Belgrade, 16 July 1991, *FBIS-EEU*-91-137, 17 July 1991.

33. *Tanjug*, Belgrade, 24 October 1991, in *FBIS-EEU*-91-206, 24 October 1991.

34. Consult the interview with DCHV Chairman Andras Agoston, in "Increasing Anti-Hungarian Sentiments in Vojvodina," *Nepszava*, Budapest, 26 February 1991.

35. Reported in *Nepszava*, Budapest, 15 February 1991.

36. See *Borba*, Belgrade, on 1 February 1991.

37. For a valuable analysis of Hungarian policy check Alfred A. Reisch, "Hungary's Policy on the Yugoslav Conflict: A Delicate Balance," Radio Free Europe, *Report on Eastern Europe*, Vol. 2, No. 32, 9 August 1991.

38. *Budapest Domestic Service*, in Hungarian, Budapest, 22 April 1991, *FBIS-EEU*-91-079, 24 April 1991.

39. For a background history of Bulgaria consult R.J. Crampton, *A Short History of Modern Bulgaria* (Cambridge: Cambridge University Press, 1987).

40. For Macedonian history consult Stoyan Pribichevich, *Macedonia: Its People and History* (University Park: Pennsylvania State University, 1982).

41. Hugh Poulton, *The Balkans: Minorities and States in Conflict* (London: Minority Rights Publications, 1991), p. 97.

42. Dragan Nikolic, "Red Black Guerrillas," *Borba*, Belgrade, 4-5 November 1989.

43. Dragan Nikolic, "New Government, Weak Government," *Borba*, Belgrade, 22-23 December 1990.

44. For some Bulgarian accusations see Nikolay Zagorichonov, "What is Macedonism, And Does it Have a Basis in Bulgaria?" *Duma*, Sofia, 12 May 1990.

45. See Duncan Perry, "The Macedonian Question Revitalized," Radio Free Europe, *Report on Eastern Europe*, Vol. 1, No. 34, 24 August 1990.

46. See *Duma*, Sofia, 25 April 1991, in *JPRS-EEU*-91-091, 25 June 1991.

47. See Dobrin Michev, Stoyan Germanov, and Anton Purvanov, "Once Again Separatism on National Grounds," *Duma*, Sofia, 15 February 1991.

48. "Skopje is Sending Help to the Illegal Illinden Organization," *Duma,* Sofia, 16 February 1991.

49. See "Most Responsibility Toward All Open Questions," *Nova Makedonija,* Skopje, 13 July 1990.

50. Radio Free Europe/ Radio Liberty, *Daily Report,* No. 166, 2 September 1991.

51. *Tanjug,* Belgrade, 17 January 1991.

52. *The Financial Times,* 20 September 1991. For the results of the Macedonian referendum see *Tanjug,* Belgrade, 10 September 1991.

53. Miroslav Lazanski, "New Information: Macedonians Buying Arms in Poland," *Politika,* Belgrade, 5 September 1991.

54. For example, see Milovan Drecun, "The 'Fraternal' Embrace of Bulgarian Expansionism," *Narodna Armija,* Belgrade, 9 January 1992.

55. For an elaboration of the Greek position on Macedonia see Evangelos Kofos, *The Macedonian Question: The Politics of Mutation* (Thessaloniki: Institute for Balkan Studies, 1987).

56. *Tanjug,* Belgrade, from Athens, 19 June 1990, in *FBIS-EEU*-90-119, 20 June 1990; and *Tanjug,* Belgrade, from Athens, 21 June 1990, *FBIS-EEU*-90-121, 22 June 1990.

57. See Milan Andrejevich, "Yugoslav Macedonians Demand Recognition of Aegean Macedonians," Radio Free Europe, *Report on Eastern Europe,* Vol. 1, No. 22, 1 June 1990.

58. *Tanjug,* Belgrade, 17 June 1991, *FBIS-EEU*-91-117, 18 June 1991.

59. *The Financial Times,* 20 September 1991.

60. According to *Tanjug,* Belgrade, in English, 16 October 1991, in *FBIS-EEU*-91-201, 17 October 1991.

6

Other Balkan Conflicts

While domestic and international disputes in central Europe revolve primarily around political, constitutional, and economic questions, in the Balkan region such problems have fueled more serious inter-ethnic and inter-national enmities. The collapse of the Soviet bloc and the unravelling of domestic Communist control have contributed to releasing deeply rooted historical tensions and exposed numerous unresolved points of conflict over territories, minorities, and resources. In some instances, former Communist forces have adopted nationalist programs and tried to exploit social and ethnic cleavages to preserve their positions and privileges. In other cases, radical populists and ultra-nationalist groupings have emerged and endeavored to capitalize on deteriorating economic conditions and continuing political instability by deliberately exacerbating cultural, religious, regional, and nationality frictions. Simultaneously, minority communities in several countries have raised their political aspirations for cultural autonomy and territorial or local self-government. Such demands have, in turn, heightened tensions with majority populations and with some neighboring states concerned over the fate of their co-ethnics abroad. In assessing the intensity of those nationality conflicts in the Balkans that do not directly involve the former Yugoslavia, it is useful to begin with an historical perspective for each of the current instances of hostility.

Hungary, Romania, and Transylvania

The chief source of friction between Hungary and Romania has been the Transylvanian region west of the Carpathian mountains.[1] Both sides claim it as their historical heritage but there is no definitive answer as to which ethnic-linguistic group first settled the area. Transylvania fell under Ottoman Turkish domination during the 16th and 17th centuries, but retained some degree of local autonomy. Ethnic and linguistic divisions between Hungarians and Romanians in the province were aggravated by religious and class differences. The Hungarians were largely Catholic or Protestant and constituted most of the noblemen landholders, while the Romanians were predominantly Orthodox Christians and peasants. As Ottoman power receded in the 18th century, Austria strengthened its controls over Transylvania with the support of the Hungarian gentry. Under Hungarian stewardship, the Romanian population, in contrast to the Magyars and Saxon Germans, was denied full legal status and equal educational or occupational opportunities.

Romania achieved independence from the Ottomans in 1862 with the union of Wallachia and Moldavia, but many Romanians remained outside the new borders in Transylvania and Russian Bessarabia.[2] After 1867, when Hungary was given a significant measure of autonomy by Vienna, Transylvania was left primarily in Hungarian hands and tensions heightened with Romanians struggling for political and cultural freedoms. A prime foreign policy objective of the Bucharest government was the annexation of Transylvania and other lands containing a large Romanian population. After World War One, Hungary was obliged to surrender two thirds of its pre-war territories, including Transylvania which was annexed by Bucharest. The Romanian regime depicted this as the fulfillment of historical destiny. However, the loss of the Transylvanian dominions spurred bitter resentment in Budapest, while Bucharest's policies in Transylvania inflamed an already poor inter-ethnic situation. Within months of unification, discriminatory policies were implemented and the Magyar and German populations lost many of their privileges and were excluded from the nation's political life. The Romanian government became increasingly dictatorial and degenerated into a quasi-fascist regime based on suppositions of national and racial superiority over other nationalities.

As an ally of Nazi Germany during World War Two, Hungary received a large portion of Transylvania under the 1940 Vienna Award. Bucharest subsequently allied itself with Germany to forestall a further partition of Transylvania and in order to gain territorial spoils from the Nazi conquest of the Soviet Union in 1941. In August 1944, after fighting alongside German troops, Romania switched sides and assisted the Red Army in its sweep through Hungary and Czechoslovakia. With Moscow's blessing, the Allied powers returned all of Transylvania to Bucharest after the war, partly as compensation for the Bukovina and Moldavian regions annexed by the Soviet Union. Over 1.5 million Hungarians were left in Transylvania, forming a majority in some eastern and central areas of the province. Their position became a simmering point of dispute between the two states.

Under the 1952 Romanian constitution, a Hungarian Autonomous Region was established in the Szeklerland area of eastern Transylvania where local Magyars were allowed to use their native language in schools and in dealings with the government. But this proved to be the high point in Communist Romania's lenient policies toward its large minority. In the late 1950s, the regime increasingly used nationalism as a legitimizing device and began to apply more repressive policies toward the Hungarians. The Autonomous Region was eliminated and all key posts in the local administration were filled by Romanians. During the Ceausescu years, from the mid-1960s onward, an assimilationist drive was pursued by the Communist authorities. The proportion of minority members in Party and state positions decreased, while hundreds of thousands of Romanian workers were resettled throughout Transylvania. The development of a "socialist mass culture" and the program of "village reorganization" during the 1980s, in which over 6,000 villages were slated for demolition, were designed to romanize the Magyars and eliminate their cultural and linguistic distinctiveness. The Communist regime in Budapest periodically revived the minority issue to apply pressure on Bucharest and to offer some protection to its ethnic compatriots. This occasionally strained relations with the hard-line Ceausescu dictatorship before the 1989 revolution.

Immediately after the Romanian uprising in December 1989, relations between Hungary and Romania visibly improved. Inter-ethnic contacts within Romania also appeared to be steered on a hopeful course, as both Hungarians and Romanians took part in the protests which toppled the dictatorial rule of Nicolai Ceausescu. But during the first few months of 1990, relations between the two states began to deteriorate again as mutual accusations intensified and inter-ethnic animosities increased in Transylvania. Hungarian spokesmen charged that the revolution in Bucharest had been hijacked by reform Communists, who not only prevented the emergence of a democratic system but were willing to employ nationalism and exploit anti-Hungarian sentiments to elicit domestic legitimacy.

Romania's ruling National Salvation Front (NSF) was also blamed by Budapest for tolerating and sanctioning the activities of extremist nationalist forces. Some of these groups were not averse to exacerbating nationality tensions and employing violence against the Hungarian minority in parts of Transylvania. Budapest also became impatient with the slow progress made by the Romanian government in recognizing the rights of different nationalities on its territory. It feared that democracy in Bucharest was simply understood as majority rule in a uni-ethnic state and not as political pluralism with guaranteed minority rights.

Various Romanian political activists also remained deeply suspicious about the long-term objectives of Hungarian organizations in Transylvania, as well as the policies of the Budapest administration. Claims abounded that minority parties received substantial material aid from Hungary, in addition to propaganda materials and subversive political instructions. Hungarian demands for schooling in Hungarian and the official use of the Magyar language in minority areas, were depicted as preliminary measures designed to gain regional autonomy and the eventual separation of Transylvania from Romania. Although such fears were clearly exaggerated, they have continued to have an impact among some sectors of Romanian society experiencing economic hardships and susceptible to political manipulation. Further ethnic hostilities in Transylvania will, in turn, adversely effect inter-state relations with Hungary.

Conflicts between Hungarians and Romanians exist at both the local and inter-governmental levels. The dispute revolves around the approximately 2 million strong Magyar community, which constitutes about 8% of Romania's total population and resides mostly in Transylvania. Hungarians live in compact areas in some parts of the territory, such as the Szeklerland area, but in most districts there is a pronounced ethnic mixture. However, in the Transylvanian region as a whole, the Magyars remain in the minority.

Ceausescu's repressive policies were calculated to undercut ethnic identity among the Hungarians by restricting language use and media access, shrinking the Magyar educational system and minimizing contacts between Transylvanians and Hungary. During the 1980s, the rearrangement of village settlements was clearly intended to destroy Hungarian cultural traditions and to homogenize the population.[3] The objective was to liquidate or combine smaller towns and villages in order to establish several hundred "agro-industrial centers." The program was abandoned in the wake of Ceausescu's fall in December 1989, when the Hungarian minority began to organize and campaign for its human rights and cultural freedoms.

Both Hungarians and Romanians participated in the rallies and demonstrations that contributed to toppling the Ceausescu regime, and the initial revolutionary phase was marked by pronounced cooperative efforts. Hungarians were soon legally permitted to establish their own organizations, and in early 1990, the Democratic Alliance of Hungarians in Romania (DAHR) was formed. By mid-year it claimed about 200,000 members, making it the largest Magyar organization in the country. In its statements and documents, DAHR did not seek the secession or re-incorporation of Transylvania into Hungary, but it spoke out for the protection of Magyar cultural, educational, linguistic, economic, and political liberties. DAHR leaders insisted on the introduction of a new law on national minorities to improve and regulate their legal status and complained that none of the Romanian parties possessed a comprehensive minorities program. DAHR took part in the general elections of May 1990, and finished in second place, capturing 7.2% of the vote and gaining 29 parliamentary deputies in 15 counties and 12 Senators in 10 counties of Transylvania.[4] The majority of the Hungarian population evidently voted along ethnic lines.

At its second congress in May 1991, DAHR claimed 533,000 members, reaffirmed its alliance with the Romanian democratic opposition, and set out its strategy for the future.[5] DAHR depicted itself as an umbrella organization for various political, professional, and civic groups, including three Hungarian political parties—the Christian Democrats, the Smallholders, and the

Independent Party. It consisted of two broad wings; younger members and former dissidents seeking close links with the Romanian liberal opposition and favoring more vehement protests against any anti-Hungarian manifestations, and older members supporting a "small steps" approach and collaboration with the Iliescu government to secure ethnic rights. DAHR leaders continued to complain that the authorities in Bucharest had failed to formally codify the "collective national rights" of minorities. Such rights evidently included the use of the Hungarian language in the administrative and judiciary systems in minority areas, the full restoration of the Magyar educational system, and proportional minority representation at all levels of the administration. DAHR leaders also asserted that they would refuse to participate in any government coalition unless Bucharest established a distinct ministry for nationality affairs.

Even though the position of minorities in Romania has substantially improved since December 1989, many of the gains were considered reversible because they lacked firm legal safeguards. DAHR leaders also expressed concern over some provisions of Romania's draft constitution that could actually restrict minority rights. These included the definition of the country as a "unitary national state," the outlawing of activities falling under the flexible rubric of "separatism," plans to make Romanian the exclusive official language, and a possible ban on ethnic-based parties. As post-Soviet Moldova has moved toward independence and established closer links with Romania, Hungarian organizations in Transylvania have also formed contacts with the Csango Association (CA)—created in August 1991 to represent the Hungarian population (Csangos) in the Moldovan republic and to campaign for their educational and cultural rights.[6]

After Hungary's multi-party elections in March 1990, the new government in Budapest became more active in speaking up for the Magyars in Transylvania. The election victors, the Hungarian Democratic Forum (HDF), had been at the forefront of campaigns for Magyar rights abroad since the party's inception in 1987. As ethnic relations in Transylvania deteriorated during the spring of 1990, the Budapest authorities complained that the Romanian government did not adopt a strong enough stance opposing extremist propaganda, agitation, and violence against Magyar communities.[7] They wanted the Romanian regime to more actively combat anti-Hungarian radicalism and to disarm or outlaw groups that stirred up racist passions. Virtually all political parties in Hungary have urged Budapest to press for minority rights in Romania and to sign agreements on the mutual protection of minorities similar to the accords codified between some west European countries.

Hungarian government officials have maintained that any substantive improvements in Romanian-Hungarian relations hinge on the restoration of full nationality rights to the Magyar minority. Many believe that Romania will not have a functioning democracy as long as its minorities continue to suffer from discrimination and inter-communal relations remain conflictive. Frequent complaints were heard that after a promising start, Hungarian aspirations have been neglected or stifled. Budapest wanted the Romanian authorities to declare the country a multi-national state and to enshrine collective minority rights in the new Romanian constitution.

Budapest has put forward numerous proposals during the past three years to help its co-nationals in Transylvania. These have included: opening consulates in cities with large Hungarian communities, such as Timisoara, Cluj, and Brasov; introducing the Hungarian language alongside Romanian in regions with sizable minorities; promoting tourism, family contacts, and opening new border crossings; building Hungarian cultural centers; increasing Hungarian television broadcasts; creating bilateral commissions to examine school books and historical texts in order to eliminate gross distortions; reopening Magyar educational facilities closed down by Ceausescu; and changing the names of towns and villages to their pre-Communist appellations.

The declared long-term aim of Hungarian organizations is a guarantee of "autonomous self-administrative rights" for eastern Europe's largest minority. But there have been no evident intentions of forcing border changes or reclaiming any Transylvanian territories. Some Hungarian political leaders support the reinstatement of an autonomous Hungarian region in Transylvania, although enlarged in comparison to the post-war territory, in order to include most of the current Magyar inhabited areas. Others have suggested more extensive administrative decentralization in minority areas, in which bilingualism would prevail in official dealings and where local self-government would become more meaningful. DAHR leaders have, in fact, opposed "territorial autonomy," in contrast to cultural and local autonomy, because many Hungarian communities in mixed population areas would be left outside the "autonomous regions" where they would be unable to benefit from their "collective rights." Romanian spokesmen of various political orientations have strongly objected to any notion of Transylvanian autonomy, pointing out that despite the substantial Hungarian presence, ethnic Romanians outnumber them in the region by roughly three to one.

The Romanian government has publicly objected to statements by high-ranking Hungarian officials implying that Romania's integration into Europe is dependent on its protection of minorities.[8] Bucharest considers such comments as a deliberate and unacceptable interference in its internal affairs. On at least one occasion, Romania's Foreign Minister Adrian Nastase accused Budapest of territorial revisionism and of stirring up anti-Romanian feelings among the Magyar population.[9] Bucharest has not openly condemned the current Hungarian administration, although it periodically criticizes some of its statements and policies. However, government spokesmen contend that Budapest could, in the future, become more nationalistic and anti-Romanian. They have also charged that Hungarian émigrés in the West remain at the forefront of the anti-Romanian campaign and have established contacts with ultra-nationalist forces in Hungary, including the Hungarian Holy Crown Association (HHCA), that, in turn, channel aid to Magyar radicals in Transylvania.

The authorities in Budapest complained that Romania was not fully committed to protecting its minorities, despite the fact that far-reaching concessions in educational and cultural affairs have been granted. They remained dissatisfied with delays in opening up Hungarian consulates and in re-establishing a Hungarian university in Cluj. In August 1990, the new Hungarian Foreign Minister, Geza Jeszensky, accused Bucharest of assimilationist pressures and even of weighing the possibility of expelling large numbers of Magyars to Hungary.[10] This was depicted as evidence of Romanian paranoia over the Transylvanian issue. Hungary has opposed any mass movement of refugees from the region because it would place an enormous strain on Hungarian resources and denude Transylvania of indigenous Magyar communities. Although by the close of 1990, Hungary only reported some 50,000 refugees from Romania, apprehensions grew that the trickle could turn into a flood if economic conditions continued to decline, if the political system remained unstable, and if ethnic conflicts escalated in Transylvania.

To resolve the minority problem, some Hungarian politicians have pushed for protective agreements with Bucharest. This has been envisaged in the framework of a series of bilateral concords between east European states containing large minorities. But, despite some high level discussions, by early 1992 no concrete agreements were reached. Budapest's proposal for an inter-governmental national minority committee was opposed by Bucharest, while the creation of a bilateral Hungarian-Romanian national minority charter was rejected outright. Romanian officials continued to treat the minority issue as an exclusively internal affair. They underscored that the country was an uni-national state containing some ethnic minorities and not a multi-national state, such as Yugoslavia or Czechoslovakia, with administrative provisions for a balance of power between distinct nationalities. The idea of turning Romania into a federation has been vehemently opposed by all political parties and was depicted as part of a Hungarian revisionist campaign designed to truncate Romanian territory.[11]

Relations between Romanian and Hungarian communities in Transylvania have not been beset by constant hostility and incessant conflicts. Nevertheless, the likelihood of communal frictions and violent provocations increased shortly after the revolution in December 1989. The activities of newly formed extremist groups served to aggravate ethnic tensions amidst mounting political turmoil and economic uncertainty in the country. In fact, much of the racist hostility in Romania and elsewhere in eastern Europe has been directed against the substantial Gypsy or Rom population. However, because the Roms neither have a history of state formation nor a separate territory or government to act as a magnet and source of protection, they are unlikely to figure prominently in future international or inter-state conflicts.

Romanian ultra-nationalists have established several political and cultural organizations during the past three years. Although they avowedly promote the national interests and socio-economic development of all Romanian citizens, some are also visibly and actively anti-Hungarian.[12] The nationalist *Romania Mare* group has issued vitriolic, anti-Magyar polemics in its widely circulated weekly publication. In August 1991, *Romania Mare* announced a one month suspension of its publication in protest against a government warning that its writings could be banned because of their provocative racist and chauvinistic attacks on minority groups. In May 1991, the group announced plans to establish its own political organization, the Greater Romania Party (GRP), with a distinct anti-minority platform. The GRP held its first nationwide conference in October 1991 claiming a membership of some 100,000 and elected Corneliu Vadim Tudor, a former pro-Ceausescu journalist, as the party's president.[13] It proposed the creation of a National Committee for the Investigation of Anti-Romanian activities to "punish all acts of national treason, destabilization, and sabotage committed by Romanian or foreign citizens." The GRP also called for the imposition of a military government to "overcome the crisis" in Romania and to ensure the country's territorial integrity which was purportedly in peril.

The largest nationalist front in Romania is *Vatra Romaneasca,* (Romanian Cradle), which together with its radical political wing, the Romanian National Unity Party (RNUP), has organized a number of anti-Hungarian manifestations. *Vatra* has claimed several million members, although this assertion proved impossible to verify and was probably exaggerated. It stood in the general elections of May 1990 as a social and cultural movement and not as a political party. Although it only received 2.1% of the vote, gaining nine parliamentary deputies for the Chamber of Deputies and two for the Senate, it performed reasonably well in Transylvania's Cluj and Mures counties inhabited by large Hungarian populations. Leaders of *Vatra* have opposed granting what they perceive as "national privileges" to the Magyar minority, including any Hungarian language classes that were restored to some schools in Transylvania during 1990. They have complained about alleged Hungarian demands for "cultural separatism" and "cultural autonomy." This would purportedly culminate in pressures for political autonomy, secession, and the forced expulsion of Romanians from Transylvania.

Extremist nationalist leaders have preyed on popular fears among Transylvanian Romanians, that Magyar aspirations will weaken their own economic position, undermine their control over local government, and threaten their educational system. Marketization and economic reform have also been depicted as an essentially Hungarian plot, in which Romanians will lose their jobs and Magyars will gain control over the local economy and apply discriminatory measures.[14] Such charges carry some resonance among the thousands of Romanians who were resettled in Transylvania during the Ceausescu years. Many appear to harbor latent anti-Hungarian sentiments based on trepidations over potential economic competition and growing unemployment. *Vatra* has clearly sought to exploit these popular fears. In order to counter any increase in Hungarian political and economic influence, *Vatra* opposed granting proportional representation to DAHR and other ethnic-based parties in the Romanian legislature. Furthermore, it supported a ban on all national minorities from forming their own political parties and attempted to incorporate such provisions in the new Romanian constitution.

Numerous accusations have been levelled against the Magyar minority in an attempt to fan public hostility. These included charges that Hungarian revolutionaries were actually responsible for imposing Communism in Romania and were now seeking to tear Transylvania away from the country. According to *Vatra* reports, Romanians are being forced to leave various Transylvanian counties so that Magyars can achieve majority status prior to territorial annexation. *Vatra* has also attacked Budapest for stirring up anti-Romanian sympathies and for allegedly sanctioning communal conflicts. These, in turn, purportedly provide Hungary with a pretext for military intervention in order to protect its co-ethnics. Romanian nationalists also asserted that the 25,000 strong Romanian minority in Hungary was subjected to "national deprivation" and threatened by physical assaults.[15] In fact, Budapest's policies toward its smallest national minority have been relatively benign. After the March 1990 elections, Budapest established an Office for National and Ethnic Minorities to maintain contacts with and to draft laws to protect the country's national minorities. Romanian Hungarians have also established new independent organizations to campaign for equitable political representation, wider cultural liberties, and contacts with Romania. Leaders of the Federation of Romanians in Hungary (FRH) calculate that the number of Romanians in the country may be underestimated as they have feared disclosing their identity in the past.

In *Vatra* estimations, coordinated actions have been planned between the Budapest regime and Hungarian leaders in Transylvania, in order to destabilize the country. DAHR is depicted as a revisionist organization with a secret agenda to divide Romania, while the Hungarian army is apparently being bolstered in preparation for possible intervention.[16] *Vatra* leaders have also claimed that the Transylvanian Hungarians (or Szeklers) are, in reality, Magyarized Romanians who were pressurized to adopt Magyar identity during the Hungarian occupation. In November 1990, an organization was established with links to *Vatra* whose purpose was to help restore Romanian family names among "Magyarized Romanians" believed to number about one million.[17] Such proposals were viewed by Hungarian leaders as a despicable provocation.

Vatra has evidently been tolerated if not supported by factions within the ruling National Salvation Front. High level links were believed to exist between the two organizations as Bucharest found it advantageous to periodically play the nationalist card. *Vatra* also enabled the Front to have access to a potentially very substantial voting constituency in Transylvania. Hungarian groups suspected that much of the Ceausescu old guard and former *Securitate* members continued to be active in *Vatra* and other similar nationalist associations. *Vatra* has also reportedly conducted a recruitment drive among military personnel, especially non-commissioned officers and soldiers, and has established branches in some army and Interior Ministry militia units. By posing as a social-cultural organization rather than a political party, *Vatra* can claim that it is not conducting political activities in the country's armed forces—something that has been formally barred since the ouster of Ceausescu.[18] The ultra-nationalist groups appeared to increase their support during the local elections in February 1992, gaining over 10% of the vote and scoring well in some areas of Transylvania. In some constituencies, the NSF formed electoral alliances with nationalist parties obviously seeking to capitalize on populist and nationalist sentiments.

Hungarian leaders have warned about rising anti-Magyar sentiments in Transylvania coupled with a sense of disappointment and frustration among the minority population. Tensions and cleavages have, in some instances, resulted in violence. The most dramatic incident took place in Tirgu Mures and Satu Mare in Transylvania in March 1990, during which eight people died and 300 were injured in inter-communal clashes. Attacks have also been staged periodically on DAHR offices in various parts of the country. After the March incidents, both sides claimed that rival political groups had provoked the violence with the assistance of outsiders. Although the clashes were criticized by Bucharest, Hungarian spokesmen felt that too little was done by the Romanian authorities to investigate the incidents and to bring the culprits to justice. Bucharest, in turn, accused the Magyars of bearing much of the responsibility for inciting ethnic tensions in Transylvania.

A major controversy erupted in the fall of 1991, after delegates of a local branch of the DAHR, styled as the Szeklerland Political Group, proposed holding a referendum in Transylvania's Covasna and Harghita counties regarding Szekler territorial autonomy. DAHR leaders quickly dissociated themselves from this local initiative and asserted that no Szeklerland political groupings existed within the Alliance.[19] But the DAHR statements were deemed unsatisfactory by the NSF and by nationalist parliamentarians who wanted the Hungarian leadership to openly condemn the Transylvanian initiative. DAHR National Chairman Geza Domokos suggested that the entire incident was a provocation designed to alarm Romanian society, mobilize the public against the Hungarian minority, and increase support for ultra-nationalist organizations.[20]

Future economic decline, fueled by an economic reform program that frees prices and cuts state subsidies to industry and consumers, could provoke wider social unrest in Romania, as witnessed in the second miners' rampage through Bucharest in September 1991. It could also lead to a breakdown of law and order and increase ethnic polarization in Transylvania. Communal tensions could be further exploited by radical nationalist organizations trying to garner popular support, as well as by a government seeking to deflect public anger from its own shortcomings and toward the perennial Hungarian scapegoat. Worsening economic conditions provide fertile ground for extremism among Romanians and Hungarians alike. The ultra-nationalists seek to polarize political life along ethnic lines, to marginalize the democratic opposition, and to scapegoat all Hungarian leaders as separatists. Such provocations could be used to justify a government crackdown, to slow down the reform process, and even to impose a new populist authoritarianism.

Any major increase in official repression or sustained nationalist attacks against Magyar organizations or communities, would almost certainly embroil the government in Budapest. Although the chances of direct Hungarian intervention in Transylvania currently appear to be slim, the authorities would undoubtedly become more active on the international arena to try and impose sanctions on Romania and isolate Bucharest in order to achieve significant policy changes.

If armed clashes in Transylvania mushroomed and the Romanian authorities seemed unable or unwilling to effectively intercede, a radicalization among Hungarian political organizations can be expected. Some Magyar groups may even seek to arm themselves for defensive purposes, possibly with direct Hungarian assistance. A scenario of escalating conflict could then unfold by way of military crackdowns,terrorist attacks, economic sabotage, and other armed actions. If the conflict continued to escalate, Hungary could become more directly embroiled. For example, Hungarian territories may be used as base and supply areas by Magyar rebels, while the Romanian armed forces became engaged in hot-pursuit and scorched earth operations against Hungarian guerrillas. In such a situation, public opinion in Hungary would probably demand government intervention and a local conflict could rapidly degenerate into a serious, inter-state confrontation.

Such worst-case scenarios may have already been considered in both capitals. Even before the fall of Ceausescu, Budapest defined Romania as its greatest security threat and transferred troops from its south eastern regions to the Romanian border.[21] In August 1990, the commander of the Romanian army in Transylvania issued a declaration of loyalty to Bucharest, underscoring his determination to defend all Romanian territory from both external and internal threats.[22] In March 1990, Hungary's Defense

Minister, Ferenc Karpati, claimed that in addition to extremist nationalist groups, members of the Romanian army's officer corps were also inspired by anti-Hungarian chauvinism and deliberately ignored or covertly supported attacks on Magyar communities in Transylvania.[23] The commitment of sectors of Romania's armed forces and security services to democracy, pluralism, and human rights cannot be taken for granted, especially if there is an extensive breakdown in law and order in the country. In October 1991, the Romanian Defense Minister, General Nicolae Spiraiu, declared that the army would be prepared to intervene to subdue social unrest if other institutions could not fulfill their responsibilities.[24] Relations between civilian and military authorities will therefore need to be carefully watched, as well as the army's role vis-à-vis inter-ethnic relations in Transylvania. The military itself is heavily Romanian and this has spurred resentment among Magyars fearful of a major crackdown. Conversely, Romanian spokesmen remain suspicious about Budapest's long-term objectives and the stance of the Hungarian armed forces. For instance, Budapest's arms sales to Croatia in late 1990, raised anxieties in Romania and led to accusations that Hungary could, in future, supply weapons to Hungarian secessionists in Transylvania.

Bulgaria and Romania

Throughout most of the 19th century, Bucharest remained on reasonably cordial terms with Bulgaria, from where many exiles fled Turkish rule and took refuge in Romania. After Romania achieved its independence in the 1870s, Bucharest sought to enlarge its southern coastal possessions bordering on Bulgaria in the Dobrudja region. This ethnically mixed area became the main point of contention between the newly independent neighbors. During the Second Balkan War in 1913, Romanian forces invaded the area and annexed a substantial portion of the territory. After World War One, Bucharest was able to enlarge its share of the coastal territories at the expense of Bulgaria, which had allied itself with the defeated Central Powers. Under the Neuilly peace treaty of 1919, the agriculturally productive southern Dobrudja region was awarded to Romania.

During World War Two, Bulgaria again allied itself with Germany. In 1940, under Nazi pressure, the Romanians surrendered southern Dobrudja and a few smaller border zones to Bulgaria. Southern Dobrudja was retained by Sofia at the close of World War Two, but it did not become a major source of conflict between the two states. Both Communist governments, evidently under some pressure from Moscow, accepted the border as legitimate. On the Bulgarian side, the issue of Romanian-held northern Dobrudja, has periodically been aired but no serious territorial claims were pursued by the Marxist-Leninist regime.

In the post-Communist era, relations between Sofia and Bucharest have remained fairly steady. With few pressing border or minority questions to be settled, the main discordant notes have been economic. The controversy has centered on cross-border environmental pollution along the Danube river frontier region. Both sides have blamed each other for the unregulated pollution and subsequent ecological damage and a workable resolution has still to be found between the two capitals. The environmental conflict may also be symptomatic of more deeply rooted hostilities between the two states that could again, come to the fore as political tensions increase throughout the Balkans.

Environmental disputes between Bucharest and Sofia have focused on the city of Ruse, situated on the Bulgarian side of the border. The Bulgarian authorities have claimed that the town is heavily polluted by chlorine gas emissions from the Giurgiu Chemical Combine on the Romanian side of the Danube frontier. The pollution has sparked protests in Ruse and led to the creation of an environmental protection group. Periodic demonstrations and sit-ins have also occasionally blocked the bridge border across the Danube. Throughout 1990, the Bulgarian authorities called for the closure of the Giurgiu plant, and periodic public protests were held against Bucharest's failure to shut down the chemical works. In August 1990, the Bulgarian Health Minister reported 70 confirmed cholera cases among people who had drunk Danube river water and he blamed Romania for the pollution. Sofia temporarily banned travel to Romania, ostensibly for fear of cholera spreading throughout the country. In October 1990, following several demonstrations against Romanian pollution and apparent Bulgarian government inaction, a mass meeting of citizens announced that the Ruse population would leave the city and seek "ecological asylum" in another country. Several hundred Ruse residents subsequently did seek asylum in Greece.

The Romanian regime claimed that their neighbors had exaggerated the pollution threat and that most of the poisonous emissions did not emanate from Romanian territory but from industrial plants in Ruse itself. Bucharest asserted that the Bulgarian administration refused to accept the results of previous commission inspections that reportedly concluded that the pollution did not originate in Romania. As a result, demands to close the Giurgiu chemical works were considered unjustified.

To counter Bulgarian attacks in this cross-border environmental contest, Bucharest complained about the potential danger to its citizens from the Kozloduy nuclear power plant near the Romanian border, a plant which is similar in design to the notorious Chernobyl reactor in northern Ukraine.[25] Sofia admitted to the danger but tried to minimize its potential impact. The nuclear power issue proved to be the major obstacle to holding an environmental convention between the two states. However, in early 1991 the ecological dispute somewhat subsided. High-level talks were held to frame some collaborative efforts in environmental protection along the Danubian border area and on the Black Sea coast. Meanwhile, several further disputes loomed ahead with regard to the delineation of the sea shelf between the two countries and over guarantees for the non-pollution of territorial waters during future oil prospecting operations by both states.

A joint commission was created to settle the Ruse problem and the dispute was submitted to an international team of experts for resolution. However, the environmental dispute heated up again in September 1991, when Sofia cancelled a scheduled visit by Romanian President Iliescu and postponed the signing of a new cooperation treaty, evidently in protest against Romania's failure to stop emissions of chlorine gas polluting Ruse. According to Bulgarian estimates, concentrations of chlorine in Ruse had reached 2.7 times the maximum safety levels, while Romania continued to reject the charges that it sanctioned harmful emissions from its chemical combine.[26] Bulgaria considered recalling its ambassador to Bucharest in order to underscore the seriousness of the incident. The dispute was pacified somewhat over the following months and in December 1991, the Environmental Ministers from both states signed a long-delayed environmental agreement.

As elsewhere in the region, there is a latent danger that domestic social unrest and serious political instability in either Romania or Bulgaria will have a negative impact on bilateral relations. Nationalist groups in either state as well as government leaders seeking a foreign policy cause to gain public credibility, could restoke some historical animosities and revive claims over the once disputed Dobrudja area. In June 1991, the Bulgarian Foreign Ministry asserted that the government was gravely concerned over statements by Romanian Foreign Minister, Adrian Nastase, that Bucharest lost southern Dobrudja to Bulgaria as a result of the "illegal" Ribbentrop-Molotov pact. A speech by President Iliescu on Romania's National Day in December 1991, declared that the frontiers of "Greater Romania" traditionally included southern Dobrudja, while the country's borders were unjustly reshaped during World War Two.[27] Such remarks were interpreted as attempts to violate Bulgaria's territorial integrity and state sovereignty. To counter Romanian insinuations, some Bulgarian politicians underscored the presence of large numbers of ethnic Bulgarians in northern Dobrudja.[28] Despite these verbal controversies, by the close of 1991, the likelihood of a major conflict over Dobrudja appeared slight, especially as both states were embroiled in much more pressing minority and political problems with other neighbors.

Bulgaria, Turkey, and Greece

The Bulgarian state was weak and fragmented when the Turks overran the country at the end of the 14th century and initiated nearly 500 years of

Ottoman rule. Periodic Bulgarian revolts were brutally suppressed and large-scale massacres of Bulgarian peasants in the 19th century created a great deal of sympathy for the country throughout Europe. As Russian imperial interests expanded into the Balkans, Tsarist forces came to the aid of Bulgaria and dictated the terms of the Treaty of San Stefano in 1878, which created an independent Bulgarian state. The Congress of Berlin reversed many of the San Stefano decisions because of European fears over growing Russian influence in the Balkans. Bulgaria had to surrender several newly gained territories, including eastern Rumelia (the Thrace coast), which became an autonomous region of the Ottoman empire. Bulgaria, itself, was made into a semi-autonomous Ottoman principality. These border adjustments were bitterly resented by Bulgaria which proclaimed its full independence from the Turks in 1908, after several more popular uprisings.

Bulgaria's territorial losses led to two major Balkan wars in 1912-1913, and set the stage for major border disputes and irredentist demands. In the first Balkan War, Bulgaria, Romania, Serbia, and Greece combined their forces to drive the Turks out of most of the Balkans. Bulgaria's unsuccessful campaign against Serbia and Greece in the Second Balkan War resulted in the loss of Thrace, the eastern portion of which was returned to Turkey and the western part to Greece, as well as Macedonia, which was divided between Greece and Serbia. These measures left a lasting sense of injustice in Bulgaria with regard to its rightful frontiers. During World War One, Sofia allied with the Central Powers to regain its lost territories but with the defeat of Germany and Austria, it was again forced to accept a harsh peace treaty. Turkey retained Erdine Thrace, while Bulgaria lost all access to the Aegean with western Thrace reverting to Greece. During World War Two, Sofia capitalized on the German-Italian conquest of Greece by occupying parts of the Thracean coast and several nearby islands, but its territorial advances were once again reversed at the close of the war.

Under the Communist regime, Bulgaria formally renounced its claims to Greek Macedonia and did not press any claims for Greek or Turkish Thrace. The major point of conflict with Ankara revolved around the large Muslim Turkish minority in Bulgaria, which has been subjected to assimilationist pressures.[29] Soon after the Communist takeover, all national privileges in education and culture were abolished and about 150,000 Turks were pressured to leave the country; these were primarily the least assimilable and the most devout Muslims. Even though Bulgarian Turks have not campaigned for autonomy or aspired for close links with Turkey, periodic assaults were mounted by the authorities to eradicate their distinct identity. The 1984-1986 "rebirth" campaign, under Zhivkov's direction, was officially justified as a means of enlarging the Bulgarian population that was allegedly threatened by an excessive Turkish demographic growth. The government forced the Turks to Bulgarize their names and desist from numerous Islamic religious rituals and cultural traditions, while pressuring several thousand people to emigrate. The campaign provoked rioting and armed clashes and several dozen Turks were reportedly shot dead by the Bulgarian police. About 310,000 Turks left the country by 1989; after the democratic changes in Bulgaria, nearly half of that number returned. The confrontations greatly aggravated tensions between Sofia and Ankara in the closing years of Communist rule. The Bulgarian regime accused Ankara of pan-Turkic designs on Bulgarian territory, while Turkey charged Sofia with cultural genocide.

Bulgaria's relations with Turkey improved substantially after the ouster of Communist leader, Todor Zhivkov, in November 1989. Since early 1990, Bulgaria's human rights violations have eased and most Turkish minority rights have been restored. But the position of the Muslim population will remain the barometer of evolving relations between Sofia and Ankara. Turkish authorities are carefully monitoring the degree of political and economic stability in the country, as well as the activities of Bulgarian nationalist groups and their impact on the Turkish community. The Bulgarian side remains concerned about the potential growth of Turkish nationalism and Islamic fundamentalism among its minority groups, and of autonomist and separatist trends supported by organizations in Turkey. It is, therefore, likely to place some restrictions on the Turkish reawakening in Bulgaria, mindful of its deleterious effects on inter-ethnic relations. It also remains watchful about any exploitation of the minority issue by extremist nationalist Bulgarian associations.

According to Bulgarian statistics, about 750,000 Turks live in compact communities in north eastern and south eastern Bulgaria. Turkish sources usually double this figure, claiming that Turks constitute well over 10% of the country's nine million population. A further 300,000 Pomak Muslims also live in Bulgaria. These are ethnic Bulgarians who converted to Islam under Ottoman rule, and were also subjected to integrationist pressures under the Communist regime, together with Muslim Gypsies and ethnic Turks. After the November 1989 democratic turnaround in Bulgaria, relations between Sofia and Ankara markedly improved, as did the treatment of Bulgaria's Turkish minority. All repressive campaigns were halted; Turks were allowed to restore their original names and religious practices, to open all their mosques, and to legally establish their own social and cultural organizations. Nonetheless, Bulgaria continued to define itself as a uni-national state and the position of the Turkish minority, recognized primarily as a religious, cultural, and linguistic grouping rather than a distinct nationality, remained at the heart of relations between Bulgaria and Turkey.

In February 1990, Turkish activists established the Movement for Rights and Freedoms (MRF) which was promptly legalized. Prior to this, some members of the group operated illegally under the name of the National Turkish Liberation Movement and organized anti-government protests before

Zhivkov's ouster. The MRF initiated campaigns for educational, religious, and linguistic rights, and pressed for the political representation of all minority groups. By early 1991, MRF leader Ahmed Dogan claimed a membership of some 120,000, together with more than one million sympathizers. This made the MRF the fourth largest political organization in the country. The MRF won 23 seats in the Bulgarian parliament during the June 1990 elections and finished third in the ballot. However, it could not contest the elections as a distinct political organization representing the Turkish community. The Socialist regime had arrived at an agreement with the main oppositionist group, the Union of Democratic Forces (UDF), that parties organized along ethnic or religious lines would not be registered.

To avoid accusations of being an exclusively Muslim-Turkish party, the MRF decided to open the organization to all ethnic, religious, and cultural groups while renouncing any autonomist or separatist ambitions. Even so, over 90% of the MRF's membership were ethnic Turks. In August 1991, the MRF announced that it was establishing a separate political party—the Rights and Freedoms Party (RFP) to stand in the upcoming national elections. But, the Sofia city court refused to register the organization on the grounds that according to the country's constitution, parties cannot be formed on the basis of ethnicity or religious conviction as this would threaten the "unity of the nation."[30] However, the MRF was allowed to register as a multi-ethnic movement despite the protests of Bulgarian nationalists. The MRF won 7% of the vote in the 1991 elections and gained 24 seats to the National Assembly, as well as several mayorships in predominantly Turkish towns and villages. Its future role in the Bulgarian parliament generated serious consternations among nationalist groups.

The success of the MRF spurred suspicions among some Bulgarian nationalists that Turkish self-organization was aided and abetted by Ankara with the aim of undercutting Bulgaria's territorial integrity. The campaign for restoring Turkish cultural and religious identity was viewed by radicals as the first step toward political autonomy and territorial secession, and that Turkish annexation would be accompanied by the expulsion of Bulgarian Christians from Turkish regions. It was purportedly fanned by Islamic religious fundamentalism and expansionist pan-Turkism. Additional allegations have been made by nationalists that the influx of Turkish capital into minority areas will result in major economic disparities between Christians and Muslims and fan Bulgarian resentment and ethnic conflict. Some Bulgarian nationalists also feared that the religious resurgence among the Pomaks would lead to closer Turkish-Pomak links in a common front against Bulgaria's Christians.

In the early stages of Bulgarian democratization, the ruling Communists-Socialists capitalized on commonplace anti-Turkish feelings in an attempt to gain broad popular support. Party officials, in provincial cities and rural areas, sought to tap on nationalist feelings. They were fearful of losing their jobs, of having to return property seized during the Turkish exodus, and of being held responsible for the sometimes brutal anti-Turkish campaign during the early 1980s. They also manipulated latent anti-Turkish sentiments among Slav Bulgarians in Turkish inhabited areas who were descendants of refugees who fled Turkish and Greek Thrace during the Balkan wars. Several demonstrations were organized around the country in January 1990, to protest the introduction of new legislation enabling Turks to restore their former names. These protests fanned ethnic tensions, deflected attention from the continuing *nomenklatura* grip over rural residents and increased feelings of insecurity among the Turkish minority.[31]

Since early 1990, various Bulgarian ultra-nationalist organizations have been formed and attempted to stir racial conflicts in order to restrict the newly acquired rights of the Turkish minority. Among them were the Bulgarian National Radical Party (BNRP) and the Fatherland Labor Party (FLP), the political arm of the Committee for the Defense of National Interests (CDNI). They claimed a combined membership of over 40,000 people and established branches in regions heavily populated by Turks. Delegates at the first congress of the FLP in April 1991, prided themselves on being described as "anti-Turkish" and "anti-Islamic." Suspicions have been raised that the FLP, the CDNI, and other radical nationalist associations have been created or financed by local Socialist activists, while their leaders are implicated in assaults on Turkish spokesmen. An indication of the close ties between Socialists and nationalists was the forging of a "pre-election union" in October 1991, between the Socialist Party and five nationalist parties, including the FLP, in the run up to the national ballot. Although the BNRP, the FLP, and other nationalist groups obtained less than 1.5% of the vote, they claimed to possess an extensive infrastructure and substantial local sympathy in mixed population areas.[32]

Ultra-nationalists have deliberately stirred anxieties among Bulgarians in areas with a large Turkish presence, claiming that a turkification campaign was underway that would deprive Bulgarians of their rights and eventually dispossess their lands. Radical nationalists also asserted that the MRF was a secessionist movement with terrorist connections that should be declared illegal and banned from parliament. The MRF's human rights agenda was viewed as a clever disguise and simply as the thin end of a wedge for Turkish expansion and domination.

Bulgarian nationalist forces have also tried to benefit from difficult economic conditions and continuing political uncertainty in the country. In November 1990, as the Socialist government faced massive social unrest and mounting political opposition, nationalist groups in the north eastern Razgrad area, inhabited by large numbers of Turks, declared an independent Bulgarian republic. They refused to recognize Sofia's authority in the region because the government had purportedly displayed too much leniency toward the Turks. Protests were staged against the restoration of Turkish family names and nationalist leaders called for acts of civil disobedience to counter alleged Turkish radicalism. The CDNI and other groups opposed giving Turks the status of a national minority because this would have supposedly threatened Bulgaria's integrity. In late November, the "Razgrad republic" was renamed as the Association of Free Bulgarian Cities, linking several towns containing large Turkish minorities. A civil parliament was to be formed to counterbalance the National Assembly, which the CDNI accused of favoring the Turkish minority and betraying Bulgaria's national interests. In recognition of mounting tensions fuelled by the nationalist initiative, Bulgaria's President, Zhelyu Zhelev, appeared on national television to appeal for calm.

The "Free City" campaign subsided during the following weeks, but in February 1991 several nationalist groups created the Bulgarian National Union (BNU) and refocused their attention on the language issue. The BNU specifically opposed the introduction of optional classes in Turkish to schools attended by large numbers of Muslims. The program was depicted as an ominous turkification of Bulgarian education. For the next few weeks, various protest actions were staged, including boycotts, hunger strikes, and blockades of schools in a dozen Bulgarian cities. The wave of protests subsided when the National Assembly decided to postpone the introduction of Turkish as an optional subject during the 1991 school year. The move was condemned by the MRF as unconstitutional and the group asserted that it would organize Turkish classes outside the state school system and conduct protest meetings throughout the country.

The language controversy has clearly played into the hands of nationalists, who seek to keep the Turkish issue on the agenda while underscoring Bulgarian grievances against minority demands. The beginning of the school year in September 1991 was marred by boycotts in some Turkish areas, in protest against government failures to meet demands for Turkish language instruction proposed by the MRF. In October 1991, the National Assembly passed laws prohibiting the teaching of minority languages in state schools. This essentially anti-Turkish legislation was proposed by nationalist deputies and drew overwhelming support from the Socialist parliamentary majority. In November 1991, the new Bulgarian government decreed that ethnic minority pupils in municipal schools could receive instructions in their native languages as an optional subject for a few hours a week. The Socialist Party attacked the decree because it countered the earlier decision that prohibited the teaching of Turkish in Bulgarian schools.

The UDF coalition, which won the general elections in October 1991, has condemned the previous Communist policy of forced assimilation while supporting Turkish demands for civic equality and full cultural rights. On occasion, it has cooperated with the MRF in parliament, particularly in opposition to the Socialists. Nonetheless, even some Bulgarian democrats and moderates have voiced apprehensions about the rise of Turkish aspirations and the potential for intensified ethnic hostilities. Much of the criticism, on all sides of the political spectrum, has focused on the high Turkish birth rate. There is a widely held perception that ethnic Bulgarians could become a minority in the country within the next two generations, especially given their current negative growth rate.

The authorities in Ankara remain displeased over official Bulgarian statements that there are no ethnic minorities in the country, as happened during the February 1991 visit of Prime Minister, Dimitur Popov, to Athens. In Turkish estimations, such a position could hinder the gradual improvement of Bulgarian-Turkish relations and the development of valuable economic links. At the inter-state level, fears persist among various political groups in Bulgaria that Ankara may play up the minority issue to its advantage. For example, some contend that Turkey could deliberately exaggerate the size of the Turkish community and claim severe official discrimination as a pretext to apply pressure on Sofia and actively interfere in the country's internal affairs. To guard against any separatist tendencies, the Bulgarian government has denounced any possibility of border revisions and outlawed all activities that encourage territorial autonomy and separatism. Ankara, for its part, remains concerned that any deterioration in ethnic relations in Bulgaria could lead to a new exodus of Turkish refugees and this, in turn, could aggravate Turkey's precarious social and economic conditions.

Some Bulgarian politicians have also expressed misgivings about growing Turkish power in the Balkans. With the disintegration of the Warsaw Pact and the dissolution of the Soviet protective umbrella, Bulgarian officials have stressed the need to maintain a strong independent military posture. This has been justified by underlining the country's critical position between Europe and Asia, and as the front line Christian nation against an apparently resurgent Islamic threat.[33] Bulgarian commentators have complained about the size of the Turkish army in eastern Thrace, in comparison to Bulgaria's forces, and questioned the logic of providing modern weaponry to Ankara from the U.S. and NATO. They argued that this policy could destabilize the Balkans and even prove threatening to Bulgaria.[34]

The Bulgarian authorities have expressed reservations about Turkey's growth as a regional economic and military power and the threat that this could pose to Bulgaria's security. Bulgaria has, therefore, pursued closer relations with Greece to counterbalance growing Turkish influence in the region. However, the country must beware of being sucked into the long-simmering and often bitter Greek-Turkish conflict and of adopting potentially damaging anti-Turkish or anti-Greek positions. Indeed, international realignments throughout the Balkans will need to be carefully watched as proposals for closer Balkan integration may be debilitated by renewed inter-state rivalries for regional predominance.

Bulgarian-Greek relations have steadily developed during the past two years, reinforced by frequent high-level contacts between the two governments. But there are some fears in Greece that post-Communist instability in Bulgaria could endanger the "special relationship" between Athens and Sofia and even resuscitate the Aegean Macedonian issue. This danger was accentuated after Macedonia gained independence and Bulgarian Macedonian activism increased, amidst calls for Macedonian reunification under some kind of Bulgarian patronage. Any major alterations in bilateral inter-state relations would, of course, profoundly affect the balance of power throughout the region.

Continuing instability in the Balkans could also promote the formation of new regional alliances that pit Orthodox Christian states against Islamic countries and Muslim minorities. In fact, as far back as 1986, Bulgaria signed a protocol of friendship with Athens, committing both countries to assist each other in combatting internally generated or externally sponsored agitation among Turks, Muslims, and Macedonians in both states. However, the lingering Macedonian problem could damage Greek-Bulgarian relations in the near future. With the unravelling of Yugoslavia, the question of Macedonia's statehood and territorial dimensions will preoccupy all of the republic's neighbors. Several possible scenarios could materialize that closely involve both Bulgaria and Greece: a sovereign Macedonia could claim special links with the Aegean area; or Bulgaria may press for some form of protection or sovereignty over Vardar Macedonia. These developments could also envelop an anxious Greek government that would seek guarantees of security on its northern borders. This, in turn, could bring Athens into a more direct confrontation with Sofia.[35]

Albania and Greece

In the post-Ottoman era, tensions developed between Greece and its northern neighbor over the disputed territory of Epirus. Athens upheld a long-term goal of annexing the southern part of Albania which contained a substantial Greek minority. Conversely, toward the end of the 19th century and periodically during this century, Albania has also claimed for itself a part of Greek Epirus. During World War Two, the Axis powers almost doubled Albania's territory and population by assigning large parts of occupied Greece and Yugoslavia to Tirana under German-Italian supervision. These policies were reversed at the end of the war when Greece regained its former Epirean territories from Albania. The two states formally remained in a state of war until the 1987 agreement between Tirana and the Papandreou government.

Recent democratic developments in Albania have also helped to improve Tirana's relations with Greece. In early 1991, the relaxation of Communist state controls, coupled with unpredictable political developments, sparked an exodus of predominantly Greek refugees from southern Albania. Suspicions were also raised that Tirana deliberately encouraged or tolerated this outflow to decrease the size of the Greek minority and thereby limit demands for Greek self-determination in Albania. The refugee exodus soured contacts between Tirana and Athens, with the Greek side voicing protests over the treatment of its minority in Albania and opposing the depopulation of Greek minority areas. The minority issue is likely to figure prominently on any future inter-state agenda and it could even rekindle calls among some political groups for territorial revisions in the border areas. In the past two years, the Cameria Albanians, many of whom were expelled from Greece after World War Two, have also become more active and may increasingly pressurize Tirana to intervene on behalf of the Albanian minority in Greece.

The Epirus or Cameria area in southern Albania and northern Greece constitutes the main potential focus of dispute between Athens and Tirana. Both states have traditional claims to this region: the Greeks call the southern extremity of Albania northern Epirus, while the Albanians call the northwest corner of Greece southern Cameria. Although neither government has pressed for territorial revisions in recent memory, both regions are inhabited by minorities whose conditions and treatment have given rise to some concern and inter-state discord. Several thousand Albanians live in the mountains of Greek Epirus. Claims over their numbers currently range from 90,000 to over one million; the lower figure appears to be closer to reality. Their numbers are believed to be underestimated because Athens does not consider the local Albanians to be a separate ethnic group and has comprehensively hellenicized the majority of Albanians who are Orthodox Christians. They have not been entitled to any special minority rights and, thus far, do not seem to have established any educational, cultural, or political associations within Greece.

Since the democratic breakthrough in Albania in early 1991, the Albanian Cams have begun to organize as a pressure group within Albania on behalf of their co-ethnics in Greece. In March 1991, the first national conference of the Cameria Political Association (CPA) was held in Tirana, with many of its activists drawn from the Albanian community expelled from Greece after the war. The CPA intends to bring to international attention the neglected linguistic, cultural, and educational rights of Orthodox Albanian Cams who have been subjected to a policy of Greek assimilation. The group has also launched campaigns on behalf of Cam exiles in Albania. It encouraged the expansion of contacts with compatriots in Greece, the return of exiles to their family areas, and the payment of compensation for the property and land that was illegally taken from them during their expulsion. The CPA claimed to have several thousand members as well as the support of a broad cross-section of Albanian political life. However, some suspicions were initially voiced about the CPA's links with the former Labor Party. Indeed, some elements of several political parties could increasingly play the nationalist and revisionist card against Greece if Albania continues to be embroiled in political and economic turmoil.

During 1991, Albanian activists across the political spectrum have become more outspoken on the Cameria issue vis-à-vis Greece. Historical grievances have been aired over Greek repression of Orthodox and Muslim Albanians earlier this century and Athens has been criticized for its ongoing assimilationist pressures against Orthodox Albanians still resident in the Cameria/Epirus region. While the Greek authorities claim the Cam problem is non-existent, Cam spokesmen continue to urge the Albanian government to take up the issue with Athens at the highest bilateral levels.[36]

Southern Albania also contains a sizable Greek minority, ranging from 58,000 (according to Tirana) to over 400,000 (in some Greek estimations). About 100,000 people would probably assert Greek nationality, if a proper census were taken in the country, although Athens tends to claim people that are Christian Orthodox by religion as Greek by ethnicity. Under the Communist regime, Greeks were subjected to repressive campaigns to albanianize their names and adopt Albanian culture. With the onset of liberalization in Albania, a Greek-based political party, the Democratic Union of the Greek Minority (DUGM), or Omonia, was formed and registered. Omonia won five seats in the March 1991 general elections, amidst some accusations that it was a Labor Party front organization designed to subdue or dilute demands for minority rights and to divide the opposition movement. In fact, Omonia proved itself to be a genuine and legitimate political body and occasionally cooperated with the Democratic Party against the Socialists in the Albanian legislature. However, the future status of Omonia came under question when Albania's new law on political parties prohibited the formation of parties based on ethnic criteria.

Tirana's election law for the parliamentary elections of March 1992 precluded the participation of ethnic or regionally-based parties. This created a furor among Greek activists and led to strong protests by Athens. The controversy was partially eased when the Albanian authorities agreed to register the Unity Party for Human Rights (UPHR) and allowed it to stand in the general elections. Although the UPHR depicted itself as a multi-ethnic organization, it was principally based among the Greek community and succeeded in gaining two seats to the newly constituted National Assembly.

Athens has consistently voiced concerns about the position of the Greek minority and the deprivation of basic cultural liberties. Some extremist Greek political groups have even raised questions about the current border with Albania. Albanian activists suspect that they have been courted and supported by certain Greek politicians. According to Tirana, in September 1990, Greek Deputy Premier, Athenasios Kanellopoulos, demanded a reconsideration of the frontier and criticized the previous Papandreou government for its accomodationist policy and inadequate pursuit of Greek minority interests.[37] Albanian authorities have protested to Athens over speeches made by various Greek officials, claiming that the border was being questioned and that anti-Albanian propaganda had been intensified.[38] On some occasions Tirana has demanded that the Greek government dissociate itself from the "chauvinistic statements and attitudes" of certain political and clerical circles.

In the estimations of some Greek commentators, if unrest continues in Albania, one of the first targets could be the Greek minority.[39] This presents Athens with a difficult problem, regarding how best to protect co-nationals across the border. The loosening of human rights restrictions by Tirana in late 1990 and early 1991, sparked a flow of refugees to Greece. Over 10,000 reportedly fled across the border and the majority were ethnic Greeks. Athens promptly accused the Albanian regime of deliberately encouraging Greeks to leave in order to solve its minority problem and to defuse any potential claims to northern Epirus. The newly formed Albanian Democratic Party (ADP) opposed the exodus, partly on the grounds that many of the refugees would have voted against the Communists. Although Athens tried to discourage the depopulation of Greek areas, most of the refugees refused to return to Albania and remained skeptical over assurances that they would not suffer any recriminations. By early 1992, over 100,000 Albanian citizens had found refuge in Greece, with about half claiming to be ethnic Greek. The numbers could further swell if economic conditions in Albania remain dire.

The refugee crisis undermined Greek-Albanian relations for a while, and Tirana rejected Athenian proposals for a United Nations delegation to visit the minority areas and for Greece to establish a consulate in the region. It also repulsed Greek accusations about the mistreatment of minorities and began to raise serious questions about the condition of the Albanian minority in Greece. The visit of Greek Prime Minister, Constantine Mitsotakis, to Albania in January 1991 took some steam out of the dispute but did not resolve it altogether. In the early part of 1992, relations between the two countries were again strained over the reported mistreatment and expulsion of Albanian refugees from Greece and over restrictions on Greek political organizations in Albania. As the law and order situation in Albania deteriorated, there were attacks on Greek-owned stores in the southern town of Saranda, with suspicions that both Albanian and Greek radicals were deliberately stirring ethnic conflicts.

Any forthright moves by Greece to protect its minority in Albania could seriously jeopardize relations with Tirana, which continues to be beset by political and social instability amidst rapidly declining economic conditions. Escalating conflicts could also embroil other Balkan neighbors. For instance, any form of Greek intervention on behalf of co-ethnics in Albania could act as a precedent for Turkey to defend its minorities in Greek Thrace and elsewhere. If Athenian pressures on Albania were to increase, a closer Albanian-Turkish relationship could also develop, especially if Islam undergoes some resurgence in Albania where about 70% of the population are nominally Muslims. Such an alliance could, in turn, promote the formation of a closer Greek-Bulgarian front and further embroil the republics of Macedonia and Serbia in regional disputes.

Notes

1. For some background check Stefan Pascu, *A History of Transylvania* (New York: Dorset Press, 1982). See also George Schopflin, *The Hungarians in Romania* (London: Minority Rights Group, 1978).

2. For a history of Romania see Gerald Bobango, *The Emergence of the Romanian National State* (Boulder, Colorado: East European Quarterly, 1979).

3. For useful accounts of Ceausescu's repressive politics consult Helsinki Watch, *Violations of the Helsinki Accords: Romania* (New York: Helsinki Watch Report, November 1986).

4. Judith Pataki, "Ethnic Hungarians Contest Romanian Elections," Radio Free Europe, *Report on Eastern Europe,* Vol. 1, No. 22, 1 June 1990.

5. Edith Oltay, "The Hungarian Democratic Federation of Romania: Structure, Agenda, Alliances," Radio Free Europe, *Report on Eastern Europe,* Vol. 2, No. 29, 19 July 1991.

6. Aranka Rehak, "Csangos Speak Hungarian," *Nepszabadsag,* Budapest, 7 August 1991.

7. See the letter from the Hungarian Foreign Minister Gyula Horn to the Bucharest authorities published in *Nepszabadsag,* Budapest, 31 March 1990.

8. See the interview with Romania's Foreign Ministry State Secretary Romulus Neagu, on *Bucharest Domestic Service,* Bucharest, 26 July 1990, in *FBIS-EEU*-90-145, 27 July 1990.

9. From the "Press Communique" issued by the Romanian Foreign Ministry, *Bucharest Domestic Service,* Bucharest, 25 August 1990, in *FBIS-EEU*-90-166, 26 August 1990.

10. Contained in the interview with Geza Jeszensky in *Magyar Nemszet,* Budapest, 16 August 1990.

11. See the Romanian Foreign Minister's condemnation of Hungarian government statements in *Rompres,* Bucharest, 4 October 1990, in *FBIS-EEU*-90-194, 5 October 1990.

12. A useful analysis of Romanian ultra-nationalist ideology can be found in N. M. "Extremist Ideology and Political Gamble," *Romania Literara,* Bucharest, 15 August 1991.

13. See Michael Shafir, "The Greater Romanian Party," Radio Free Europe, *Report on Eastern Europe,* Vol. 2, No. 46, 15 November 1991.

14. For a valuable overview see Dennis Delefant, "The Role of *Vatra Romaneasca* in Transylvania," Radio Free Europe, *Report on Eastern Europe,* Vol. 2, No. 5, 1 February 1991.

15. See the "Appeal to the Country," issued by the National Conference of the *Vatra Romaneasca* Union, in *Dimineata,* Bucharest, 9 May 1990.

16. See Constantin Duica, "Are We Naive Again?" *Dimineata,* Bucharest, 21 July 1990.

17. See the interview with Senator Radu Ceontea, President of *Vatra,* in *Tineretul Liber,* Bucharest, 11 November 1990, *FBIS-EEU*-90-236, 7 December 1990.

18. See Constantin Vranceanu, "*Vatra Romaneasca's* Tentacled Grasp at the Army," *Romania Literara,* Bucharest, 6-7 July 1991.

19. For some details on the controversy see "Political Life: Towards Autonomy for the Szeklers Land?" *Rompres,* Bucharest, 11 October 1991, in *FBIS-EEU*-91-199, 15 October 1991; *Kossuth Radio Network,* Budapest, 10 October 1991, in *FBIS-EEU*-91-201, 17 October 1991.

20. See the statements by Domokos in *Romaniai Magyar Szo,* Bucharest, 10 October 1991, in *FBIS-EEU*-91-200, 16 October 1991.

21. Bruce D. Porter, *Red Armies in Crisis* (Washington, DC: Center for Strategic and International Studies, 1991), p. 17.

22. See the "Appeal of the Army in Transylvania," *Adevarul,* Bucharest, 29 August 1990, in *FBIS-EEU*-90-187, 26 September 1990.

23. *Nepszabadsag,* Budapest, 22 March 1990, in *JPRS-EER*-90-060, 4 May 1990.

24. Radio Free Europe/ Radio Liberty, *Daily Report,* No. 203, 24 October 1991.

25. See the interview with Romanian Foreign Ministry spokesman Traion Chebeleu on "Romanian-Bulgarian Cooperation in the Field of Environmental Protection," *Bucharest Domestic Service,* Bucharest, 27 August 1990, in *FBIS-EEU*-90-167, 28 August 1990.

26. *Khorizont Radio Network,* Sofia, 28 September 1991, in *FBIS-EEU*-91-189, 30 September 1991.

27. Radio Free Europe/ Radio Liberty, *Daily Report,* No. 228, 3 December 1991.

28. *BTA,* Sofia, 26 June and 27 June 1991, in *FBIS-EEU*-91-124, 27 June 1991.

29. See Bilal Simsir, *The Turks of Bulgaria (1878-1985)* (London: Rustem & Brother, 1988).

30. Radio Free Europe/ Radio Liberty, *Daily Report,* No. 164, 29 August 1991.

31. See "Deep Tensions Continue in Turkish Provinces, Despite Some Human Rights Improvements," *News From Bulgaria,* in *News From Helsinki Watch,* August 1990. For some reports on ethnic unrest see Petur Iliev and Lazar Dimov, "The Great Game of Patience," *Demokratsiya,* Sofia, 25 July 1990.

32. Kjell Engelbrekt, "Nationalism Reviving," Radio Free Europe, *Report on Eastern Europe,* Vol. 2, No. 48, 29 November 1991.

33. Major Aleksandur Gerginov, "Do We Need a Strong Army?" *Narodna Armiya,* Sofia, 15 June 1990.

34. Check the interview with Chavdar Chervenkov, chief of the Disarmament Inspectorate at the General Staff of the Bulgarian Peoples Army, in *Narodna Armiya,* Sofia, 11 January 1991.

35. *BTA,* Sofia, in English, 23 October 1991, in *FBIS-EEU*-91-206, 24 October 1991.

36. *ATA,* Tirana, in English, 17 September 1991.

37. *Tirana Domestic Service,* Tirana, in Albanian, 3 September 1990, in *FBIS-EEU*-90-171, 4 September 1990.

38. For example, see Shaban Murati, "Chauvinist Calls Which Damage Greek-Albanian Relations," *Zeri i Popullit,* Tirana, 6 September 1990.

39. See Panos Loukakos, "Greece and the Balkans," *Kiriakatiki Elevtherotipia,* Athens, 15 July 1990, p. 80.

7

Regional Cooperation

Post-Communist eastern Europe has been subject to both centrifugal and centripetal pressures. While the prospects for inter-state and sub-state conflicts have markedly increased in some parts of the region, new opportunities have also emerged for furthering international cooperation in various realms. In some cases, cordial relations have developed between states unencumbered by any significant traditional hostilities or in instances where points of conflict do not occupy a central role and can be amicably resolved. In other cases, the perceptions of threat from an openly hostile, a potentially threatening, or an increasingly unstable neighboring state may even bring together governments that harbor some mutual historical animosities.

Bilateral and multilateral cooperative arrangements have developed in parts of eastern Europe. In some instances, these have been based on subregional linkages that were established prior to the final collapse of the Soviet-enforced alliance system. In practice, cooperative ties have evolved more rapidly in the central European area, between Poland, Hungary, and the Czech and Slovak Federal Republic. By contrast, international relations in the south east European or Balkan area have been clouded by mutual suspicions and enmities. However, even in this region, some cooperative bilateral ties have developed, particularly with some Yugoslav republics during the progressive disintegration of the federation. An overall exploration of evolving regional cooperation throughout eastern Europe can be conducted in three key areas—in the emerging political realignments, in the forms of economic collaboration, and in the development of security linkages.

Political Realignments

The Soviet bloc was not an alliance of equal states that voluntarily formed a regional pact to defend their national and mutual interests. It was an enforced union imposed on the region by a dominant Soviet state and implemented by generally subservient local Communist Parties. Far from bringing the east European states closer together politically or economically, the

Kremlin-controlled bloc both prevented manifestations of inter-state conflict and precluded the development of genuine bilateral or regional cooperation. In many respects, the countries of eastern Europe remained as isolated from each other as they were from the Western states, while most channels of foreign policy decision-making passed through the Kremlin. Even the more independent minded Romanian government needed to pay close attention to Soviet responses before undertaking any major policy initiatives. Only Albania and Yugoslavia, standing outside the Soviet bloc, were able to pursue their own independent international agendas.

All Soviet administrations since World War Two sought to ensure and balance bloc-wide cohesion with the domestic viability of east European regimes.[1] Moscow feared either an economic collapse and social explosion or unrestricted national diversity resulting in the dissolution of the "socialist camp." In the late 1980s, Gorbachev's Kremlin realized that internal political controls had to be significantly loosened and structural economic reforms needed to be implemented in order to preserve domestic stability and overall alliance cohesion.[2] But the reform process rapidly accelerated beyond Moscow's early expectations. As Communist rule began to disintegrate, the artificial multi-national union on which it rested also began to unravel as the new democratic governments pressed for national independence. Unwilling to forcefully roll back the region's democratic revolutions and facing its own mounting internal problems, the Soviet government had little choice but to adjust to the new international realities and endeavor to establish cooperative ties with its former satellites.

The new east European governments have followed a two track policy on the international arena, pursuing close ties with the west European states while renegotiating their relations with the Soviet Union and later the Commonwealth States. In addition, they have endeavored to reformulate their realignments with their ex-Pact neighbors on the basis of national equality and mutual interest. Soon after the democratic breakthroughs, several neighboring states sought to place their relations on a new footing and strengthen their bilateral political ties. In some instances, the new relationships were proclaimed in symbolic gestures of post-Communist reconciliation. For instance, in March 1990 Czechoslovak President Vaclav Havel met with Solidarity leader Lech Walesa on the border between the two states. The two leaders issued a joint communique calling on both countries to coordinate their "return to Europe" as a "friendly union of free nations and independent democratic countries."[3]

A number of high level meetings between state leaders have taken place around the region. For example, in May 1990 Bulgarian Prime Minister, Andrei Lukanov, visited Prague and urged the adoption of a "new system" for regulating and encouraging bilateral relations.[4] In August 1990, Hungarian and Czechoslovak Foreign Ministers agreed to establish a bilateral committee to develop stronger mutual relations in various spheres, including minority rights and the Danube dam project.[5] Declarations of friendship and cooperation have also been signed between a number of states during the past two years, pledging non-aggression and the enhancement of political, economic, and cultural ties. Lower level bilateral cooperation has also become more commonplace between ministers, parliamentarians, and political party leaders and activists.

The east European states were among the first to establish direct links with neighboring republics in the Soviet Union. Several governments pledged to formalize diplomatic relations with republics that aspired toward independence and separation from the USSR, once they elected democratic pro-independence administrations and held national referendums on secession. Before the failed Soviet coup, a number of cooperation agreements or consular conventions were signed. These included links between Czechoslovakia and Russia in March 1991, and between Hungary and Ukraine in June 1991. But full diplomatic recognition for these republics was not afforded until after Moscow's agreement was assured, for fear of unduly antagonizing the Kremlin. The independence of all three Baltic states was swiftly recognized by each east European state in August 1991, and further progress was made in signing treaties with the Soviet government and recognizing the sovereignty of several non-Baltic republics.

All the east European administrations have stressed that any closer bilateral or multilateral links between them should not interfere with or be viewed as a substitute for closer integration with west European states and institutions. Indeed, a good deal of anxiety has been displayed by the new governments over recreating some new Eastern bloc that would keep apart the two halves of Europe rather than bringing them closer together. As a result, propositions by some western leaders that some states in the region should form federations or confederations have been viewed with skepticism and as a ploy to delay their integration into the EC and other multi-national organizations. For instance, in January 1990 the Czechoslovak Foreign Minister indirectly dismissed the idea of a Polish-Czechoslovak confederation by asserting that Prague wanted a pluralistic Europe and not the "creation of new blocs."[6] The Czech-Slovak and Hungarian governments were also hesitant in agreeing to Poland's entry into the regional Pentagonale Group because the country was viewed as potentially anti-German, expansive, and a drain on its neighbors' resources. State leaders have underscored that their bilateral and multilateral ties must serve to enhance not hinder their entry into pan-European bodies.

In January 1990, Czechoslovak President, Vaclav Havel, addressed both the Polish and Hungarian parliaments and urged the three states to coordinate their efforts to "return to Europe."[7] Indeed, since early 1990 Warsaw, Prague, and Budapest have pursued trilateral cooperation on a number of important foreign policy issues. In April 1990, such cooperation was taken a step further during a three-way meeting in Bratislava billed as a central European mini-summit.[8] Although the session itself did not produce any dramatic new initiatives, and even revealed some rifts between the delegations, it helped to formalize and regularize the process of trilateral collaboration. The Czechoslovak Foreign Minister affirmed that cooperative relations between the three states would be one of the most important safeguards against the emergence of a security vacuum in the region, even though a separate regional security structure was not needed.[9] By helping to stabilize the region, such cooperation would also serve to encourage western aid and investment. During the Visegrad mini-summit in Hungary in February 1991, leaders of the three states drafted a joint declaration emphasizing their desire to cement ties to western Europe through institutions such as the EC and the Council of Europe.[10] Polish Foreign Minister, Krzysztof Skubiszewski, defined the region's new "triangular group" not as a formal international organization but as a "loose mechanism for cooperation."[11] In the opinion of all three states, the Visegrad summit helped to establish a framework for the common effort of the "triangle" or "troika" to integrate with western Europe.

Leaders of the "troika" countries held another two day summit meeting in Krakow, Poland in October 1991. Presidents Walesa and Havel, and Premier Antall issued a joint declaration at the close of the proceedings declaring their principal aim as full membership in all the European political, economic, legal, and security systems.[12] At the same time, Poland signed agreements on "good neighborhood, solidarity, and cooperation" with Czechoslovakia and Hungary. A similar Czechoslovak-Hungarian treaty was delayed because its text had not yet been approved by the Czech and Slovak republican parliaments and governments. The three sides agreed to intensify cooperation, consult on various pressing issues, and develop coordination on their foreign policy initiatives. Working groups were also established to improve economic, cultural, and scientific cooperation between the three states. However, the three state leaders reiterated that they were not establishing a permanent body, a supranational organization, or a joint bureaucracy.[13]

Political cooperation and inter-governmental coordination have proved much more difficult to arrange in the Balkans, where many outstanding issues have still to be resolved between any number of states. Even so, efforts have been undertaken to improve the consultation process in the region. For instance, in October 1990, foreign ministers of six Balkan countries met in Tirana, amid calls for the creation of a more permanent body with its own secretariat, to mediate regional disputes and to represent the six states in meetings and negotiations with other European regional groupings.[14] The conference concluded with a declaration that pledged the six governments to pluralism, the rule of law, and a market economy. However, no mechanisms were established to promote regional integration or a Balkan confederation. Formal bilateral ties between some neighboring states have also been pursued even though some contentious issues remain unresolved. For instance, in January 1992, Romania and Bulgaria signed a treaty of friendship, cooperation, and good neighborly relations to replace the 1970 agreement. The document called for the peaceful settlement of bilateral disputes, and for cooperation in communications, transportation, fighting organized crime, terrorism, and smuggling, and for joint efforts on controversial environmental issues.[15]

Economic Cooperation

The development of cooperative economic arrangements between the east European states during the past three years has been influenced by several critical events. In particular, these have included the dissolution of the Soviet-directed Council for Mutual Economic Assistance (CMEA), the collapse of the previously guaranteed Soviet market, the shift to hard currency payments in trade with the USSR, and recurrent difficulties in restructuring intra-regional economic links.

The CMEA (or Comecon) consisted of a cumbersome network of bilateral ties that neither facilitated economic growth nor enhanced genuine international cooperation. It was an artificial multilateral formation created by Stalin to help guarantee Soviet economic control over the east European satellites.[16] The CMEA isolated member countries from the rapidly developing west European economies and resulted in the adoption of an unsound and increasingly anachronistic, Soviet-type, heavy industry model in each country. Most inter-state economic agreements were based on ideological and political decisions, rather than on rational economic calculations about comparative advantage. The CMEA did not develop into a viable Communist integrated market and the centrally planned east European economies experienced increasing stagnation, breakdown, and decline vis-à-vis their expanding European Community counterparts.

As Communist Party rule and the centrally planned economies collapsed throughout eastern Europe in the fall of 1989, all existing multi-national Soviet bloc structures began to evaporate. Trading agreements between all states in the region came under increasing strain as various governments embarked on programs of market reform, restructuring their industries and bureaucracies, cutting down subsidies to state-run enterprises, and reorienting their foreign trade priorities. In addition, marketization and the transformation of command economies was accompanied by a great deal of administrative confusion, supply backlogs, and unfulfilled contracts. The rapid economic merger of East Germany into the German Federal Republic also had a profound impact on several east European states. The closure of unprofitable East German industries and the increasingly western orientation of the restructured economy resulted in the unfulfillment of various contract deliveries and the severing of numerous bilateral links with the east European economies.

The CMEA relationships quickly outlived their usefulness and several of the newly elected democratic governments pushed to formally dismantle all the outdated Comecon institutions. Gorbachev's early efforts to enhance Comecon integration proved to be a failure, and the east European governments concluded that restructuring the organization into a workable commercial body was neither feasible nor desirable. At the 45th Session of the CMEA Council in Sofia in January 1990, top officials from a number of states openly questioned the rationale of maintaining the institution. The Council initially agreed to temporarily preserve some CMEA functions while scaling down its linkages and bureaucracies. The CMEA was primarily required to uphold the supply of Soviet energy and raw materials in return for east European manufacturing goods. This would evidently preserve some supply stability during the difficult transition to market economies, while the reforming states endeavored to produce and export competitive products for hard currency payments.

As market reforms accelerated in the region, the remaining CMEA institutions fell into disuse. At a meeting of the CMEA Executive Committee in January 1991, it was decided to wind down and disband the cumbersome institution.[17] Renewed emphasis was placed on developing bilateral ties through market-based trade between individual enterprises and largely bypassing the government bureaucracies. The final meeting of the CMEA Council was held in Moscow in May 1991, when a decision was passed to disband the institution. Comecon was formally dissolved during a meeting in Budapest in June 1991 and technically ceased to exist by September 1991. Proposals were also put forward to establish an informal consultative committee between former CMEA members to help prevent the rapid collapse of all trading networks. Poland, Hungary, and Czechoslovakia, in particular, adopted a cooperative approach to coordinate the disbanding of Comecon. But, the Soviet-proposed successor to CMEA—the Organization for International Economic Cooperation—proved to be a non-starter.

Throughout 1990, the east European economies were further burdened by serious shortfalls in Soviet oil and gas supplies. In some instances, the provisioning of oil only reached 40% of the amounts contracted for the year. As the Soviet economy continued to decline and chaos reigned throughout the production and distribution process in the USSR, the east European states found their traditional Soviet markets disappearing with few immediate alternatives to dispose of their non-competitive products. In fact, during the first part of 1991, Soviet imports from eastern Europe fell by about half. The changeover from barter deals and subsidized Soviet oil to hard currency purchases at world market prices, further undermined the post-bloc economies and pushed the governments to seek alternative suppliers. The monetization of trade with the Soviet Union and the replacement of the transferable ruble with hard-currency transactions were positive developments toward market-based exchange. However, in the short term they seriously handicapped east European economies dependent on a single supplier and short of hard-currency reserves. The hardest hit were east European companies exclusively dependent on exports to the Soviet Union.[18]

The energy shock did have the effect of bringing some of the east European governments together to discuss their common difficulties and to seek alternative arrangements. Several high level meetings were held between the Finance Ministers of Poland, Czechoslovakia, and Hungary to find ways to handle the Soviet economic crisis, but they were unable to adopt a concerted economic policy toward the USSR. Moscow was also involved in the talks and various agreements were reached with the three states to resume some barter deals between individual enterprises. For instance, in October 1990, Czechoslovakia's "Chemapol" enterprise signed an agreement with a Soviet company in Tyumen *oblast* for the delivery of 500,000 tons of oil in exchange for manufactured goods.[19] This initial barter deal was intended to evolve into broader oil-for-goods contracts. In June 1991, a joint-stock company, "Dialog Ural," was formed in Prague to enhance barter trade with the USSR. Some clearing arrangements were also initiated, in which trade accounts were kept in national currencies in the respective states and were balanced periodically through barter or hard-currency payments.[20]

Various inter-governmental economic deals have also been concluded. The Czech-Slovak and Soviet governments signed an agreement for Soviet oil deliveries for 1991, partly in exchange for drilling equipment from Prague. In July 1991, Czechoslovakia and the Soviet Union signed a trade agreement allowing mutual payments in a mixture of hard currency, local currency, and barter deals.[21] Barter trading was resumed more widely during 1991, because the USSR itself was suffering from severe hard currency shortages making it difficult to pay for imports from eastern Europe. For instance, in May 1991, the Hungarian Foreign Minister signed a cooperation agreement with the Soviet government outlining new terms for bilateral trade with a temporary return to barter contracts.[22] Warsaw also agreed to sell grain and meat to the USSR in mixed hard currency and barter transactions.[23] Some Soviet debts to individual states were also arranged to be repaid in energy supplies because Moscow found it difficult to make up its trade deficits with hard currency payments. In June 1991, Budapest and Moscow signed a protocol for Soviet compensation for Hungary's construction of the Yamburg gas pipeline: Hungary's contribution was to be repaid through the delivery of 14.6 billion cubic meters of natural gas during the following year.[24] At the close of 1991, Warsaw arranged a deal with Moscow to increase trade between the two states; a portion of the trade was to be conducted in barter deals between individual enterprises.

The economic and political breakup of the USSR has also accelerated progress in the development of direct ties between the east European states and individual Soviet republics. The collapse of trade with the central government in Moscow has spurred Warsaw, Prague, Budapest, and other capitals to develop bilateral trading arrangements for specific goods, particularly with the Baltic states, Ukraine, and Russia. For example, in November 1990 a preliminary Hungarian-Soviet trading agreement contained provisions for the fulfillment of shortfalls in Soviet oil supplies through direct deals with republican governments. A similar arrangement was reached between the Czech-Slovak and Soviet governments, whereby Prague could make contracts for oil deliveries with specific republics and regions.[25] Warsaw arranged a deal with Moscow at the close of 1991 to increase trade between the two states. In the long term, the liberalization of Commonwealth commerce is likely to result in the increasing purchase of east European goods and growing trade between the two regions.

Several bilateral economic agreements were signed between the east European and Soviet republican governments, even before the failed coup severed most of the Union bonds. For example, Poland and Ukraine reached an accord in January 1991, whereby Warsaw would export industrial and construction goods and import iron ore and other raw materials.[26] This was the first such foreign agreement concluded by the sovereign Ukrainian republic. In June 1991, Hungary signed the first direct economic pact with the Russian republic and enhanced trade links with other republics to make up for commerce lost with the central government in Moscow. Hungary concluded an accord with Ukraine in May 1991.[27] Poland and Russia signed a bilateral economic pact in September 1991, and a Polish-Russian Chamber of Industry and Commerce was created to help enhance and coordinate international trade between the two states.

During 1991, Czechoslovakia became the first country to reach inter-governmental agreements on economic relations and scientific exchanges with all three Baltic states, and Prague also concluded various inter-firm arrangements. Economic cooperation was to take place directly between enterprises and not through the governments. Furthermore, in July 1991 the Soviet republics were formally given direct jurisdiction over exports and imports into their territories without central government interference. During 1991, several joint ventures were also established between east European and Soviet companies. The most notable one involved the Hungarian bus manufacturer "Ikarus" which signed an agreement with a Soviet consortium, ATEX, together with the Turin-based Central European Investment Company.

Problems resulting from de-stabilizing Soviet developments have spurred a search for protective economic policies, especially among the "troika" states. In the early part of 1991, Warsaw, Prague, and Budapest expressed profound fears that the USSR would become the major recipient of Western credits, aid, and favorable trade arrangements at the expense of eastern Europe. Direct Western aid would have also further undercut the "troika's" eastern market. The three states launched a strong campaign to convince western aid-granting organizations to either channel assistance through eastern Europe or establish triangular deals in which western funds would reinforce Soviet trade with eastern Europe. Such proposals met with some success. In March 1991, it was agreed that Poland would participate in a major EC aid program to the USSR: a proportion of the cash was to be spent in Poland for the purchase of various agricultural products for the Soviet Union.[28] Several other similar triangular deals were planned with Western partners. For instance, in September 1991, Hungarian grain exporters signed a large deal to export wheat and flour to the USSR; the sale was financed by a bank consortium headed by the Central European International Bank and an unnamed Swiss firm.[29] Further deals were struck to unload agricultural surpluses and alleviate food shortages in some states. In September 1991, the EC agreed to buy surplus Hungarian wheat in order to supply the Albanian government with desperately needed produce.[30] This was the first triangular operation involving the EC aid program within eastern Europe. EC Commissioners also considered buying the Soviet Union's currency debt with all the east European states.

A number of bilateral economic arrangements have been established between most states in the region following the collapse of the CMEA. These have included transport protocols easing border customs clearances and visa requirements, as well as scientific and technological exchanges and agreements between individual enterprises regarding direct trade and barter deals. However, parallel to the sharp decline in the Soviet market, the intra-east European market has also shrunk during the past three years. This has been the result of a number of factors; the unattractiveness and low standard of east European goods, the similarity of goods produced in each state, the increasing budgetary constraints on state-subsidized firms, and the changeover to hard-currency trade among the dollar poor post-CMEA states. While foreign trade has been liberalized throughout eastern Europe and the intermediary foreign trade organizations have been curtailed, the more successful firms have sought to establish links with new partners in the west or to market their products outside the region. It became clearly unprofitable for the east European states to trade with each other, except with regard to products that could not be easily sold in western markets for competitive prices.

A few attempts have been initiated to broaden regional cooperation between the east European states, but moves toward any genuine economic integration have been limited to the "troika" countries. Even here, however, there has been a general reluctance or even resistance to formally band together, through some new multi-national institutions, and thereby reestablish a restrictive and unproductive trading bloc. For example, suggestions by the vice president of the European Bank for Reconstruction and Development (EBRD) regarding the creation of a central payments union, that would facilitate regional trade by making up for trade shortfalls or surpluses, was strongly opposed by the Czech and Slovak government.[31] Prague considered that such arrangements, and the early formation of a free trade zone in central Europe, would be tantamount to creating a "poor-man's club" separating eastern Europe from the Western economies and further restricting their access to Western markets.

In September 1991, a Soviet proposal to establish a loose "economic community" between the Soviet republics and the east European nations was not well received in central Europe.[32] The new governments feared that such a trading bloc would obstruct their economic progress by continuing to keep their products uncompetitive in Western markets. Similar fears have also been voiced in the Balkan area, where economic progress has proved even slower. The proposed formation of a "Black Sea Economic Zone" between the USSR, Bulgaria, Turkey and Romania, has been criticized by the Sofia administration because rather than assisting integration into Europe's economic structures it would reorient each state "in the opposite direction."[33] The Bulgarian authorities also feared that the new trading bloc would give undue influence to Turkey throughout the Balkans.

Despite the understandable hesitancy to re-establish any strong multilateral regional economic structures, several states have tried to maintain high-level consultations on the region's economic options. For example, proposals were lodged in July 1991 to set up a European Consultative Economic Forum as an inter-governmental association composed of the former CMEA countries.[34] But more substantive cooperation has remained limited because multilateral economic institutions have not been created to replace the defunct Comecon bodies. Instead, leaders of Poland, Czechoslovakia, and Hungary have tried to coordinate their projected entry into the European Community and to enhance their cooperation within the Hexagonale (formerly the Pentagonale)—a regional grouping that also includes Italy, Austria, and Yugoslavia. The Hexagonale has promoted collaboration on such issues as transportation and environmental protection, and changed its name in December 1991 to the Central European Initiative.

The "troika" states of central Europe have also made some progress in synchronizing their customs tariffs, as a first step toward an eventual customs union and even a free trade zone. At the end of November 1991, Warsaw, Prague, and Budapest signed a memorandum on liberalizing mutual trade over the next five years, specifying which goods would be allowed into the region's markets.[35] If these endeavors prove successful, the "troika" could eventually become the backbone of a new trading network embracing most of eastern Europe.

Moves have also been made to develop some kind of sub-regional or inter-regional economic cooperation between areas within neighboring Central European states. Some plans have focused on specific border areas, such as the Oder-Neisse region between Poland and Germany, while others have been wider ranging. For instance, a Danubian or Carpathian grouping has been promoted by Hungary to include southern Poland, subcarpathian Ukraine, eastern Slovakia, north eastern Hungary, and parts of Romanian Transylvania.[36] Such proposals have also sparked major controversies in Bucharest, where government spokesmen depicted these plans as an underhand maneuver to sever the Transylvanian territories from Romania. A report published by a Polish newspaper in September 1991 based on a study prepared for the Polish Foreign Ministry led to a vehement protest by Bucharest. The study proposed expanding the Hexagonale by including the Transylvanian region but not Romania's entire territory. The Romanian government was outraged and charged that such proposals undermined the principles of territorial integrity and undercut east European cooperation.[37] The Polish authorities denied that the study represented the official position of the Warsaw administration, but the incident clearly exposed the sensitivities of the Romanian leadership to any territorial questions.

With eventual Romanian support, in January 1992 officials from Hungary, Poland, Romania, Slovakia, and Ukraine agreed to establish a new regional economic community. This Carpathian-Tisza grouping would endeavor to promote multinational cooperation in the fields of trade, science, tourism, culture, demographics, and environmental protection.[38]

Security Linkages

In assessing the restructuring of security networks in eastern Europe, it is important to consider the changing military postures of each state following the dissolution of the Warsaw Treaty Organization (WTO), or Warsaw Pact. Moscow seemingly did not anticipate the speed at which the Pact would dissolve, and even its attempts to preserve some multilateral political structures to assure overall Soviet supervision proved to be unrealistic.[39] At the June 1990 summit, the first steps were taken to disassemble the WTO. The east European governments were willing to maintain some of its structures in the interim, in order to develop a broader European security framework and to participate in arms control negotiations with NATO. In this transitory period, the east European leaders still feared provoking a hard-line reaction in Moscow. They primarily sought a dissolution of the military aspects of the alliance, to ensure that it could not be used against any member state, as well as a substantial revision in bilateral military agreements with the Soviet

Union.[40] The Soviet controlled WTO Joint Command was to be transformed into a coordinating secretariat arranging high level meetings between foreign and defense ministers, but with no supra-national command over the armed forces of any participating state. East European leaders were suspicious about any Soviet proposals for transforming the Pact from a military to a political alliance, in which Moscow would continue to exercise major political influence.

As the danger of Soviet military pressure to reverse the democratic reforms in eastern Europe rapidly receded, the new governments became emboldened and pushed to dismantle the WTO. Despite Moscow's delaying tactics, in February 1991, the Foreign and Defense Ministers of the Warsaw Pact states signed a statement in Budapest declaring the WTO's military institutions to be dissolved as of the end of March 1991.[41] Numerous WTO military treaties were abrogated and the Pact was left with a temporary consultative role, but devoid of Soviet overlordship. In July 1991, the WTO's political mechanisms were formally terminated at a final meeting in Prague of the Political Consultative Committee.[42]

Since early 1990, all governments in the region have been engaged in transforming their militaries from Soviet-oriented politicized institutions into armed forces serving specifically national interests and responsible to democratically elected governments. In fact, since the early 1980s, east European leaders have been concerned about falling behind NATO technologically: they began to reconsider their national defense doctrines given their increasing sense of vulnerability within the Soviet coalition. Military doctrines were adjusted from a focus on coalition warfare and first strike ground-attack operations aimed against NATO, to essentially independent and sovereign defensive postures, employing scaled down military forces sufficient to deter outside aggression. The emphasis was changed from a definition of NATO as the prime enemy, to an avoidance of declaring any state as a real or potential military foe. Military forces were redeployed in each country from the western regions facing NATO and more evenly distributed along state borders, including those with the Soviet Union.[43]

All the east European administrations have taken important steps to cut down the size of their militaries and decrease their military expenditure. Tight budgetary constraints have promoted this process, but they have also prevented the acquisition of more sophisticated modern weaponry. Measures have been taken to de-Sovietize and de-Communize all branches of the military and security services, thereby terminating Soviet control and supervision and rooting out Communist Party penetration. Civilian-military relations have been drastically altered and all services have been placed under parliamentary and government control. Military defense ministers have been replaced by non-Communist civilians, and many senior-ranking Communist officials have been retired, with a view to building a loyal, non-political officer corps. Former commissars and political directorates in the military have been assigned non-ideological tasks in providing education and welfare for conscripts. In many cases, military service has been cut back and plans have been laid for the professionalization and modernization of all military branches. Most governments have also tried to diversify their arms suppliers; but they remain constrained by excessive costs and continuing dependence on weaponry and spare parts from the former Soviet Union.

Even before the collapse of Communist rule, Poland's military analysts stressed that with the new East-West detente and the demilitarization of international relations, each east European state had to reorient its military toward defensive objectives.[44] After the democratic changeovers, Poland's new military doctrine placed emphasis on defensive operations and the effective deterrence of any potential aggressor.[45] Poland adopted its new military doctrine in February 1990; the first such security document in post-Communist eastern Europe. During 1990, Warsaw began to redistribute troops between western, central, and eastern regions, although realizing that this would be an extremely costly operation because the proper military infrastructure was lacking. More forces were deployed on the eastern border with the USSR as a precaution against any spill-over of Soviet unrest. The stress was on achieving military self-sufficiency, in terms of an ability to repel direct aggression.[46] Cuts were initiated in Poland's military forces with a view to constructing a smaller modernized army. The authorities realized that this would be an expensive, long-term proposition if antiquated equipment was to be modernized, given Warsaw's serious budgetary constraints.[47] By the end of 1990, the armed forces were reduced by some 12%, from 347,000 to under 315,000, with plans to cut to about 250,000 during the next two years, with a further half a million reservists.

The restructuring of civilian-military relations was delayed in Poland because the Communists retained the defense and internal affairs ministries after the June 1989 elections. A civilian deputy defense minister was appointed when the new government was formed in September 1989, but a former Communist appointee was retained as defense minister in order not to aggravate Moscow before it became clear that the Warsaw Pact was disintegrating. The new administration was initially cautious in its approach to security matters, including the question of the Soviet troop presence, partly in response to Bonn's ambiguous stance over the border issue on the eve of German reunification. But as the German danger subsided and the potential Soviet threat receded, Warsaw pressed forward for the withdrawal of all Red Army troops and the comprehensive de-Communization of its military forces. The depoliticization of the army gathered pace during 1990 and 1991 with the removal of political officers and Communist Party cells from all military branches. By August 1991, preparations were made to appoint a civilian defense minister, while all military commanders (including the chief of the general staff and the general inspector) were professional soldiers appointed by the supreme commander of the armed forces, the Polish President.

Czech-Slovak military doctrine has also emphasized defensive aspects since the political breakthrough in late 1989. Quickly abandoned were the principles of coalition warfare through large-scale joint exercises, planning for multi-national missions and the use of Czech-Slovak forces outside the country. In February 1990, Moscow agreed to withdraw all of its 80,000 troops from the country by mid-1991: the evacuation was largely completed on schedule.[48] Prague underscored that it would not participate in any new security bloc that would, in any way, undercut national control over the armed forces. Troops were redistributed throughout the country with more substantial concentrations than before in Slovakia and along the Soviet border as potential protection against turmoil in the east.[49] Prague also initiated the creation of a professional border police, which was to consist of 2,000 troops by the end of 1992. Budget cuts were accompanied by a planned 30% reduction of the armed forces from nearly 200,000 in 1989 to about 140,000 personnel by 1993. Basic military service was shortened, the call-up of reservists was reduced, and steps were taken to create a smaller professional army and a territorial defense system staffed by a civilian reserve. The military was steadily de-politicized with the removal of Communist cells, the termination of any domestic security functions, the replacement of key officers tied to the defunct Warsaw Pact command structure, and the creation of new parliamentary agencies to oversee the armed forces.

Since the revolutionary developments of 1989, Hungary has been forthright in pressing for the removal of all Red Army contingents and for a full withdrawal from the WTO. In fact, its strategically peripheral position has provided Hungary with greater room for maneuver than its two northern neighbors. Most of the 60,000 Soviet troops stationed in Hungary were evacuated by July 1991. Budapest also quickly removed its forces from the Warsaw Pact joint command and placed them under full national control.[50] Hungary's new military doctrine was exclusively defensive, and troops have been redeployed equally between the western and eastern parts of the country to reflect new security priorities and the absence of a singular enemy. Budapest has also acknowledged that Yugoslavia will remain a persistent trouble spot and that Hungary must shape its defense policy accordingly. Despite the threat on its southern borders, Hungary's defense budget has been substantially curtailed and its troop strength was planned to decrease from approximately 90,000 in 1990 to under 65,000 by the end of 1992: an overall reduction of about 35% since 1989.[51] Compulsory military service was shortened, the number of active duty officers was gradually reduced, and the military was scheduled to become an all-volunteer and professional force to replace the conscript-based army. Even before the March 1990 elections, military depoliticization proceeded apace with a ban on all political party activities and a greater reliance on a younger non-Communist officer corps.

Unlike other WTO states, since the early 1960s Romania has upheld a more independent military doctrine, emphasizing self-sufficiency and a defensive strategy based on the protracted territorial "war of the entire people." The objective was to preclude any return of Soviet troops, the use of Romanian territory by WTO forces, or the employment of Romanian troops outside the country. In fact, Bucharest did not participate in any joint Warsaw Pact military maneuvers after the early 1960s. Romanian military leaders played a more prominent role in the democratic revolution in 1989 than in any other east European state. During and after the overthrow of Ceausescu, most military commanders sided with the anti-Communist forces and some were suspected of having participated in the planning of the coup that accompanied the popular revolt. Older line officers were replaced after the revolution and in February 1990 the new defense minister indicated that he would purge the army of Communist activists who had defended Ceausescu.[52] Although Bucharest underscored that the military would no longer serve the interests of any political party and officers would be selected according to merit and performance and not ideological fidelity or political loyalty, strong suspicions continued to be voiced that Romania's security forces remained under the control of the ruling National Salvation Front.

Romania's military doctrine and military forces structure are unlikely to change significantly in the near future, as they serve the country's essentially defensive needs. Nonetheless, the low quality of military hardware will handicap the Romanian army vis-à-vis potential adversaries. The armed forces are poorly equipped and organizationally inferior even by east European standards. The situation is unlikely to improve in the near term, because of Romania's dire economic conditions and its slim prospects for obtaining any large infusion of foreign funds. Budgetary problems and the squeeze on military expenditure could, in turn, fuel disgruntlement among army officers against the country's civilian leaders.

Bulgaria's Socialist government sought to preserve its security ties with Moscow even while the WTO began to unravel. Likewise, Bulgaria's military doctrine has been the slowest to change in the region; for example, there were no early calls for the termination or even the reorganization of the Warsaw Pact. But during 1990, Sofia placed increasing stress on defensive operations and initiated cutbacks in military spending and personnel.[53] As in Romania, the curtailment of funds for the Bulgarian military could breed resentment among some army commanders. The officer corps could support military reorganization and lower force levels, but it has also shown concern that the armed forces may be placed in a grossly inferior position vis-a vis Turkey and other potential adversaries in terms of weaponry and military preparedness.[54]

While the Soviet government tried to forge links with its former satellites through bilateral military treaties, the new east European governments opposed any provisions prohibiting either partner from forming military alliances with third parties. Such stipulations would have prevented possible future entry into NATO or other pan-European security structures. On the other hand, each state has tried to establish security guarantees with its superpower eastern neighbor while continuing to be dependent on the USSR for a great deal of military hardware, fuel, and spare parts.

Only Romania initially agreed in March 1991 to sign a 15-year treaty of cooperation with the Soviet Union, stating that neither country would participate in an alliance directed against the other party.[55] The government came under intense criticism from the democratic opposition for arranging the treaty so hastily and for surrendering too much of Romania's sovereignty. The treaty was due to be renegotiated after the failure of the Moscow coup and the collapse of the Soviet Union. In June 1991, Poland refused to sign a treaty of cooperation with the USSR that would have included a pledge not to join any "hostile military alliances," including NATO.[56] In October 1991, Polish and Soviet officials agreed to drop the controversial security clause from the treaty that was scheduled to be signed later in the month.[57] In June 1991, the Czech-Slovak government also rejected a clause, proposed by the Soviets in a new treaty, preventing either state from entering military alliances that the other might consider hostile. Meanwhile, in September 1991 Hungarian and Soviet foreign ministers finally agreed on security clauses in a new bilateral treaty.[58]

All the former WTO members have pursued bilateral and multilateral regional agreements on military cooperation. Bilateral ties have been preferred over any new regional structures that could resuscitate the dominance of stronger parties, create new "spheres of influence," and even hinder the creation of an all-European security framework. Officials calculated that the establishment of any military-political mini-blocs may not offer long-term stability if they do not enhance the process of European security integration.

A series of cross-cutting bilateral accords have been reached during the past few years in eastern Europe. In January 1991, Czechoslovak and Hungarian defense ministers signed a military agreement establishing a framework for bilateral security policy and the exchange of information on military movements along their common frontier.[59] In February 1991, Poland and Czechoslovakia signed an agreement calling for cooperation in various military matters.[60] The following month Poland and Hungary initiated new defense agreements stressing cooperation in officer training, disarmament policies, and arms purchasing.[61] Three-way sessions between "troika" leaders have also been held following the first post-Communist meeting in Bratislava and much of the discussion has focused on pressing security issues.

The three central European states appear to have made more progress than the Balkan countries in holding regular high level meetings on defense issues and arriving at various security agreements. Nevertheless, some bilateral cooperation has also been evident in the Balkans, even between countries embroiled in conflictive disputes. For example, in October 1990, Hungarian and Romanian defense ministers agreed on a framework of collaboration to boost military ties through the mutual exchange of information and regular meetings between senior officers.[62] Romanian and Bulgarian leaders have also discussed regional security issues in the Balkans at both bilateral and multilateral levels. Bucharest has proposed creating a Central and East European Union patterned after the security-oriented West European Union.[63] Understandably, such plans have been approached cautiously as the new governments oppose any separate security status or special security zones in eastern Europe. Warsaw and other capitals underscore that they do not intend to be an intermediate buffer area or a "grey zone" between NATO and the post-USSR. According to their calculations, security cooperation in the region must run in tandem with the construction of a pan-European security umbrella.

Notes

1. See J. F. Brown, *Eastern Europe and Communist Rule* (Durham: Duke University Press, 1988), pp. 30-61, and Charles Gati, *The Bloc That Failed: Soviet-East European Relations in Transition* (Bloomington: Indiana University Press, 1990).

2. For an evaluation of Gorbachev's policies toward the region see Ronald D. Asmus, J. F. Brown, Keith Crane, *Soviet Foreign Policy and the Revolutions of 1989 in Eastern Europe* (Santa Monica: Rand Corporation/ National Defense Research Institute, 1991), pp. 1-31.

3. Radio Free Europe, "Weekly Record of Events," *Report on Eastern Europe,* Vol. 1, No. 13, 30 March 1990.

4. Radio Free Europe, "Weekly Record of Events," *Report on Eastern Europe,* Vol. 1, No. 20, 18 May 1990.

5. Radio Free Europe, "Weekly Record of Events," *Report on Eastern Europe,* Vol. 1, No. 36, 7 September 1990.

6. Radio Free Europe, "Weekly Record of Events," *Report on Eastern Europe,* Vol. 1, No. 4, 26 January 1990.

7. Radio Free Europe, "Weekly Record of Events," *Report on Eastern Europe,* Vol. 1, No. 6, 9 February 1990.

8. Radio Free Europe, "Weekly Record of Events," *Report on Eastern Europe,* Vol. 1, No. 16, 20 April 1990.

9. See Jiri Dienstbier, "Central Europe's Security," *Foreign Policy,* Summer 1991, No. 83, pp. 119-127.

10. Radio Free Europe/ Radio Liberty, *Daily Report,* No. 33, 15 February 1991.

11. Radio Free Europe/ Radio Liberty, *Daily Report,* No. 75, 18 April 1991.

12. *PAP,* Warsaw, 6 October 1991. See also Jan B. de Weydenthal, "The Cracow Summit," Radio Free Europe, *Report on Eastern Europe,* Vol. 2, No. 43, 25 October 1991.

13. See the press conference by Walesa, Havel, and Antall in Cracow on 6 October 1991, in *Radio Warsaw Network,* Warsaw, 6 October 1991, *FBIS-EEU*-91-195, 8 October 1991.

14. Radio Free Europe/ Radio Liberty, *Daily Report,* No. 204, 25 October 1990.

15. Radio Free Europe/ Radio Liberty, *Daily Report,* No. 18, 28 January 1992.

16. An excellent analysis of the inbuilt flaws in the CMEA can be found in Vlad Sobell, *The CMEA in Crisis: A New European Order?* (New York/Washington: Praeger/CSIS, 1990).

17. Vladimir Kusin, "CMEA: The End is Nigh," Radio Free Europe, *Report on Eastern Europe,* Vol. 2, No. 5, 1 February 1991.

18. Patrice Dabrowski, "East European Trade (Part I): The Loss of the Soviet Market," Radio Free Europe, *Report on Eastern Europe,* Vol. 2, No. 40, 4 October 1991.

19. See Radio Free Europe/ Radio Liberty, *Daily Report,* No. 195, 12 October 1990.

20. Patrice Dabrowski, "East European Trade (Part II): Creative Solutions by the Former Eastern Bloc," Radio Free Europe, *Report on Eastern Europe,* Vol. 2, No. 41, 11 October 1991.

21. Radio Free Europe/ Radio Liberty, *Daily Report,* No. 132, 13 July 1991.

22. Radio Free Europe/ Radio Liberty, *Daily Report,* No. 98, 24 May 1991.

23. Radio Free Europe/ Radio Liberty, *Daily Report,* No. 86, 11 May 1991.

24. Radio Free Europe/ Radio Liberty, *Daily Report,* No. 117, 21 June 1991.

25. Radio Free Europe/ Radio Liberty, *Daily Report,* No. 223, 26 November 1990, and Radio Free Europe/ Radio Liberty, *Daily Report,* No. 239, 18 December 1990.

26. Radio Free Europe/ Radio Liberty, *Daily Report,* No. 19, 28 January 1991.

27. Radio Free Europe/ Radio Liberty, *Daily Report,* No. 147, 5 August 1991.

28. Radio Free Europe/ Radio Liberty, *Daily Report,* No. 46, 16 March 1991.

29. Radio Free Europe/ Radio Liberty, *Daily Report,* No. 174, 12 September 1991.

30. *The Financial Times,* London, 5 September 1991.

31. *The Guardian,* London, 18 April 1991.

32. *The Financial Times,* London, 5 September 1991.

33. Radio Free Europe/ Radio Liberty, *Daily Report,* No. 240, 19 December 1990.

34. Radio Free Europe/ Radio Liberty, *Daily Report,* No. 131, 12 July 1991.

35. Radio Free Europe/ Radio Liberty, *Daily Report,* No. 227, 2 December 1991.

36. Check the interview with Hungarian Foreign Affairs Minister Geza Jeszenszky in *Nepszabadsag,* Budapest, 11 October 1991.

37. See "Diplomatic Activities: A Communique from the Foreign Ministry on a Polish Study", *Rompres,* Bucharest, in English, 8 September 1991, in *FBIS-EEU*-91-174, 9 September 1991.

38. Radio Free Europe/ Radio Liberty, *Daily Report,* No. 16, 24 January 1992.

39. For a useful assessment of the WTO in the pre-democratic era, see *The Warsaw Pact and the Question of Cohesion, A Conference Report,* Kennan Institute for Advanced Russian Studies, Wilson Center, May 1985. For an analysis of changing Soviet military doctrine on the eve of the East European revolutions see Pal Dunay, *Military Doctrine: Change in the East?* (New York: Institute for East-West Security Studies, 1990).

40. Douglas Clarke, "Warsaw Pact: The Transformation Begins," Radio Free Europe, *Report on Eastern Europe,* Vol. 1, No. 25, 22 June 1990. See also Wilfred Gruber, *The Future of Europe's Security* (Santa Monica: Rand Corporation, February 1990).

41. See Vladimir Kusin, "Yet Another End for the Warsaw Pact," Radio Free Europe, *Report on Eastern Europe,* Vol. 2, No. 11, 15 March 1991.

42. Douglas Clarke, "The Warsaw Pact's Finale," Radio Free Europe, *Report on Eastern Europe,* Vol. 2, No. 29, 19 July 1991.

43. Douglas Clarke, "A Realignment of Military Forces in Central Europe," Radio Free Europe, *Report on Eastern Europe,* Vol. 2, No. 2, 8 March 1991.

44. See General Tadeusz Cepak and Jerzy Nowak, "The Reduction of Conventional Fores in Europe - A Polish View," in *European Security: Views From Eastern Countries* (Rome: Studie Richarche del Centro di Studi Strategici, 1989).

45. Colonel Michal Glinski, "Toward a Real and Imagined Future," *Zolnierz Rzeczypospolitej,* Warsaw, No. 14, 16 September 1990.

46. See "Poland's Military Doctrine in the Future Political Situation," *Honor i Ojczyzna: Niezalezne Pismo Wojskowe,* Warsaw, No. 3, 1990.

47. Ewa Wilk, "The State of the Army," *Tygodnik Solidarnosc,* Warsaw, 22 June 1990. For a valuable analysis of the restructuring of the Polish military see Thomas S. Szayna, *The Military in a Postcommunist Poland* (Santa Monica: Rand Corporation, 1991).

48. Jan Obrman, "Withdrawal of Soviet Troops Completed, " Radio Free Europe, *Report on Eastern Europe,* Vol. 2, No. 30, 26 July 1991.

49. See *Czechoslovak Radio Network,* in Slovak, Bratislava, 7 August 1991, in *FBIS-EEU*-91-153, 8 August 1991.

50. See *MTI,* Budapest, in English, 8 June 1990, in *FBIS-EEU*-90-112, 11 June 1990.

51. For useful background see Ivan Volgyes and Zoltan Barany, "Hungarian Defenders of the Homeland," in Jeffrey Simon (Ed) *European Security Policy After the Revolutions of 1989* (Washington DC: National Defense University Press, 1991), pp. 351-374.

52. For a useful account see George W. Price, "Romanian Armed Forces," in Jeffrey Simon (Ed) *European Security Policy After the Revolutions of 1989* (Washington DC: National Defense University Press, 1991), pp. 457-477.

53. See the interview with Colonel General Khristo Dobrev, first deputy minister of national defense and commander of the general staff of the Bulgarian People's Army in *Narodna Armiya,* Sofia, 11 January 1990.

54. Daniel N. Nelson, "Political Dynamics and the Bulgarian Military," in Jeffrey Simon (Ed) *European Security Policy After the Revolutions of 1989* (Washington DC: National Defense University Press, 1991), pp. 479-512.

55. Radio Free Europe/ Radio Liberty *Daily Report,* No. 59, 22 March 1991.

56. Radio Free Europe/ Radio Liberty *Daily Report,* No. 116, 20 June 1991.

57. Radio Free Europe/ Radio Liberty *Daily Report,* No. 192, 9 October 1991.

58. Radio Free Europe/ Radio Liberty *Daily Report,* No. 185, 27 September 1991.

59. Radio Free Europe/ Radio Liberty, *Daily Report,* No. 15, 22 January 1991.

60. Radio Free Europe/ Radio Liberty, *Daily Report,* No. 42, 28 February 1991.

61. Radio Free Europe/ Radio Liberty, *Daily Report,* No. 157, 21 March 1991.

62. Radio Free Europe/ Radio Liberty, *Daily Report,* No. 201, 19 October 1990.

63. Radio Free Europe/ Radio Liberty, *Daily Report,* No. 86, 3 May 1991.

8

European Integration

The long-term objective of all the east European states is their full incorporation into all multilateral European institutions. Political integration would enhance the legitimacy, credibility, and equilibrium of the emerging pluralistic democracies. Economic integration would provide many tangible benefits by way of trade, aid, and investment, and help buttress the process of market transformation. Security integration would help to stabilize the region in the wake of the Warsaw Pact collapse by providing guarantees for the military defense of national independence and the territorial integrity of all participating states. The east European governments have also pursued closer bilateral ties with specific west European countries, as well as with the United States, partly in order to further their access and entry into pan-European and trans-Atlantic institutions.

However, the process of European integration has neither been rapid nor smooth. Political collaboration has proved least troublesome, once individual east European states displayed their commitment to party pluralism, regular free elections, and democratic institution building. But in the economic arena, the EC countries have been hesitant in providing full membership to the new European democracies, contending that the Community needs to deepen its own integrative process before widening its reach to embrace new members. The west European governments have also hesitated in lifting various restrictions on east European imports and in establishing free trade agreements with the region. Similarly, in the area of security the NATO states have avoided giving formal military guarantees to the east European countries or in extending the NATO umbrella despite the requests of several states. It remains uncertain whether NATO or any other essentially western institution can successfully restructure and expand its reach in the region, or whether new military networks will need to be established to provide security guarantees to a larger group of member states. Whatever the outcome, European security no longer revolves around a Soviet military threat, but on a complex set of problems in a "multi-polar" Europe in which local conflicts over territories, minorities, resources, and comparative military advantage may undermine domestic and regional stability. In such a situation, conflict prevention and mediation will figure as a high priority for both old and new European bodies.

Political Alliances

The development of political cooperation between western and eastern Europe during the past three years has proceeded along two tracks: bilateral and multilateral. The post-Communist governments quickly endeavored to re-establish good relations with their immediate western neighbors and with countries that they maintained close ties with in the pre-Communist era. They also calculated that a network of strong bilateral relations with specific western powers would help speed up their membership in various European institutions. The central European states (Poland, Czechoslovakia, and Hungary) achieved faster progress in those efforts largely because of their achievements in building stable pluralistic democracies and free market economies, and because they had strenuously cultivated western contacts.

Poland moved swiftly to re-establish good relations with its traditional Western allies, France and Great Britain, as well as with other EC states. Agreements on mutual cooperation, friendship, and solidarity were signed during 1990 and 1991.[1] These concords also assisted Warsaw in its dispute with the German government regarding Bonn's final acceptance of Poland's western borders. With French and British support, Poland was included in some of the "four plus two" talks during 1990 dealing with German reunification, particularly in discussions on security and territorial questions. Paris and London evidently exerted some pressure on Bonn to alleviate Polish concerns and move more rapidly toward a new inter-state treaty. Although Polish-German relations remained strained, by the close of 1990 the frontier issue was virtually settled and an agreement was finally signed in November pending parliamentary ratification. In June 1991, Warsaw and Bonn-Berlin signed a comprehensive treaty recognizing each others' territorial integrity and pledging mutual cooperation.[2]

The Czech-Slovak government established firm relations with West Germany early in 1990, following President Havel's visit to Berlin and Bonn in early January; this was his first official visit abroad as President.[3] Havel publicly supported German reunification and appeared to underscore Czechoslovak-German reconciliation as the cornerstone of his new European foreign policy and of economic integration with the West. A broad cooperation and friendship treaty was initialled between Prague and Bonn in October 1991 and formally signed in February 1992. It addressed most of the unresolved issues between the two states, reaffirming existing borders and renouncing any territorial claims or the use of armed force.[4] Czech-Slovak relations with Austria also developed relatively smoothly, despite some controversy over a nuclear power plant located near the Austrian border that Vienna wanted closed down. Various agreements were signed on bilateral relations in the political and economic realms. Prague concluded similar treaties during 1991 with Italy, Great Britain, and other EC states.

Hungary began to build on its already cordial relations with a number of Western neighbors even before its first democratic elections in March 1990. Travel restrictions were eased, economic cooperation was enhanced, and inter-governmental political agreements were prepared with Austria, Italy, and Germany. A few problems surfaced with Austria with regard to Hungarian compensation for the cancellation of the Gabcikovo-Nagymaros dam project between the two countries. Budapest also signed a friendship accord with France that evidently committed Paris to support Hungary's association with the EC.[5] French backing was also sought to help improve Budapest's relations with Romania.

The Romanian authorities have made efforts to enhance Bucharest's ties to its traditional allies, particularly to France, Italy, and Spain. The reform Communist government focused on Paris and displayed markedly less interest in a rapprochement with other major western nations.[6] During 1991, treaties of cooperation were signed with France and Italy, and the French authorities also invited Romania to join the group of 44 nations belonging to the Francophone "Agence de Cooperation Culturelle et Technique." However, several west European states remained hesitant in expanding their bilateral ties with Romania or in entering new treaties, largely because of their continuing skepticism about Bucharest's commitment to political pluralism and a market economy.

Bulgaria has fared better than Romania in forging new relationships with the Western democracies. Ties with Germany have undergone the most consistent improvement during the past two years. Bonn has strongly supported Bulgaria's membership in the EC, the Council of Europe, and other all-European bodies. In October 1991, the German Foreign Minister signed a treaty with Bulgaria on "friendly cooperation and partnership in Europe," involving collaboration in legislation, culture, education, ecology, and the economy.[7] Sofia has also enhanced its contacts with its NATO-linked Balkan neighbors: a treaty on friendship, good neighborliness, cooperation, and security was signed with Greece in October 1991, followed by a defense agreement to help Bulgaria reorganize its armed forces. Bilateral relations with Turkey were also steadily improved.

Since early 1991, Albania has emerged from its international isolation and re-established contacts with several western and eastern European states. While Tirana's diplomatic progress was gradual before the first free elections in March 1991, after the balloting Albania accelerated its opening to the outside world at both bilateral and multilateral levels. Especially cordial relations were pursued with Italy, Greece, and Germany, and diplomatic ties were even revived with countries that the former Communist regime had declared as Albania's chief enemies, including Great Britain, the Soviet Union, and the United States.

By contrast with other Communist states, Yugoslavia had maintained good high-level relations with most west European states even before the emergence of multi-party systems in its constituent republics. Paradoxically, increasing republican independence after the elections of 1990 complicated Belgrade's relations with its neighbors and the EC states. Moreover, the election of republican governments that pushed for independence when agreement could not be reached on a new Yugoslav confederal arrangement presented the west European states with a new set of headaches. Aside from questions of conflict prevention, mediation, and resolution, the issue of recognizing new states that emerged from the crumbling Yugoslav federation began to preoccupy the western democracies. As the war in Yugoslavia intensified during the summer and fall of 1991, a handful of countries, including Germany, Italy, and Austria, appeared willing to unilaterally recognize Slovenia's and Croatia's declarations of independence. The majority of western nations feared that such recognition could intensify the war in Yugoslavia and set a destabilizing precedent throughout the continent. Facing an internal split over the issue, in December 1991 the EC announced it was prepared to recognize the republics if they fulfilled certain criteria on democratic rule. In January 1992, Slovenia and Croatia were formally recognized by all the EC states. Recognition of Macedonia and Bosnia-Hercegovina was placed on hold pending Greek acceptance of the former and the results of the republican referendum on independence in the latter.

The east European states have made substantial progress in gaining associate membership or participation in several multilateral institutions and thereby strengthening their claims to European integration. A key body is the Council of Europe (COE), set up in 1948 as the political arm of the European integration process which encompassed 24 states before the collapse of Communist rule. The east European governments sought inclusion in the Council as a seal of legitimacy for their political and economic reforms and as a first step or springboard toward EC membership. While the Council of Europe seeks to harmonize the policies of its members, strengthen the sense of common identity, and further European unity, it has no legislative powers or security dimension. It also possesses few sanctions at its disposal, other than expulsion from the Council, against states that violate its human rights principles. Despite these shortcomings, incorporation in the Council was viewed as an important vehicle for attaining EC membership and for consolidating international credibility.

In October 1990, Hungary gained full membership in the Council; it was the first east European state to be admitted.[8] Meanwhile, Poland was conditionally admitted pending the holding of fully free elections, while Romania was denied guest status due to a lack of progress on human rights and political pluralism. The Czech and Slovak Federal Republic joined the Council in February 1991 and Bulgaria earned guest status in July 1990, to be upgraded to full membership once its domestic political situation stabilized. Yugoslavia had been a guest member for several years, but due to the lack of democratic pluralism at the national-federal level and continuing instability in the country, full membership has been withheld. During 1991, Albania also moved toward guest status in the Council. In November 1991, a few weeks after Poland's multi-party elections, the country was formally admitted as the 26th member of the Council of Europe.

The east European states have also sought membership in regional groupings that incorporate neighboring Western nations. The largest of these is the Hexagonale Initiative. The group was first established in the late 1970s as an organization combining several border regions; it was then known as the Alpine-Adria Working Group. Under Italy's direction, in November 1989 the group was transformed into an international organization consisting of four states: Italy, Austria, Hungary, and Yugoslavia. When Czechoslovakia joined the group in May 1990, it became known as the Pentagonale, and upon Poland's admission in June 1991 it was renamed as the Hexagonale. The purpose of the organization was to bridge the two halves of Europe, to bring the east European countries closer to the EC, and to act as a counterweight to the political and economic strength of a unified Germany. In its practical activities, the Hexagonale has focused on regional cooperation in transportation, telecommunications, trade, environmental protection, and numerous cultural, scientific, technological, and infrastructural projects. The Hexagonale has also tried to coordinate its policies at the United Nations and has presented various proposals to the CSCE and other international bodies on minority rights and other pressing issues.

Several east European states have also participated in international conferences and initiatives with Western representatives, emphasizing regional cooperation in specific projects such as energy, telecommunications, the environment, migration, transportation, and technology. Efforts have also been made to revitalize continental initiatives that have remained dormant for several years. These include the European Movement (EM), an international organization designed to breathe new life into the resolutions of the 1948 European Congress in the Hague that proposed the creation of a European government dealing with questions individual countries could not handle by themselves. The EM held its first working session in eastern Europe in Prague in August 1990, followed by a first congress in eastern Europe convened in Budapest in September 1991, at which participants discussed cultural, economic, and foreign policy issues.[9] Although such initiatives are unlikely to lead to the creation of any authoritative supra-national government, they can help buttress the continent's integrative processes and provide them with long-term direction.

Economic Integration

The Western states have desisted from offering or launching any kind of comprehensive Marshall Plan for eastern Europe, partly because of their own limited resources and largely because conditions in post-Cold War eastern Europe are very different to those prevailing in post-World War western Europe. The west European states possessed developed capitalist structures and productive economies that could be quickly resuscitated despite their substantial war-time damage. Moreover, it was not simply the provision of cash that restored the western economies, but the close links that developed between financial assistance and trans-national economic cooperation through such institutions as the European Payments Union (EPU).

Following the Communist collapse in eastern Europe, Western governments calculated that they would not squander economic assistance as they did in the 1970s when massive credits were made available to the Communist governments without being tied to concrete market reform programs. Instead, they would seek to develop institutions in the east that would allow private investment from the West to be used productively, and would promote the incorporation of these states in west European economic institutions.[10] Increasing inter-state interdependence through strong international bodies would evidently mitigate against isolationism, protectionism, domestic instability, and international conflict. But the links would need to be permanent and expansive and not subject to sudden reversals that could provoke both disillusionment and domestic disorder. In fact, even after three years of deep reform, the West retained fears of economic failure in the East that could retard the development of democratic governments.

The reforming east European states have greatly enhanced their economic cooperation with Western countries and taken major strides toward integration into various multilateral financial and economic institutions. Bilateral and multilateral relations have been strengthened through government loans and debt forgiveness, commercial business investments, and expanded trading networks. For example, Poland, the most indebted country in eastern Europe, has benefited from various debt forgiveness arrangements. In March 1991, the Paris Club of foreign creditor governments agreed to halve Warsaw's debt over the next three years; part of this forgiveness remained conditional on Poland fulfilling the IMF's financial stipulations for gaining further credits.[11] In April 1991, Bulgaria was able to reschedule $2 billion of debt with the Paris Club over the next ten years, with a six year grace period. Other states, including Hungary and Yugoslavia, have concluded similar agreements with Western creditors.

During the past three years, all the east European states have gained participation in global financial institutions, including the International Monetary Fund (IMF), the World Bank (WB), and the General Agreement on Tariffs and Trade (GATT). Their membership qualified them for access to important technical and financial resources. For instance, the IMF is able to garner large supplies of finance from public and private institutions and provide technical assistance and economic policy advice.[12] The World Bank first approved loans to Poland in February 1990, partly to help modernize its export industries, and to Hungary in April 1990 to help modernize the country's financial infrastructure and agricultural sector. The World Bank also announced plans to lend the east European countries a total of $5 billion.[13] In January 1991, the IMF arranged a major $1.78 billion credit package to Czechoslovakia, tied to the implementation of price and trade liberalization, rapid privatization, and a tight monetary policy.[14] A month later, the IMF approved a loan package for Hungary, including a $1.6 billion standby loan contingent upon Budapest expanding its economic reforms and privatization program.[15] In April 1991, a three-year $2.48 billion loan agreement was reached between Poland and the IMF: Warsaw was required to uphold tight monetary and budgetary policies and pursue structural changes such as the development of private banking.[16]

To enhance and coordinate the provision of financial assistance to eastern Europe, a European Bank of Reconstruction and Development (EBRD) was established in April 1991 and headquartered in London. It began operations with $12 billion dollars from 39 countries and with stipulations that 60% of the bank's investments must be made in the private sector. In June 1991, the EBRD made its first loan to help restructure Poland's heating sector and support energy pricing reform. Funds were channeled to private heating companies and state-owned firms with privatization potential.[17] The Bank subsequently decided to focus on providing financial and technical assistance for the privatization of banking and financial institutions. Further EBRD initiatives included direct loans, investment, and technical advice to assist Bulgaria's efforts at privatization, financial reform, and agricultural and infrastructural modernization. Proposals were also lodged to create a fund financed by Western countries and administered by the EBRD to help finance Czechoslovak, Hungarian, and Polish exports to the USSR. Soviet payments were in turn to be remitted to a special EBRD account to be used for industrial restructuring in various parts of the USSR.

The east European governments have endeavored to boost their trade with Western states in order to help converge their economies and develop more rational trading patterns following the collapse of the CMEA. Increasing trade with the West was also intended to earn the hard currency necessary for servicing debts and purchasing western commodities, as well as improving the competitiveness and production standards of east European companies.

Bilateral trade with western countries has grown significantly during the last two years. For example, Hungarian-Austrian trade increased by 50% in the first six months of 1991 as compared to the same period the previous year.[18]

But despite the increase in trade, the central European states have persistently complained about western barriers on the import of their goods. These impediments take the form of prohibitively high tariffs or quotas on highly competitive east European goods such as agricultural, steel, and textile products.[19] The new governments have appealed for equitable concessions and greater access to western markets in order to compete on equal terms with western producers. This is unlikely to happen soon, because of fears of competition in France and Germany and because of the continuing impact of the protectionist EC Common Agricultural Policy (CAP). As a result, east European exports have not kept pace with imports from the west, causing an increasing trade imbalance. Western governments have suggested that most trade barriers will be lifted when the east European countries conclude their full association agreements with the EC. The east Europeans are ultimately seeking free trade agreements with the west and the successful completion of the Uruguay Round of the General Agreement of Tariffs and Trade (GATT), which would help lift barriers on agricultural and textile imports. Meanwhile, progress has been made with the Coordinating Committee for Multilateral Export Controls (COCOM), which in May 1991 agreed to cut in half the number of high technology items that could not be exported to eastern Europe and the Soviet Union without special licenses.[20]

Direct investments by western corporations in eastern Europe have steadily increased in recent years, especially in countries where market reforms have proceeded furthest and foreign investment laws have been significantly liberalized. For example, in September 1991, Budapest announced that foreign investment in Hungary would exceed $1 billion for the year and that 8,700 joint ventures were currently operational.[21] The following month, Poland reported that foreign investments in the country totalled $670 million, mostly centered on joint ventures: Germany, the U.S., and Sweden were the leading investors.[22] As with bilateral trading agreements, the Balkan states have trailed behind the "troika" in their attractiveness for Western investments.

Bilateral agreements have been reached between traditional Western and Eastern allies with regard to direct investments and other economic benefits. In September 1991, Germany promised Bulgaria an increase in investments and credit guarantees as well as support for the rescheduling of Sofia's foreign debt and the country's associate membership in the EC.[23] A treaty between the two states was signed in October 1991. France and Czecho-slovakia also initiated a friendship treaty pledging economic cooperation and French support for Czech-Slovak membership in the EC.[24] France signed a similar treaty containing comparable pledges with Hungary.

Some observers calculated that EC membership could be enhanced through association with the European Free Trade Association (EFTA), a grouping that includes the non-EC west European states. This would offer free trade arrangements and help assure greater access to EC markets. But although EFTA can complement east European linkages with the EC, it cannot offer either a large volume of trade or substantial economic assistance. Suggestions have also been made to revive plans for a "European Economic Space," culminating in the creation of a common market between the EC and EFTA that would prove beneficial for eastern Europe. This could help to synchronize economic policies between the two regions, coordinate western European aid, and even prepare the "troika" for full EC membership.

While the east European governments pushed for speedy associate membership in the EC, the west European states were divided on their approach to potential new members. The majority have favored "deepening" before "widening" the organization, and have offered membership only upon the fulfillment of certain important conditions, including a proven stable democracy and a functioning market economy. In fact, no new applicants were allowed to enter the EC until after 1992, and three steps were laid out for membership: bilateral agreements with EC states, association status, and eventual full membership. In addition, the previously unaffiliated states of Austria and Sweden, both prosperous capitalist democracies, also applied for EC membership and were likely to be accepted before the east European countries.

The EC signed trade and cooperation agreements with all the east European states by October 1990. The agreement with Hungary was actually concluded before the collapse of Communist rule in September 1988.[25] The Community has also supplied financial loans and grants to individual states for specific reconstruction purposes such as environmental clean ups, industrial and trade projects, health care improvements, management training, and the restructuring of finance and business sectors. The new governments have also benefited from agreements with the European Investment Bank, a non-profit arm of the EC that finances development projects.

The three central European states qualified for EC associate status much more rapidly than the Balkan countries. During the process of affiliation, Poland, Hungary, and Czechoslovakia were to be allowed to participate in selected EC activities. But complaints continued to be lodged in some capitals that the EC states were obstructing the entry of east European goods on to western markets. At one point, the Polish authorities even threatened to cancel talks on an association agreement if the Community could not significantly ease access for their agricultural products.[26] In fact, the Community was involved in a program of gradually removing quotas and other restrictions on a range of east European products. However, a system of "safeguards" has remained in place as a protective measure against imports that could seriously hurt domestic producers in the EC.[27] Trade in the less sensitive products was liberalized with Hungary, Poland, Czechoslovakia, Bulgaria, and Romania being accorded the Generalized System of Prefer-ences (GSP) that provided tariff free access for manufacturers, with the exception of textiles, steel, coal, and agricultural goods.

In December 1991, the three central European states signed association accords with the EC in an important step toward full membership. The ten year "Europe Agreements" offered the "troika" various trade concessions and economic assistance programs and were described as a trial run for EC entry. The central European countries wanted further trade liberalization, technical assistance, and foreign investment to constitute the centerpiece of EC association, eventually resulting in a full free trade area. Indeed, the "Europe Agreements" will provide a more stable framework and an advantageous climate for the development of trade and investment. In addition, the benefits of association can be revoked if any Associate were to abandon its commitment to democracy and a market economy. Full membership for the "troika" could take up to a decade, as this much time may need to elapse before the east European economies become internationally competitive without special protective measures.

The Balkan states may also be afforded association with the EC, but the process is likely to take longer and will remain contingent on the direction and consolidation of domestic reforms. In the interim, they will benefit from trade and cooperation agreements with the Community, together with the lifting of various import quotas. It is clearly in the long term interest of the EC that the economies of eastern Europe become stable and productive; otherwise, mounting social and economic problems could lead to a large outflow of refugees seeking job opportunities or welfare in the West, and the resulting chaos may prove more costly for the EC in the long term.

Some debate has been evident in the region regarding the strategy of east European integration into the EC, especially on whether this should be pursued independently or collectively. Individual and separate entry into the EC has been criticized because it would eliminate all economic protection and expose the country's uncompetitive export sector to world market forces, leading to further economic deterioration. By contrast, it has been claimed that some form of coordinated entry would prove more rational and profitable, particularly if it was accompanied by the expansion of regional trading networks within which imports would be cheaper than those on the world market. The maintenance of local trade would purportedly help preserve sufficient domestic economic equilibrium to attract foreign investment. Critics of such regional arrangements argue that the preservation or strengthening of intra-east European trade may actually retard economic development by keeping open various unproductive industries and even obstructing the process of economic integration into the EC.

Conflict Resolution

While the likelihood of East-West confrontation has substantially receded if not disappeared during the past three years, new sources of insecurity have emerged in a "multi-polar" Europe. According to some analysts, "multi-polar" systems are prone to instability because there are fewer restraints on each state to stay in line with any alliance commitments.[28] In such a situation, governments may seek to maximize their power relative to their neighbors in order to maintain their means for self-defence and to weaken potential adversaries. Attempts to gain military advantage, particularly when coupled with serious international disputes, could contribute to escalating regional conflicts. Moreover, the question of security in post-Cold War Europe cannot be understood simply in military terms, as many of the regional threats stem from a range of non-military factors—economic de-stabilization, mass migrations, the collapse of energy distribution and trading networks, man-made disasters, and escalating social unrest.

The two superpowers and western Europe's medium powers have proved to be extremely hesitant in becoming directly involved in the multifarious intra-state and inter-state conflicts that have mushroomed in eastern Europe. They have not seen a direct threat to their national or security interests and are wary of becoming embroiled in seemingly intractable local conflicts. Nevertheless, the outbreak of armed hostilities in Yugoslavia, the threat of similar unrest in other parts of the region, and the danger of cross-regional spill-overs, has sensitized most European states to try and devise methods for preventing conflicts or containing hostilities in the east European area.

Prior to the east European revolutions, there was no tried and tested international process for resolving inter-state or intra-state conflicts in the region. Neither NATO nor the EC were equipped or prepared to handle "out of area" conflicts, while the only all-European institution, the Conference on Security and Cooperation in Europe (CSCE), did not possess any verified mechanisms for conflict mediation or any levers to enforce its decisions. Nevertheless, because of its breadth, scope, and legitimacy in human rights, confidence building, and other dimensions, the CSCE has been proposed as the most suitable organization to grapple with regional disputes. It could also attempt to fulfill a number of functions not executed or only partially performed by other organizations, including arms control verification, human rights oversight, environmental inspection, as well as various peacekeeping functions.[29]

The Paris CSCE summit in November 1990, which produced the "Charter of Paris for a New Europe," began to expand Conference structures and establish more specialized institutions. A CSCE administrative secretariat was located in Prague, thus answering some of the criticisms that the organization lacked permanent institutions. A Council of Foreign Ministers was also created as well as a parliamentary assembly whose members were to be elected or appointed by national parliaments and were scheduled to meet annually. A Committee of Senior Officials was also required to gather on an *ad hoc* basis. An Office of Free Elections (OFE) was set up in Warsaw to provide East European nations with an election information clearing house. The OFE was subsequently expanded into an "Office for Democratic Institutions" with a broader mandate to support developing democratic institutions. A Conflict Prevention Center (CPC) was also established in Vienna to undertake conciliation and mediation efforts, particularly in the east European region.

The CSCE has both positive attributes and obvious shortcomings. On the positive side, it enjoys broad legitimacy, has substantial flexibility, and incorporates all the European states, including Albania which was accepted in the summer of 1991 and the three Baltic states of Estonia, Latvia, and Lithuania which were admitted in September 1991. On the negative side, it has lacked permanent institutions, a standing army, or any other means or sanctions to bring any state into line in the event of conflict. Indeed, its size and all-inclusiveness could prove cumbersome in reaching difficult yet important decisions.

The CSCE Conflict Prevention Center consists of a consultative committee and a small secretariat. Its initial brief was to arrange consultations over unusual military activities, exchange military information, and hold assessment meetings over the implementation of Confidence and Security Building Measures (CSBMs). But the CPC has lacked developed mediation or arbitration services, is inexperienced in muting or resolving inter-state conflicts, and has no peacekeeping forces at its disposal that could intervene in any dispute. However, some observers believed that in the longer term, it could assume greater responsibility in preventing or containing local conflicts. For instance, it may provide an arbitration service between states, have a role in verifying conventional arms control compliance, engage in fact-finding missions, and provide mechanisms for bringing together regional groupings and other European institutions to resolve growing local tensions.

Despite its overall desirability, there are several problems with outside mediation that will require careful handling, understanding, and perseverance. Some east European governments may prove unwilling to surrender any component of their regained sovereignty, even in resolving a dispute involving a troublesome minority, region, or republic. Such reluctance may be sharpened if one of the initiating powers is a neighboring state that is perceived to harbor long-standing political or territorial designs on that country. The February 1991 report of the CSCE Valletta Meeting, regarding the peaceful settlement of disputes, stipulated some basic ground rules for inter-state negotiations and outside mediation.[30] But the report assumed initial agreement on means and ends in addition to a mutual willingness to compromise. In reality, some nationality disputes remain so polarized that foreign arbitration will prove extremely problematic or even counterproductive where it stiffens resistance against perceived foreign influence in a country's internal affairs.

The CSCE has been proposed as the most credible instrument for resolving inter-state disputes, once it could establish more permanent organizational structures. Nevertheless, its standing resolutions may still fall short in several critical respects. The CSCE's 1975 Helsinki Final Act and the various follow-up conferences stipulate that all European borders are inviolable, or cannot be changed by force, thus seemingly confirming a virtual *status quo* on all territorial issues. On the other hand, it does envisage the possibility of peaceful border changes, if such revisions are mutually agreed upon, are in keeping with international law, and take account of the rights of the affected population to self-determination.[31] Such specifications assume the full agreement of neighboring states, but do not provide any meaningful input in the process for compact national minorities residing in border areas and do not establish any acceptable precedents for frontier adjustments.

Moreover, there is an absence of any internationally agreed provisions regarding either the creation of new borders or the establishment of new independent states. This constituted a serious omission and a major impediment to the peaceful and regulated fracturing of multinational federal states such as Yugoslavia, Czechoslovakia, and the Soviet Union. For instance, no mechanisms were envisaged for negotiations between a federal state and its constituent republics, or for the voluntary separation of compact ethno-cultural communities that have unilaterally opted for national independence through general elections or a republican referendum. Such developments have been taking place in eastern Europe in a legal and international vacuum. The stance of most Western governments against the splitting of states, regardless of their viability, cohesion, and stability, has not provided long-term answers or resolutions.

The CSCE could assume practical peacekeeping functions if its members can agree to establish some multi-national armed units. Indeed, the CSCE agreed to send observers to Yugoslavia in the summer of 1991 to monitor troop movements and the various short-lived cease-fire agreements. It was argued that such formations could act as a buffer between contestants, with troops from selected states supervised by some overall coordinating body. In its peacekeeping missions, the CSCE could benefit from the experience of the UN in various global trouble spots as well as from governments, such as the British and French, that have engaged in peace-keeping tasks and have issued valuable peace-keeping manuals. But the question of unanimous agreement by all participating states may prove problematic in specific conflicts: at present the dissension of any single government could block the dispatch of projected CSCE forces to a particular conflict zone. The institution would then find itself paralyzed unless the stipulations for consensus are altered. Although some modifications have been made in CSCE procedures including the convocation of emergency sessions when a threatening situation is developing between or within member states, all substantive decisions still require the consensus approval of all member states, thus allowing one dissenting party to veto any proposed actions.[32] Some kind of majority agreement could ensure a faster reaction to a conflict scenario. But this in turn could create further resentment among some of the affected parties and even exacerbate animosities within the CSCE structure and effectively paralyze the process of conflict resolution.

The war in Yugoslavia has raised serious questions about the absence of any all-encompassing European security umbrella or any effective conflict prevention and peace-keeping mechanisms. The CSCE Council of Foreign Ministers meeting in Berlin in June 1991, established an Emergency Meeting Mechanism. The Mechanism was to be engaged if any participating state considered an emergency situation to be developing.[33] During the Yugoslav crisis in the summer and fall of 1991, the CSCE Valletta Mechanism on the peaceful settlement of disputes could not be employed since this was not considered a dispute between states unless and until the conflict spread beyond Yugoslavia's borders. However, the CSCE Emergency Meeting Mechanism was implemented in a series of meetings in Prague. The sessions condemned the use of force in Yugoslavia and offered to establish a Good Offices Mission upon Belgrade's invitation to facilitate political dialogue between the warring sides. CSCE countries convening in Prague supported the deployment of a UN peace corps to Croatia and even proposed sending a contingent of human rights monitors to Yugoslavia under CSCE auspices. But the CSCE was clearly not equipped to handle the crisis on its own without the goodwill and support of all parties to the conflict and without some viable pressures at its disposal.

In the immediate future, the CSCE is unlikely to obtain any meaningful security dimension or an effective force structure. It appears that only such agreements could help guarantee or restore stability by interceding to forestall or contain armed confrontations within and between states. In addition, some commentators have argued that any efforts to militarize the CSCE, the EC, or other multilateral European institutions could in practice undermine the NATO structure before anything more effective has been constructed in its place. Such moves could unwittingly contribute to destabilizing the continent. Moreover, the failure of any initial CSCE peace-keeping mission will seriously undermine the credibility of the organization and mitigate against involvement in any subsequent regional conflicts. These and other issues will need to be carefully considered during the Helsinki follow-up meeting scheduled for the spring of 1992 that could set in motion new institutional initiatives. A new European security and disarmament forum is planned to convene after the CSCE meeting.

An additional vexing issue for CSCE is the question of collective or group rights in the newly liberated east European states.[34] These have proved to be a major source of dispute in the region since the collapse of Communism. As we have seen in previous chapters, governments that may comprehensively guarantee individual human rights for their citizens may balk at providing special provisions for the "collective rights" of ethnic or national minorities. Government officials may fear that granting distinct privileges and financial assistance to minority populations may actually aggravate inter-ethnic relations. Such measures could breed resentment among the majority, while stimulating aspirations for territorial and political autonomy among certain minorities. Moreover, some political leaders seem willing to manipulate and exploit inter-group tensions to their advantage. The use of scapegoats can deflect attention from pressing economic and social problems and increase the popularity of nationalist leaders.

CSCE agreements and resolutions have only contained general provisions for protecting collective minority rights; indeed these are generally understood and defined as the rights of individuals to engage in group activities. CSCE officials are well aware of the difficulties involved in defining minorities, in delineating clear distinctions between individual and group rights, in deciding on the parameters of minority "self-determination," and in reaching international consensus on the extent of minority rights and the obligation of governments. The CSCE Copenhagen Document, produced in 1990, included several passages confirming the rights of individual members of minorities to participate in collective activities such as using their "mother tongue," forming religious and other associations, engaging in cross-border contacts, and participating in public affairs and the local administration. Although the document moved beyond the traditional focus on individual human and civil rights, it fell short of forging any concrete agreements on minority group protection. The July 1991 CSCE meeting in Geneva dealt specifically with minority issues as a result of growing ethnic tensions in eastern Europe. Although the Geneva Report stated that issues regarding minority rights did not constitute an exclusively internal affair of the respective state, the meeting produced little consensus and few new initiatives.[35] Controversy surrounded such questions as the definition of a national minority, the distinctions between individual and group rights, and the degree of government help to protect minorities. The Concluding Document simply stressed the importance of non-governmental organizations in resolving ethnic conflicts and promoting tolerance between ethnic, cultural, and religious groups.

Security Restructuring

All the European states have been grappling with the long-term problem of establishing some new continental security order following the demise of the Cold War. The future challenge to European stability is not a major East-West confrontation or a Soviet invasion, but a series of local incidents escalating into regional conflicts and embroiling the larger European powers. The absence of firm regional alliances in eastern Europe, coupled with the surfacing of numerous hostilities over territories, minorities, and resources, has increased perceptions of insecurity among all the post-Communist states.

In general, democratic, publicly accountable, and freely-elected governments do not wage war with other democracies or engage in aggressive acts against neighboring dictatorships. However, even a democratically elected administration may evolve into a quasi-dictatorship, capitalize on radical nationalist sentiments, and threaten its neighbors in order to preserve itself in power. Moreover, a democratic, non-expansionist government may either take preventative action against another state to forestall aggression, or it could intervene to offer direct protection to its co-ethnics suffering repression and threatened with violence. The likelihood of war is heightened where there are substantial military disparities between hostile neighboring states and insufficient deterrents to prevent or preclude an attack. Furthermore, a government anxious about its own weakness and vulnerability may seek coalitions with stronger parties and traditional allies, and thereby increase the chances that a local conflict could escalate into a regional conflagration.

In addition to voicing concerns over domestic instability and potential confrontations with neighbors, the east European governments have been anxious in the past over the exposure of their territories as potential war zones between NATO and the Soviet Union. They feared that even if they declared themselves as neutral states and did not allow their territories to be used for offensive operations, NATO and Soviet forces would not issue watertight guarantees that the region would be spared military activities. The danger of a NATO-Soviet clash has, of course, all but disappeared during the past few years.

Some apprehensions have also been expressed in Poland over Germany's future military position. Officials in Warsaw felt that decisions on the German military should not be an internal NATO matter, but must involve potentially vulnerable neighbors such as Poland. Warsaw has sought long-term warranties that German forces will maintain a strictly defensive orientation and will not assume greater responsibility in future NATO planning or obtain nuclear arms and other sophisticated weaponry. Before the final disbanding of the Warsaw Pact, NATO and the WTO signed a Paris treaty in November 1990 under the rubric of the Conventional Forces in Europe (CFE) negotiations. It limited the holding of offensive weapons, initiated exchanges of military information, and formalized on-site inspections. There was also agreement on assigning arms quotas to participating governments in which ceilings were placed on the volume of weapons and their distribution was balanced between states.

The nuclear weapons issue has also preoccupied the new east European administrations. Reservations have continued to be voiced over the nuclear capability of the Commonwealth of Independent States, as well as fears that some of the neighboring post-Soviet republics will acquire some part of Moscow's nuclear arsenal. Indeed, in the long term the east European states may have a strong incentive to develop their own nuclear, chemical, or biological weapons capability as protection against potential nuclear blackmail by Russia or a military threat from neighboring republics. Even without nuclear weapons, Russia, Germany, and other states could achieve overwhelming conventional strength in the region. Such prospects could lead to unregulated and even mismanaged nuclear proliferation as new governments search for a relatively inexpensive deterrent where the cost of modernizing and professionalizing their conventional forces proves far too high for their modest budgets. Uncontrolled proliferation would clearly be a dangerous and destabilizing development. It could even lead to a new arms race in Europe, as states will endeavor to prevent their neighbors from obtaining an unfair advantage.

The ultimate goal of the east European governments is either membership in NATO or in whatever effective security organization emerges in the years ahead to span the continent. Simultaneously, they have also pursued bilateral security links with several west European states. For example, in December 1990, Hungarian and French Defense Ministers signed a military cooperation treaty that established regular high-level contacts between the two ministries and consultations among military experts.[36] Further agreements on military cooperation were signed by the French and Hungarian Chiefs of Staff in June 1991. France reached similar accords with the Poles and the Czechs and Slovaks, while Budapest concluded a bilateral military agreement with Vienna in October 1991. In early 1990, proposals were made in both Warsaw and Bonn to form joint Polish-German military units along the model of the existing Franco-German brigade. The idea was to help create a climate of confidence, form a basis for security cooperation between border units, and further the process of Polish integration with Western military forces.[37] Several east European governments have also sought Western help in modernizing their military forces. For instance, in October 1991 Romania reportedly reached such an agreement with the French.[38] In addition, several western military academies opened their doors to accept east European cadets.

Practically all the east European governments have expressed their endorsement of NATO as the one effective and proven security organization in Europe. Although they realized that immediate NATO membership was highly improbable, they nevertheless pursued closer links with the Alliance calculating that through a series of concrete steps, NATO's security umbrella would be gradually extended to encompass their territories. Relations between NATO and the three central European or former "northern tier" states have developed the furthest during the past two years. As early as September 1990, NATO's Secretary-General visited Poland and proposed direct bilateral relations with individual former WTO members. The Soviet Union and its former satellites were invited to establish liaison missions at NATO headquarters in Brussels. NATO's London Declaration in June 1990 announced an end to the Cold War and opened the way for diplomatic relations and formal consultations in areas of mutual interest. Shortly afterwards, the east European states appointed ambassadors and despatched liaison missions to Brussels.

In November 1990, NATO's parliamentary wing, the North Atlantic Assembly, invited parliamentarians from Poland, Czechoslovakia, Hungary, Bulgaria, and the USSR to take part in the capacity of associate delegates at the Assembly's annual meetings. As associates they could participate in debates involving representatives from the legislatures of NATO members even though they could not vote on its resolutions. Only Romania was excluded because of western dissatisfaction with the slow pace of political reform in the country. Interestingly enough, the Romanian armed forces maintained contacts with NATO in the pre-revolutionary era and have since been seeking to expand cooperation in military training and the purchase of modern equipment. Despite NATO resistance, Bucharest has continued to press for a closer association with the Alliance. NATO signed non-aggression pacts and defensive agreements with individual members of the defunct WTO and high-level political contacts were expanded through a number of mutual visits and joint conferences in several east European capitals. NATO's governing political arm, the North Atlantic Council (NAC), which includes heads-of-state, foreign ministers, and ambassadors, approved various measures to enhance east European involvement. These have included programs for the advanced training of officers in the military academies of NATO members and the exchange of views on military restructuring.

Before the Soviet coup attempt, Moscow staunchly opposed east European membership in NATO, while the Western states did not want to antagonize Moscow by expanding Alliance membership.[39] The Soviet position appeared to soften somewhat in late 1991. The coup itself spurred the former WTO countries to seek more rapid and comprehensive NATO connections, largely as protection against any future destabilizing Soviet developments. At their Krakow summit in October 1991, the "troika" leaders issued a joint appeal to NATO to allow them to participate formally in Alliance activities.[40] NATO leaders continued to oppose granting associate membership to the east European states because this could apparently complicate NATO operations and enmesh the Alliance in difficult "out-of-area" conflicts.[41] Critics of this position argued that NATO membership itself may help to mitigate against any escalation of east European conflicts, as it would provide a defensive shield for each state against any threat of outside aggression. NATO may also have an important role to play in managing the growing refugee crisis by providing valuable humanitarian and relocation assistance. NATO already has in place an emergency planning structure, the Senior Civil Emergency Planning Committee (SCEPC) and the Civil Wartime Agencies (CWA), that could help coordinate a major exodus of refugees into western Europe or even between some east European nations.[42]

Despite its hesitation in accepting new members, NATO has made various moves to support the new east European governments and has displayed a strong security interest in the region. In June 1991, NATO Foreign Ministers declared that any coercion or intimidation of the east European states would be treated as a "direct concern" of the Alliance. In November 1991, the NATO summit in Rome decided to create a North Atlantic Cooperation Council (NACC) to provide an opportunity for all the Eastern states to interact directly with NATO.[43] The initiative was positively received in all the east European capitals as a move in the right direction, but it was not viewed as an ultimate solution to the region's security vacuum. The new governments continued to seek more formal ties with the Alliance and eventual membership of an expanded or modified NATO structure.

The search for a comprehensive European security system has led to some alternative proposals for either expanding the nine member West European Union (WEU) or the CSCE, and equipping these organisms with a military apparatus. Several east European leaders have expressed an interest in joining the WEU, which unlike the EC does have a security component. A WEU meeting in Paris in December 1991 raised the possibility that the "troika" states would be invited to take part in the activities of the WEU military satellite center and cooperate in armaments questions. However, suggestions that the WEU should serve as the military arm of the EC have run into difficulties. There are fears that it could undermine the NATO alliance before it can evolve into an effective defensive system. Moreover, some EC members or aspiring members, such as Ireland, Sweden, and Austria, are essentially neutral states that will probably avoid any regional military entanglements.

Some observers have proposed transforming the CSCE into a new European Treaty Organization, once the Conference is fully institutionalized and the Helsinki Final Act becomes a binding international treaty. For example, Czech-Slovak President Vaclav Havel proposed the creation of a European Security Commission as a first step toward a continental security arrangement.[44] But serious reservations remain whether a security system that embraces all the European states can properly function by integrating dozens of national military structures and effectively dividing up responsibilities between them.

Notes

1. Radio Free Europe/ Radio Liberty, *Daily Report,* No. 69, 9 April 1991.
2. Radio Free Europe/ Radio Liberty, *Daily Report,* No. 114, 17 June 1991.
3. For a useful assessment see Peter Martin, "Czechoslovakia's New Foreign Policy," Radio Free Europe, *Report on Eastern Europe,* Vol. 1, No. 10, 9 March 1990.
4. Radio Free Europe/ Radio Liberty, *Daily Report,* No. 191, 7 October 1991.
5. Radio Free Europe/ Radio Liberty, *Daily Report,* No. 174, 11 September 1991.
6. See Vladimir Socor, "Foreign Policy in 1990," Radio Free Europe, *Report on Eastern Europe,* Vol. 1, No. 52, 28 December 1990.
7. Radio Free Europe, "Weekly Record of Events," *Report on Eastern Europe*, Vol. 2, No. 42, 18 October 1991.
8. Radio Free Europe/ Radio Liberty, *Daily Report,* No. 199, 18 October 1990.
9. Radio Free Europe/ Radio Liberty, *Daily Report,* No. 166, 31 August 1990, and *Daily Report,* No. 188, 2 October 1991.
10. For a valuable development of this position see Jack Snyder, "Averting Anarchy in the New Europe," *International Security,* Vol. 14, No. 4, Spring 1990, pp. 5-41.
11. Radio Free Europe/ Radio Liberty, *Daily Report,* No. 54, 18 March 1991.
12. For an overview of IMF involvement in Eastern Europe see John M. Starrels, *Assisting Reform in Eastern Europe* (Washington, D.C.: International Monetary Fund, 1991).
13. Radio Free Europe, "Weekly Record of Events," *Report on Eastern Europe*, Vol. 1, No. 9, 9 March 1990.
14. Radio Free Europe/ Radio Liberty, *Daily Report,* No. 247, 8 January 1991.
15. Radio Free Europe/ Radio Liberty, *Daily Report,* No. 38, 22 February 1991.
16. Radio Free Europe/ Radio Liberty, *Daily Report,* No. 76, 19 April 1991.
17. Radio Free Europe/ Radio Liberty, *Daily Report,* No. 120, 26 June 1991.
18. Radio Free Europe/ Radio Liberty, *Daily Report,* No. 153, 13 August 1991.
19. See Patrice Dabrowski, "East European Trade (Part III): Getting the West Involved," Radio Free Europe, *Report on Eastern Europe*, Vol. 2, No. 42, 18 October 1991.
20. *The New York Times,* 25 May 1991.
21. Radio Free Europe, "Weekly Record of Events," *Report on Eastern Europe*, Vol. 2, No. 41, 11 October 1991.
22. Radio Free Europe, "Weekly Record of Events," *Report on Eastern Europe*, Vol. 2, No. 41, 11 October 1991.
23. Radio Free Europe, "Weekly Record of Events," *Report on Eastern Europe*, Vol. 2, No. 37, 13 September 1991.
24. Radio Free Europe, "Weekly Record of Events," *Report on Eastern Europe,* Vol. 2, No. 41, 11 October 1991.
25. See Tibor Palankai, *The European Community and Central European Integration: The Hungarian Case,* Occasional Paper Series No. 21 (New York: Institute for East-West Security Studies, 1991).
26. *The Financial Times,* 10 September 1991.
27. John Pinder, *The European Community and Eastern Europe* (London: Royal Institute of International Affairs, 1991), pp. 27-28.

28. See John J. Mearsheimer, "Back to the Future: Instability in Europe After the Cold War," *International Security,* Vol. 15, No. 1, Summer 1990, pp. 5-56.

29. Check Kate Holder, Robert Hunter and Paavo Lipponen, *Conference on Security and Cooperation in Europe: The Next Phase* (Washington D.C.: Center for Strategic and International Studies), Significant Issue Series, Vol. XIII, No. 7, 1991.

30. See the report of the CSCE meeting of Experts on the Peaceful Settlement of Disputes, Valletta, Malta, 8 February 1991.

31. For a valuable analysis of the territorial issue see John J. Maresca, *To Helsinki: The Conference on Security and Cooperation in Europe 1973-1975* (Durham, N.C.: Duke University Press, 1985), pp. 110-116.

32. For valuable background see Richard Weitz, "The CSCE's New Look," *RFE/ RL Report,* Vol. 1, No. 6, 7 February 1992.

33. See the conclusions of the Berlin Meeting of the CSCE Council, 19-20 June 1991.

34. For useful background see *Minority Rights: Problems, Parameters, and Patterns in the CSCE Context,* Compiled by the staff of the Commission on Security and Cooperation in Europe, Washington, D.C., 1991.

35. See the *Report of the CSCE Meeting of Experts on National Minorities,* Geneva, July 1991; and Bob Hand, "Minority Questions Prove Difficult in Geneva," *CSCE Digest,* Summer 1991, Washington, D.C.

36. Radio Free Europe/ Radio Liberty, *Daily Report,* No. 240, 18 December 1990.

37. See Ronald Asmus and Thomas S. Szayna (Eds.), *Polish National Security Thinking in a Changing Europe: A Conference Report* (Santa Monica, California: Rand/ UCLA, Center for Soviet Studies, 1991).

38. Radio Free Europe/ Radio Liberty, *Daily Report,* No. 203, 24 October 1991.

39. A useful survey is contained in Richard Weitz, "NATO and the New Eastern Europe," Radio Free Europe, *Report on Eastern Europe,* Vol. 2, No. 21, 24 May 1991.

40. For background see Jan B. de Weydenthal, "The Cracow Summit," Radio Free Europe, *Report on Eastern Europe,* Vol. 2, No. 43, 25 October 1991.

41. A valuable discussion on the future of NATO can be found in Jan Willem Honig, *NATO: An Institution Under Threat?,* Occasional Paper Series, No. 22 (New York: Institute for East-West Security Studies, 1991).

42. See Jeffrey Simon, "European (In)security and NATO Challenges," in Jeffrey Simon (Ed.), *European Security Policy After the Revolutions of 1989* (Washington, D.C.: National Defense University Press, 1991), pp. 613-619.

43. *The New York Times,* 7 November 1991.

44. See Christopher D. Jones, "Czechoslovakia and the New International Security System," in Jeffrey Simon (Ed.), *European Security Policy After the Revolutions of 1989* (Washington, D.C.: National Defense University Press, 1991), pp. 307-330.

9

Conclusions: The New Europe

All the countries of eastern Europe have entered the post-Communist era with fragile democratic systems and facing serious economic problems. The potential for domestic political turmoil coupled with the eruption of numerous long-suppressed and unresolved ethnic and international tensions, could engender various forms of conflict within and between several states in the region. The more homogeneous countries, such as Poland, Albania, and Hungary, have fewer internal rifts stemming from ethnic, cultural, religious, or regional cleavages. But in multi-ethnic countries containing large and territorially compact minorities, cultural, linguistic, religious, and regional differences will continue to fan frictions and conflicts. These disputes could turn confrontational and damaging, if economic conditions markedly deteriorate or if political reforms and administrative decentralization fail to satisfy rising minority aspirations for cultural and political self-determination.

The collapse of the Soviet bloc has released previously submerged national ambitions and led to the formulation of novel foreign policies among all the east European states. Although current and future expressions of nationalism are unlikely to repeat the often destructive inter-war conflicts, traditional animosities may, in some cases, be revived and diverse state interests could provoke fresh disputes. However, future sources of instability in the region are more likely to be manifested in political rifts, economic disparities, social divisions, and ethnic enmities, rather than in outright armed confrontations.

Nonetheless, certain domestic and international conflicts may have the potential of escalating into military threats and even low-intensity armed clashes. Political leaders searching for popular support, in the midst of often severe social and economic disruption, may seek to capitalize on nationalist feelings and exploit the presence of minority scapegoats. Extremist groupings could also attempt to take advantage of public disorientation during the destabilizing reform process. In order to gain public influence, assorted populists and militant nationalists, sometimes in league with the remnants of the Communist apparatus, may launch attacks on various domestic minorities and historical foreign adversaries. Perceived internal and external threats could thereby act as a catalyst for the emergence of authoritarian regimes demanding "national unity" and intolerant toward domestic criticism and political diversity. These developments could slow down progress toward the institutionalization of political pluralism and the emergence of productive market economies.

Ethnic and national antagonisms will continue to pose fundamental questions about human rights and inter-state relations, for which international institutions seem to have no firm blueprints. One problem revolves around the distinction and sometimes the contradiction between individual civil rights and collective group rights. Not all governments that may formally guarantee the sanctity of the former will necessarily recognize any deep or lasting commitments to the latter. State officials may fear that bestowing special privileges, increasing state funding, or conducting affirmative action programs for minority groups may actually aggravate inter-ethnic relations in parts of the country. Such policies could breed resentment among the majority population, while arousing uncontainable aspirations for territorial autonomy and even separatism among the minority group.

In multi-ethnic states, minorities frustrated by years of discrimination could further escalate their demands for cultural, religious, educational, and even regional autonomy. In a few cases, this could spur pressures for secession from the dominant state, if growing aspirations cannot be satisfied or the community is subject to harassment or repression. Nationality disputes, linked with various political and economic grievances, will also have significant international reverberations. Unsettled conflicts that were simply subdued or ignored by the ousted Communist regimes may continue to strain inter-governmental relations. Furthermore, the disintegration of Yugoslavia, the Soviet Union, and Czechoslovakia could heighten irredentist or other claims by some neighboring states, as well as boosting the political ambitions of the newly independent republics.

Three possible kinds of worst-case conflict scenarios can be envisaged in eastern Europe over the next decade, with differing implications for outside involvement and regional stability. The first form of conflict may be in the nature of an ethnic or regional dispute in any one state, possibly escalating into some violent incidents, but not exceeding the boundaries of the country in question. Outside powers could become involved by way of peace keeping, conflict mediation, or in monitoring human rights practices, but they will not harbor any outstanding claims on the destabilized state. Examples of case one could involve massive social unrest or a civil war linked with inter-ethnic, inter-republican, or inter-regional disputes, such as has already been witnessed between Serbs and Croats in parts of Yugoslavia. In extreme cases this may culminate in the weakening or collapse of the central government and the emergence of new autonomous or independent states whose relations remain conflictive.

The second form of conflict could be an internal dispute that directly involves interested parties outside the country or has some form of major spill-over effect on neighboring states. For example, if Yugoslavia continues to disintegrate through violent means, or the Serb-Croat war escalates into more extensive clashes, distressed sectors of the population will seek refuge in nearby countries. Neighboring states may be tempted or pressured to intervene to protect or rescue a co-ethnic minority, to claim some economic assets within the destabilized state, or even to take armed action to prevent further damaging overflows of the conflict. Some governments or political leaders may also use the opportunity provided by a neighbor's weakness to revive dormant irredentist and territorial claims. For instance: violent confrontations between Romanians and Hungarians in Transylvania may result in direct Hungarian intervention; clashes in Macedonia could draw in Bulgaria and Greece; and mounting conflicts in Serbia's Kosovo region may presage some form of Albanian involvement.

The third form of conflict would be a direct inter-state confrontation that may result from the previous two scenarios or it may be directly sparked by a serious bilateral international dispute. For instance, a government fearing internal unrest or seeking popular legitimation may find pretexts to initiate actions against a nearby state that could escalate into some form of military threat or even armed clashes. Examples of case three could involve various states nursing deep rooted historical and political grievances against specific neighbors. Various probable conflict pairs can be posited here including Romania and Hungary, Slovakia and Hungary, Bulgaria and Turkey, and Albania and Serbia.

The decentralization, disintegration, or re-centralization of the post-USSR will also have an immense impact on several east European countries. Growing post-Soviet turmoil will continue to disrupt important energy supplies and trading networks, and could result in a large influx of refugees whose presence would seriously exacerbate already pronounced social and economic difficulties. In the event of another coup attempt in Moscow, there is a further possibility of armed incursions and hot-pursuit border violations by military or irregular guerrilla formations from the post-Soviet republics on the territories of the east European states.

A future Russian leadership may also grow alarmed over expanding contacts between some east European countries and the increasingly independent post-Soviet republics, including Belarus, Ukraine, and Moldova. Such fears could provoke some form of threat, blackmail, or overt intervention by Moscow. Alternatively, in the event of an authoritarian backlash in Russia, a nationalistic Russian government may try to exploit and exacerbate traditional national antagonisms in the region, in order to gain leverage, advantage, and dominance over the contending parties. Russia's direct involvement in any regional inter-state disputes, even if intended to arbitrate between the contesting sides, could serve to aggravate rather than settle the hostilities. Such endeavors may be resented as renewed imperialistic initiatives calculated to re-establish a new sphere of Russian influence and control.

The decomposition of Communist regimes, the thaw in East-West relations, and the withering away of the Warsaw Pact as a Russian-controlled alliance, have provided a much wider margin of maneuver for small and medium-sized states. It will allow a broader opportunity for all the east European nations to articulate and act upon their security concerns. Changing military doctrines in the region, discarding the Soviet-imposed model of coalition warfare, have enabled the newly liberated countries to deploy their armed forces in an independent defensive mode. Military expenses have been substantially scaled down by virtually all governments in the region and state funds will be increasingly directed toward infrastructural and other economic priorities. But the evolution from a bipolar to a multipolar Europe could also prove destabilizing. As the Soviet umbrella of restraint has been removed and the new governments increasingly pursue their own distinct national interests, the prospects for inter-state frictions escalating into military actions may, in some cases, be heightened.

Any armed clashes between these small countries will clearly not be as devastating as any superpower confrontation and they are unlikely to seriously resuscitate East-West competition. There appears to be only a remote chance for any U.S. or NATO military involvement on the side of either adversary unless the Russian military becomes directly engaged in the hostilities. Nonetheless, bilateral conflicts do have the potential of broadening into regional contests by embroiling several neighboring states who may side with one or other protagonist. Conflictive international blocs could also emerge in the region, either based on historical state alliances or determined by a search for mutual defense against threatening neighbors. The west European powers may also become involved in these regional rifts, as individual east European states seek out Western patrons and protectors, while Western countries such as Germany, France, and Italy, attempt to extend their influence or to limit the influence of other EC members. Such developments could herald a new era of trans-European division, rivalry, and competition.

Concerted international involvement in conflict prevention and dispute resolution will become paramount, if the post-Communist half of Europe is to preserve sufficient stability to complete its political and economic transformation and if the region is to integrate into pan-European political, economic, and security structures. Despite the difficulties with international mediation, the European Community (EC), the Conference on Security and

Cooperation in Europe (CSCE), and other continental institutions can help to normalize or regulate the situation in eastern Europe. A two track approach is crucial in this regard: tackling some of the root causes of instability, and creating mechanisms whereby local conflicts are prevented from escalating into regional crises. More substantial material assistance and business investments, as well as quickened economic integration and equitable access to Western markets would certainly improve domestic conditions and could help to subdue some simmering disputes. The provision of humanitarian relief, and the direct involvement of international agencies to help cushion against a potential influx of refugees from unstable neighboring states, may also become a high priority in the coming years.

In the short term, east European prospects for full membership in the EC do not appear very promising or remain contingent upon the completion of vital political and economic reforms. This may change after the creation of a single market and when substantive progress is achieved toward monetary union in western Europe. The process will be accelerated once market economies are more firmly in place in individual east European countries. In this regard, the central European states have made a more auspicious start by gaining associate membership in the EC, while most of the Balkan nations face an uphill struggle before EC entry can be attained.

With the collapse of east European Communism, attempts have been made to devise a common security policy in the region. The CSCE could evolve into a new European Treaty Organization once the Conference is institutionalized and the Helsinki Final Act is given the binding character of an international treaty. But at present, there are serious reservations whether a security system embracing all the European states can properly function.

Although a CSCE Conflict Prevention Center was opened in Vienna in early 1991, its mandate has remained limited and it does not have a peacekeeping force at its disposal that could be deployed in the territory of any member state. In the immediate future, the CSCE will not obtain a clear security dimension that could help guarantee stability by interceding to prevent or contain intra-state or inter-state confrontations. Moreover, some have argued that efforts to militarize the CSCE or other non-military organizations could actually undermine NATO before anything more secure and effective is built in its place. In early 1992, no European institution was able to engage in peace-keeping operations in the Yugoslav war. In the meantime, a UN force was mandated to perform a peace-keeping role in Croatia, although its composition, deployment, role, and timetable was likely to stir further disputes.

Whether the CSCE can enhance, complement, or replace NATO, or assume UN-type peace-keeping functions in the future remains a debatable issue. The consistent monitoring of human rights practices throughout the region and progress in military confidence-building could help the CSCE evolve into a genuine system of pan-European collective security. However, it would then require permanent organs and concrete powers to impose sanctions on states that violate its international codes, as well as the capability to despatch multi-national forces to major European trouble spots. This may require the adoption of majority decision-making, otherwise the current consensus rule would paralyze most military incentives. Alternatively, the EC could develop into a European Union with some kind of security component, an element that has been specifically excluded from the Community's agenda.

The disappearance of the Warsaw Pact and the restructuring or scaling down of NATO necessitates an all-encompassing security umbrella to help resolve damaging conflicts and to regulate inter-state relations. In addition, bilateral security agreements and various multilateral and regional security arrangements in various parts of eastern Europe could help mitigate against any serious escalation of disputes. A cross-cutting network of regional alliances, economic contracts, and military agreements could significantly lessen the dangers of serious conflict. It would also help to counter the development of some new conflictive subregional alliances.

The future security role of the United States in Europe must also be defined. Several of the newly elected east European governments have underscored that they view continuing American military involvement in Europe to be imperative. It counterbalances any future Russian threats to the region and keeps all potential new aggressors in check. Furthermore, the U.S. is widely perceived in the area as a neutral state, in terms of its interests and ambitions. Washington, therefore, has a mandate to continue playing an important role in the emerging security arrangements, both by maintaining its influence in existing institutions and by helping to construct novel structures that also embrace the east European states. The U.S. itself could take the lead in proposing and forging a pan-European NATO, a strong European pillar to the Atlantic Alliance, or some other restructured but equally effective security organization. Several east European governments have already expressed an interest in inclusion, if not as full members than as committed observers or initially as non-military or low-level participants.

A central problem remains the position of the post-Soviet Union. The West has been hesitant to expand NATO membership in the past, largely because of fears that this would antagonize Moscow or provoke a hard-line reaction in the Kremlin. However, while such a stance may have been understandable a few years ago, the disintegration of the USSR will provide more flexibility and room for maneuver in extending security guarantees and building broader alliances. Western states now have significant economic and political levers at their disposal, both to apply pressure on Moscow and to reassure Russia and all the post-Soviet republics that NATO does not constitute a threat to their territory.

Western economic assistance to the Commonwealth states could also help stabilize the situation in eastern Europe. For example, the financing of Soviet imports from the east European states, whose trade with Moscow has fallen off dramatically in the past two years, would help cushion against the sudden collapse of the post-CMEA trading system and enhance future economic cooperation in the region. The desperate need for foreign economic aid and business investment among the Commonwealth states also places Western governments in a stronger bargaining position than ever before with regard to internal post-Soviet developments. The involvement of these newly independent countries in any revamped European security structure will also become desirable and possible during the next decade.

Postscript

Since this manuscript was completed in March 1992, eastern Europe has continued to evolve dynamically. Several of the conflicts explored in the text have intensified, particularly in the Balkans where the danger of escalating violence has sharply increased. Throughout the region, continuing economic decline and political volatility has undermined the stability of the post-Communist states and could spawn further ethnic antagonisms within or across state borders. Although there seems little danger of a return to Communist rule, in some cases progress toward stable competitive democracies has been slowed down by shrewd politicians unwilling to surrender their powers and willing to exploit popular anxieties.

The Yugoslav war spread to Bosnia-Hercegovina in early April. The regime in Belgrade launched a new land-grabbing operation on the pretext that Serbs in Bosnia had the right to "self-determination" and did not recognize the internal republican borders established by Tito. Yugoslav army units, supplemented by troops evacuated from Croatia and by nationalist guerrillas infiltrated from Serbia and Montenegro, began a major offensive across Bosnia-Hercegovina. The objective was to expand the territories controlled by Serbs who refused to recognize the authority of the government in Sarajevo or the legality of Bosnia's declaration of independence. The operational plan involved linking up five previously declared "autonomous republics" by forcefully expelling the Muslim and Croat populations from municipalities in which Serbs formed a relative minority of residents. In April, the Assembly of the Serbian People in Bosnia-Hercegovina, controlled by the Serbian Democratic Party proclaimed the independence of the Serbian Republic of Bosnia-Hercegovina.

With overwhelming fire power and the covert backing of Belgrade, Serbian forces rapidly gained control of approximately 65% of Bosnian territory. Bosnia's Muslim forces were caught unprepared and defenseless and suffered serious casualties across the republic. Serbian "ethnic cleansing" operations, first imposed on Croatian territory the previous year, were comprehensively applied across the republic. By early fall, well over a million refugees had been expelled from their homes and over 50,000 people had perished. Ethnic conflicts were thereby manufactured across Bosnia-Hercegovina by radical politicians and militant gunmen as a smokescreen to disguise their strategic objectives.

At the end of April, Serbian and Montenegrin leaders in Belgrade proclaimed a third and smaller Yugoslavia. They also adopted a new constitution that left open the possibility that other self-declared Serbian states in Croatia and Bosnia-Hercegovina could join the new federation. In addition, Belgrade announced that the Yugoslav army was withdrawing from Bosnia. In reality, approximately 80% of the soldiers simply switched their allegiance to the new Serbian authorities in Banja Luka while continuing to receive arms, ammunition, fuel, and other supplies from Yugoslavia.

As the war escalated, the Croatian authorities in western Hercegovina formed their own army and government structure while pledging allegiance to the government of Alia Izetbegovic in Sarajevo. In early July, Mate Boban, leader of the Croatian Defense Council, declared the autonomy of the "community of Herceg-Bosnia" with its capital in Mostar. The move heightened speculation that Zagreb was prepared to betray the Muslims by arranging secret agreements with Serb leaders to partition Bosnia-Hercegovina. Croat spokesmen contended that "Herceg-Bosnia" was merely a temporary arrangement to assure administrative continuity in war-time conditions. Croatian President Franjo Tudjman underscored his support for Bosnian independence and integrity by announcing moves toward a Croat-Bosnian military alliance against Serbian aggression. Nonetheless, suspicions remained that as Bosnia-Hercegovina splintered, Croatia would claim its share of about 20% of the republic, particularly those municipalities in Hercegovina where Croats formed absolute majorities.

The UN and EC endeavored to provide humanitarian assistance to the besieged residents of Sarajevo and other Bosnian cities. But Western governments dismissed appeals for any direct military involvement and refused to be drawn into what they contended was an intractable guerrilla war. Bosnian authorities complained that they were not seeking Western ground troops, but the lifting of the arms embargo which hardly affected the Serbian side and the provision of weapons for Bosnian forces for purposes of self-defense. Belgrade, for its part, sought to forestall any military involvement by agreeing to various peace talks and disarmament proposals while simultaneously consolidating the Serbian hold on captured territories. In early August, the government of the Serbian Republic of Bosnia-Hercegovina and the Serbian Republic of Krajina (in Croatia) announced moves toward unification, including the creation of a joint parliament and a common defense system.

Croatian authorities grew impatient with the progress of the UN in restoring Zagreb's authority in Serb-occupied areas of Croatia. There was a clear danger that the war in Croatia could restart again, this time with Croatian forces aiming to regain their lost territories. There were also signs that the war in Bosnia would assume increasing complexity. Although by late September, Serb forces controlled major towns and roads in about 70% of the republic, the countryside became a battleground between competing guerrilla forces often outside any central control. Muslim units were regrouping and rearming amidst fears that relatively moderate politicians in Sarajevo would be superseded by radicals intent on violent retribution.

The situation within the rump Yugoslavia also deteriorated. Economic conditions severely worsened as the impact of U.N. sanctions, imposed in May because of Belgrade's involvement in Bosnia, began to be felt. Political tensions also mounted in both Serbia and Montenegro. The dispute between Serbian President Slobodan Milosevic and the new Yugoslav Prime Minister Milan Panic served to strengthen the opposition movement during preparations for new republican and federal elections. Panic appeared to favor a more flexible approach to Serbian foreign policy in order to end the country's international isolation. The government in Podgorica signalled that it would not back Milosevic unequivocally. Montenegrin President Momir Bulatovic indicated that he would reconsider his relations with Belgrade, while the political opposition sought outright Montenegrin independence. Montenegro's Albanian and Muslim minorities remained supportive of the republic's sovereignty but increasingly feared the activities of Serbian paramilitary forces. As a measure of self protection, in late August the Democratic Forum of Albanians announced plans for a referendum on autonomy within the republic.

In Serbia itself, Albanian activists organized an election in Kosovo at the end of May and elected Ibrahim Rugova as President. Serbian authorities continued to apply discriminatory and repressive pressures and refused to countenance any moves toward Kosovan autonomy. Observers grew concerned that Belgrade was preparing an "ethnic cleansing" operation in Kosovo to resettle thousands of Serbian families displaced from Bosnia and to drive out thousands of Albanian residents from the province. Kosovo's Albanian leaders continued to appeal for international recognition as an independent republic, but aside from Albania itself no government was willing to take such a step and challenge Serbia's territorial integrity.

The Hungarian minority in Vojvodina also pushed toward greater autonomy and warned about the forcible resettlement of Serbs in Hungarian areas. In April, the Annual Convention of the Democratic Community of Hungarians in Vojvodina issued a "memorandum on self-rule" for eight municipalities containing a majority Magyar population, with the possibility of a future Hungarian autonomous region in northern Vojvodina. In late August, leaders of the Muslim-based Party of Democratic Action in the Sandzak area announced that the region would seek sovereignty and independence if the rump Yugoslavia was internationally recognized. Serbian radicals stepped up their pressures on the Muslim population in Serbian and Montenegrin Sandzak, amid fears that another anti-minority campaign would be launched throughout the region. Reports in early September indicated that 70,000 Muslims had already fled the area as Serbian military and irregular units became more active.

Macedonia edged closer toward open conflict. The republic failed to gain comprehensive international recognition because of Greek government opposition to the republic's name. Skopje tried to abide by UN sanctions against Yugoslavia and began to suffer the economic consequences of a major loss of trade. Athens aggravated the problem by imposing its own informal economic sanctions against Macedonia. It also stood accused of negotiating with Belgrade over a partition of Macedonia. Economic decline and political paralysis exacerbated ethnic relations in the republic, particularly between Slav Macedonians and Albanians. Local Albanian leaders remained concerned about the potential growth of Macedonian nationalism and the threat to minority rights. They sought cultural and political autonomy in municipalities where Albanians formed a majority, but they desisted from claiming outright independence. Observers feared that Serbia was intent on exploiting and provoking Albanian-Macedonian controversies in order to destabilize the republic. In one worst case scenario, Belgrade could drive out thousands of Albanian refugees into Macedonia and then intervene militarily in the republic posing as a protector against alleged Albanian expansionism.

In addition to its concerns over Kosovo and Macedonia, Albania faced growing problems with its own substantial Greek minority. During the local elections in June, Albanian leaders charged that Greece was intervening in the country's internal affairs by assisting the Unity Party for Human Rights and tolerating the activities of radical groups that campaigned for the autonomy and secession of minority areas in southern Albania. Although intercommunal relations remained calm, some Albanians feared that the prospect of obtaining Greek visas could encourage ethnic Albanians to claim Greek identity and thereby play into the hands of separatists.

Romanian-Hungarian relations in Transylvania continued to simmer in preparation for the presidential and parliamentary elections in late September. In particular, the situation in Cluj remained tense as the new nationalist mayor from the Romanian National Unity Party continued to place restrictions on Hungarian public activities. Romanian nationalists gained nearly 15% of the popular vote in the general elections, heightening anxiety that ethnic relations could be further undermined. The Moldovan issue also played a larger role in Romanian foreign policy. The government in Bucharest was increasingly drawn into the conflict and various Romanian groups seeking reunification with Moldova condemned the involvement of Russian troops in assisting separatist forces in the Trans-Dniestr region.

Central Europe was not immune to political rifts and ethnic divisions. In the Czechoslovak general elections in June, the pro-independence Movement for a Democratic Slovakia captured a majority of seats in the Slovak National

Council. This signalled a pending "velvet divorce" between the two republics. In July, Vaclav Havel resigned as Czechoslovak President having failed to win the requisite number of votes in the Federal Assembly when Slovak deputies blocked his re-election. The Slovak parliament declared its sovereignty while Czech premier Vaclav Klaus and Slovak premier Vladimir Meciar agreed to a timetable of separation. Slovak leaders announced that the republic would formally attain its independence in January 1993. But serious conflicts between Prague and Bratislava seemed unlikely and the two states were slated to conclude various political and economic agreements to coincide with their formal split.

Slovak sovereignty alarmed some Hungarian minority leaders who feared renewed discrimination by Bratislava without federal government protection. When a Slovak constitution was adopted in early September, deputies representing the Coexistence Political Movement and the Hungarian Christian Democratic Movement stormed out in protest. They demanded more explicit guarantees for minority rights, while none of their submitted amendments were accepted by parliament. In June, Magyar leaders put forward proposals for territorial autonomy in the event that Slovakia achieved independence. The long-term goal was the formation of several autonomous regions containing self-governing administrative units. The proposals were rejected by the Slovak government and Hungarian leaders complained that Bratislava had not developed a constructive minorities policy. The question of Magyar rights in Slovakia will also preoccupy the government in Budapest and have a profound impact on relations between the two states. The dispute over the long-delayed Gabcikovo hydroelectric plant on the Danube border also persisted. Bratislava rejected claims by Budapest that the variant of the project adopted by Czechoslovakia following Hungary's withdrawal would change the Slovak-Hungarian border by diverting the flow of the Danube. The controversy could precipitate some fundamental legal disputes between the two states.

Cooperative and integrative processes also continued to develop in some parts of the region. In late April, the ministers of international economic relations of the "Visegrad Triangle" (Hungary, Poland, and the Czech-Slovak Federal Republic) signed the founding document of the Central European Cooperation Committee. The objective was to eliminate trade and other economic barriers between the three states and to speed up their entry into the EC. A free trade agreement was also expected to be ratified in the near future to eliminate tariffs on all industrial and agricultural products. Several new bilateral agreements were also completed in the region. For instance, in June Poland and Belarus signed a friendship treaty accepting their common borders and guaranteeing the rights of minorities in both states.

Relations between some states in the region continued to improve: in particular Bulgarian-Turkish, Hungarian-Ukrainian, and Polish-German relations appeared to develop steadily. However, the inability of the EC and the UN to stem the fighting in Bosnia-Hercegovina cast an ominous shadow over the continent. It starkly displayed the unpreparedness and impotence of European institutions to handle a brutal low-intensity sub-regional war. NATO leaders indicated that they would be prepared to use military forces for peacekeeping missions outside the borders of NATO member states. But such proposals were unlikely to affect the south Slav war: it seemed that Bosnia-Hercegovina had fallen into the crack between the Cold War and the New World Order. Indeed, the war in Croatia and Bosnia, and potentially in Kosovo and Macedonia, could be a harbinger of periodic regional conflicts in which the international community will seek to mediate but will lack the foresight, resources, and stamina to intervene or resolve.

October 1992

List of Political Organizations

Albania

ADP	Albanian Democratic Party
CPA	Cameria Political Association
DUGM	Democratic Union of the Greek Minority (Omonia)
KPPA	Kosovo Patriotic and Political Association
MPA	Motherland Political Association
NUP	National Unity Party
UPHR	Unity Party for Human Rights

Bosnia-Hercegovina

BMO	Bosnian Muslim Organization
CDU	Croatian Democratic Union
PDA	Party for Democratic Action
SDP	Serbian Democratic Party

Bulgaria

ABA	All Bulgarian Association
BNRP	Bulgarian National Radical Party
BNV	Bulgarian National Union
CDNI	Committee for the Defense of National Interests
FLP	Fatherland Labor Party
IMRO-UMS	Internal Macedonian Revolutionary Organization–Union of Macedonian Societies
MRF	Movement for Rights and Freedoms
RFP	Rights and Freedoms Party
UDF	Union of Democratic Forces
UMA	United Macedonian Association
UTCEA	Union of Thracian Cultural and Educational Association

Croatia

CDA	Croatian Defense Association
CDU	Croatian Democratic Union

CPR	Croatian Party of Rights
SDP	Serbian Democratic Party

Czech and Slovak Federal Republic

CDM	Christian Democratic Movement
CDU-PAV	Civic Democratic Union–Public Against Violence
Egyutteles	Coexistence
FHC	Forum of Hungarians in Czechoslovakia
HCDM	Hungarian Christian Democratic Movement
IHI	Independent Hungarian Initiative
MDS	Movement for Democratic Slovakia
MIS	Movement for Independent Slovakia
MSC	Moravian–Silesian Council
MSG-SMS	Movement for Self Government–Society for Moravia and Silesia
NSM	National Salvation Movement
PAV	Public Against Violence
RMNP	Radical Moravian Nationalist Party
RP-AR	Republican Party–Association for the Republic
SCD	Slovak Christian Democrats
SFSR	Society of Friends of Subcarpathian Ruthenia
SHR	Slovak Heritage Foundation
SNP	Slovak National Party
SPP	Slovak People's Party
UGCA	Union of German Cultural Associations
UURCS	Union of Ukrainians and Ruthenians in Czechoslovakia

Hungary

ASH	Association of Slovaks in Hungary
CDA	Croatian Democratic Alliance
DASS	Democratic Alliance of Southern Slavs
FRH	Federation of Romanians in Hungary
HDF	Hungarian Democratic Forum
HHCA	Hungarian Holy Crown Association
SDA	Slovenian Democratic Alliance

Macedonia

AAM	Assembly of Aegean Macedonians
DFBY	Democratic Foundation of Bulgarians in Yugoslavia
IMRO-DPMNU	Internal Macedonian Revolutionary Organization–Democratic Party for Macedonian National Unity

MAAK	Movement for All-Macedonian Action
PDP	Party for Democratic Prosperity
SOB	Society of Bulgarians

Montenegro

ADA	Albanian Democratic Alliance
DPS	Democratic Party of Socialists
MPP	Montenegrin People's Party

Poland

APCGN	Association of Polish Citizens of German Nationality
BDA	Belarusan Democratic Assembly
CCG	Central Council of Germans
CCGUS	Chief Council of Germans of Upper Silesia
EPW	East Prussian Wolves
GFC	German Friendship Circles
Hramada	
LU	Lemko Union
MAS	Movement for the Autonomy of Silesia
MSA	Movement for Silesian Autonomy
NRP	National Rebirth of Poland
OAGM	Olsztyn Association of the German Minority
SCACS	Social Cultural Association of Czechs and Slovaks
SCAGMSO	Social Cultural Association of the German Minority in Silesia-Opole
USU	Upper Silesian Union
UUP	Union of Ukrainians in Poland

Romania

CAM	Civic Alliance Movement
DAHR	Democratic Alliance of Hungarians in Romania
GRP	Greater Romanian Party
NPP	National Peasant Party
NSF	National Salvation Front
PBBA	Pro-Bessarabia and Bukovina Association
RM	Romania Mare
RNUP	Romanian National Unity Party
RPF	Romanian Popular Front
VR	Vatra Romaneasca

Serbia

ACDP	Albanian Christian Democratic Party
AHHSY	Association of Hungarians for the Homelands of Serbia and Yugoslavia
CCAPPY	Coordinating Council of Albanian Political Parties in Yugoslavia
CL-MY	Communist League–Movement for Yugoslavia
DACV	Democratic Alliance of Croats in Vojvodina
DAK	Democratic Alliance of Kosovo
DAVR	Democratic Alliance of Vojvodina Romanians
DCHV	Democratic Community of Hungarians in Vojvodina
MNCS	Muslim National Council in the Sandzak
PDA	Party of Democratic Action (in Sandzak)
SNHF	Slovak National Heritage Foundation
SPA	Serbian Peony Association
SRP	Serbian Radical Party
SRM	Serbian Renewal Movement

Slovenia

DEMOS	Democratic Opposition of Slovenia
IDA	Istrian Democratic Assembly
ISM	Italian Social Movement
IUIR	Italian Union for Istria and Rijeka
SDA	Serbian Democratic Alliance

Other Countries

CA	Csangos Association
CCMHR	Central Committee for Macedonian Human Rights
Edinstvo	
ESGC	Eintracht Society for German Culture
HCAS	Hungarian Culture Association of Subcarpathia
HDAU	Hungarian Democratic Alliance of the Ukraine
HYAS	Hungarian Youth Association of Subcarpathia
MPF	Moldovan Popular Front
Rukh	
RR	Ruthenian Revival
SCR	Society of Carpathian Ruthenians
UPB	Union of Poles in Belarus
USIO	Ukraine State Independence Organization

Index